BELSHADE

Best wishes,

Best Sladet

First published in 1997
by Quest Books (NI)
2 Slievenabrock Avenue, Newcastle, Co. Down, N. Ireland. BT33 0HZ.

Typeset by December Publications, Belfast
Printed in Northern Ireland by
The University Press (Belfast) Limited

A CIP catalogue record of this book is available from
The British Library

ISBN 1 872027 08 3

Front cover by Carousel Design

BELSHADE

Bert Slader

A Novel

Set in the Blue Stack Mountains of Donegal,
in the French and Spanish Pyrenees
and in the pilgrimage town of Lourdes,
shortly after World War 2

Quest Books (NI)

ACKNOWLEDGEMENTS

The characters and story of Belshade are fictitious but the locations in Donegal, in the French and Spanish Pyrenees and in Lourdes at the end of the nineteen forties are as accurate as memory and research enable me to make them. Many of the incidents in the story like the sighting of the Brocken Spectre, the finding of the King's Road in the Enchanted Mountains and the thunderstorm in the Pyrenees were my own experiences. The walks, climbs and the car-touring itinerary mentioned in the text are actual routes.

I am indebted to my wife and family, Eileen, Jenifer and Dion and many of my friends for their patience and help. My particular thanks are due to Ruth Potterton, Phyl Templeton, Josephine McLoughlin, Dr Jim Gibson, C. J. Law, Sr Mary Patrick of the Lourdes Domain, Sr Raphael of Kylemore Abbey, Molly Kerr and Maurice O'Connor.

I am assured by experienced authors that fiction does not need a bibliography but I must mention the Official Record of the Second Irish National Pilgrimage to Lourdes in 1924 kindly lent to me by the Lecky Library, Trinity College, Dublin.

As a boy, I was told the story of the Allied Invasion of the South of France by my half brother, Sam Castles, who was a merchant seaman on a troopship involved in the landings. My second cousin, John Slader's book, *The Fourth Service*, on the role of the British Merchant Navy in World War 2, provided the detail of Operation Dragoon. I am grateful to both.

My thanks are due to Faber and Faber Limited for permission to quote extracts from copyright material published in *Collected Poems* by T. S. Eliot.

By the same author

AVAILABLE POST FREE FROM

QUEST BOOKS (NI)

2 Slievenabrock Avenue, Newcastle, Co. Down.

N. Ireland. BT33 0HZ

Telephone: 013967 23359

Pilgrims' Footsteps

A walk along the ancient Pilgrim Road to Santiago

Pilgrims' Footsteps

An audio tape

Beyond the Black Mountain

A journey around the Ulster of yesterday

Across the Rivers of Portugal

A journey on foot in Portugal

Footsteps in the Hindu Kush

Tales of Afghanistan

An Echo in Another's Mind

Echoes in the mountains of Ireland and abroad

For Wilfrid

and the Santiago Pilgrims

Grannie Mac's Legacy

'The Seer of Belshade was as limber as a hazel wand,
Lithe, supple, as strong as the hazel trunk.
Her hair was the colour of a roan pony's mane,
Her face was small and oval like the Queen of the Elves.
She had clear hazel eyes,
And the power to change the world.'

Anamar's grandmother always began her stories this way. She was a welcome visitor to the fireside of every house in the valley, the traditional Irish story teller, the seanscealai.

Rose MacFadden always began her tales reluctantly. She had a dread of speaking to those for whom she might be only a quaint entertainment. When she did start she could confuse her listeners, intriguing them, daring them to join her in the narrative, as if it already existed in their own heads and she was merely bringing the characters and events forward into their conscious minds. There was always a beginning to Rose's stories but there might be no middle, nor might there be an end.

They said that Rose knew the secret of leading you into her tales. Listeners were expected to become involved.

'Are you with me?' she would ask. And they always said 'Yes'.

It was easy for Anamar, she could enjoy the stories without explanation. It was as if she and Rose understood each other beyond words.

'My stories are for those who can hear with the ear inside the head,' Rose would say. 'Once I start they should be able to finish without me.'

Her cottage was only a field away from Anamar's home. She was the maternal grand-mother, tall for a Donegal woman, dressed invariably in black with black lace-up boots and a white bibbed apron made from bleached flour bags to keep her dress clean. She kept a milking goat and half a dozen hens and tended a neat garden with enough potatoes, cabbage, onions, leeks, carrots and parsnips to make her almost self-sufficient.

Rose was sitting in the sunshine on a wooden bench outside her cottage. Anamar was at her feet on a stool. They were close friends, allies, this woman of seventy-five and the child of ten. The seanscealai let the words come gently.

'The Seer of Belshade was born on a farm on the rim of the Blue Stack Mountains in Donegal in the month of August under the sign of Virgo. Her parents loved her, their only child, born when many would have thought their chance of a child had gone. At the time, the neighbours had said, this one is a gift from God.'

'But from where had she come? Her parents knew she was their child, from them but not of them, or their people. She did not speak as they did, think as they thought. When she was young some thought she was strange, odd, there were even those who said softly that she might be a changeling.'

Rose, the grandmother, the seanscealai, paused. Her face showed a life-time of hard days, and a few good ones too. It was serene. No achievement for her was higher than holding her grandchild's fascination. Anamar had heard this story before but only the beginning. Was there more? Did it have an end? Her grandmother paused and took her hand.

'Don't stop Grannie Mac,' Anamar's voice was pleading. 'Tell me the next bit. This is where you stopped the last time.'

Rose began to laugh softly.

'Hold your whist, child dear,' she said. 'Like every other young one in the country, you'd rush helter-skelter through your life to the very end if we let you.'

'This story has been born but it hasn't grown yet. You'll know it well enough. If you give it time to grow up and live, you'll know it better than any of us.' Rose stood up and led Anamar by the hand into the kitchen.

'Come on, you wee rascal,' she said still laughing. 'We've pots to scrub and bread to bake and hens to feed. Story time is over.'

The year Anamar was nine, World War Two started and, at her mother's insistence, her father bought a wireless in Donegal Town. It was powered by a big battery which had to be taken into the town every so often to be recharged.

In Ireland the war was called 'The Emergency' and although the Republic of Ireland was neutral, the conflict was on its doorstep. A few miles away across the border, County Fermanagh was in Northern Ireland, and, as a part of the United Kingdom, was now at war with Germany. A few miles in the other direction the Atlantic Ocean washed the shores of Donegal and separated the Allies in Europe from their friends in America. There the great sea battles of attrition between Allied convoys and German U-Boats had already begun.

Through the wireless Anamar immediately felt connected to a much bigger world. It brought a different sound of music into the home which she had only heard once before, on a Christmas outing to the cinema in Ballyshannon. There was news of the war, plays, comical shows and a new language of catch phrases, American slang and that music - jazz, swing, crooners.

When she was ten and after a secret conversation with her grandmother, she had changed her given name to Anamar, the Spirit of the Sea. No one questioned the change and Anamar she became as if she had been so named before she was born.

Anamar's parents, John Joseph and Una were known throughout the country as a quiet couple. They had been childless, until, at the age of forty-three, Una gave birth to a baby girl. No one knew if the mother and father were surprised or pleased. They were not given to discussing such feelings with their neighbours. But Una's mother Rose, who lived in the cottage a field away, was delighted. Whether it was by default or agreement no one could be certain, but she it was who reared the child.

Two years later Rose came back one afternoon from a trip to the town with John Joe and asked Anamar to help carry her shopping up the field to her cottage. Anamar unharnessed the pony, led him to the paddock and followed Rose with the parcels. It was a cold afternoon in the month of December. Rose put a few whin roots on the fire to make a blaze and help the fresh turf light in the ashes.

She made tea and the two of them sat, one on either side of the fire, each with her feet on one of the two smooth stones Rose had persuaded John Joe to set into the ends of the hearth. In her favourite chair, with her crossed heels on the warm stone and the dresser with her delph cups, bowls and plates behind her, Rose could see out over the half-open half-door across the field to the farm house and down the lane to Lough Eske below.

The smooth stones were always warm from direct contact with a hearth heated by a turf fire never allowed to go out, day or night, winter or summer. The Blue Stack Mountains were the earth element above the valley. The lake was the water element below and the fire at the heart of every farm house and cottage completed the elemental trilogy.

Anamar's legs were now long enough to reach the stone on her side. When she had been younger she had always wanted to sit like her Granny sat, one foot cocked over the other, leaning back in her chair, totally at ease, toes warming on the stone. She was not aware of it but to the flames of the fire she was a timeless mirror image of her grand-mother - youth and age caught together without the gap of years.

Anamar cradled her bowl of tea in her hands.

'Did you get a good price for the turkeys Grannie?' She said it like one grown-up to another.

'Not bad,' said Rose, when she meant she had been well pleased. 'Not bad at all.' There had hardly been room to breathe, sharing the trap with the turkeys on the way into town, but on the way back she had sat straight in her seat like a grand lady out for a drive.

'And that's what I wanted to see you about,' she said. 'Do you mind old Malachy Doherty?' It was not a question. Anamar would certainty remember Malachy. Who could forget him? It was just Rose's way of introducing what she wanted to say.

Malachy had lived three fields away on the low side of the valley. He had rented a cottage and a one acre field which was all the land he had ever farmed. As a traditional fiddler and singer he was one of the best known men in the south of the county, in great demand for weddings, wakes, pub parties, church socials. But that was just his social life. He made his living, as his father had done before him, as a dealing man.

Malachy Doherty bought and sold sheep and cattle. Sometimes he would have a pony or a horse for sale, occasionally a donkey or a jennet. He reared and sold chicks, ducklings and goslings, all expertly sexed. His seed potatoes were guaranteed free of any disease known to man, beast or plant. Malachy would claim his eggs for hatching were the finest in the county. 'I should know,' he would say. 'Didn't I lay them m'self'.

Rumour had it that Malachy had a small fortune hidden away in his cottage. When tackled about it, as he drank with some of his cronies in one of the local bars, he would deny it as a matter of course, but always did so with a smile, flattered that his companions took him for a man of means. But their interpretation of his cunning, dealing-man's grin was quite different. 'And what else would he say,' they would reason. 'That oul cod has a knowin' look about him but we'll never see hilt nor hare of his pot of gold.'

Malachy travelled the country in a donkey cart. One night on the way home from the pub he was stopped by two strangers just outside the town. He had noticed them in the bar earlier, drinking heavily, chatting to some locals.

The two men had heard about the hidden wealth and demanded, with threats of violence, that he take them to his home and hand it over. Once they were up on the cart beside him, Malachy produced a large bottle of poteen from under a sack, took a swig and handed it to one of the men. He let the donkey amble along at its own speed and watched the level of the poteen steadily fall as the bottle passed from hand to hand.

A few miles from home he stopped the cart and tipped the would-be robbers, now roaring drunk, into the ditch. Later he would claim that there was never any danger that the highwaymen would succeed. 'The only difficulty was them two drinkin' my share,' he would say. 'Luckily the poteen and me have always been the best of friends.' He would smile his dealing-man's smile and wink at the ceiling to let them know he was well in with the powers above. 'And, thanks be to God,' he would say in the tone he usually reserved for the confessional. 'The donkey's a Pioneer and knows his way home.'

In his later years Malachy's health failed and he was crippled with arthritis. He found it hard to get beyond his own front door and, as his nearest neighbour, Rose had taken to visiting him. Every day she had crossed the three fields to make him two good meals and keep the cottage clean. Often Anamar would have joined her grand-mother when she saw her on the path heading for the old man's cottage.

When Malachy died his only brother Sean had asked Rose at the wake to meet him at the cottage the following morning. Next day Sean told her that his brother had greatly appreciated what Rose had done for him. There was no hidden treasure but Malachy had said that she was to have the pick of anything she wanted from the cottage.

The choice was easy. Rose spotted a setting of six turkey eggs for hatching and expressed herself well pleased with her legacy. She had taken the eggs home, hatched them under a broody hen, and reared the birds for Christmas.

That very morning she had taken the turkeys to the market in Ballyshannon where she expected to get a better price than in Donegal Town. With cash in her hand the next stop had been Hartington's the Jewellers.

Rose reached into the pocket of her dress and produced a little packet.

'It's for you,' she said and gave Anamar a hug.

Anamar unwrapped the tissue paper and opened a little blue box. Inside was the most beautiful gold watch she had ever seen. She looked at Rose and her eyes prickled. She had never received a present like this before in her whole life.

'But it should be yours, Grannie Mac,' she said. 'It should be for you to wear.'

'Turn it over, child dear,' said Rose with a smile. 'And you'll understand.'

Anamar turned the watch over. James Hartington senior was well known for his skill as an engraver and on the back of the watch he had inscribed, as directed, of course, by his valued customer, Mrs Rose MacFadden,

To Anamar
From Grannie Mac
And Malachy Rice

Rose stood up and kissed her grand-daughter on the forehead.

'And may it serve you well your live-long day,' she said.

Anamar hugged her Grannie so tightly it almost hurt and not just for the gift alone. It was as if she wanted to show her love for her, from as far back as she could remember.

Later her father shook his head in disbelief when his daughter showed him her new Swiss gold watch. She knew her mother was pleased, although no one could have guessed.

'So that's what the oul one does when she has a bit of money,' she said. I'm sorry there weren't a few pounds about when I was your age.'

When Anamar was fifteen her beloved Grannie died and she grieved long and hard, but in secret. Her mother would have felt, and would have made it clear if necessary, that the display of a person's feelings was not seemly.

Coming Home

The day she was seventeen Anamar left the home which overlooked Lough Eske and walked down the lane. She had packed a few things in a carpet bag and carried it under her arm with the straps slung over her shoulder. In her pocket she had forty-five pounds given to her by Grannie Mac two days before she died. It seemed like a fortune, but Anamar knew it would soon go on travelling fares, bed and board. She would have to find work, but the money in her pocket would give a good start.

Before the bend she turned to wave, her mother a step or two outside the door, her father still inside but framed in the doorway. They had talked about dissuading her from leaving but it had seemed pointless to intervene. So they had said nothing. In their heads words formed that wished her well and hoped she would come back to see them - the father afraid of an even greater loneliness, the mother resentful of a parting not of her wish and outside her understanding.

Anamar looked up and across the field to what had once been her grandmother's cottage. When Grannie Mac had died, Anamar had cleaned and tidied every room. In a jar on a shelf beside the fire she had found the receipt for her watch on the note-paper of Hartington's The Jeweller...

> 'To one Rotary watch
> 9ct. gold, 15 jewel movement,
> with 9ct. gold expanding bracelet,
>
> | | | |
> |---|---|---|
> | Total | - | £6/17/6 |
> | less discount for cash | - | 5/0 |
> | Total Due | - | £6/12/6 ' |

Anamar had smiled as she put the receipt back in the jar. She could hear her Grannie Mac insisting on that discount. After one last look around to see that everything was in order she had closed the door and locked it with the big key. Inside, the pots sat on the dead hearth or hung by a crook from the crane. The crockery was still on the dresser. Nothing had been removed except the rubbish.

Nothing had been sold except the hens and the goat. In the back of her mind a thought was lodged. Some day she would live here. Grannie Mac's cottage would be her home.

She turned away and walked down towards the road. Someone who knew her would surely pass and offer her a lift. There was no turning back now. Now she was heading for the wider world.

A year later to the day, Anamar came back to Donegal and walked up the lane to the solid farmhouse which had once been her home. She had lived in Dublin and in France near the Pyrenees Mountains. She was the traveller returned. The home valley was even more beautiful than she remembered. The Blue Stack Mountains might well be much lower than the Pyrenees but they were a magnificent sky-line above the lake. Lough Eske's water flickered and shimmered like shards of a broken mirror stuck at random on a rough board, flashing at the sun.

Her father met her at the door. Like his late mother-in law he was tall but there the resemblance ceased. John Joe Cassidy was of sallow complexion, dark haired, slightly stooped and so thin it seemed he must be frail. To watch him work in the fields or cutting turf in the bog would have proved that such looks can be deceptive. When it was him against the land there was a frantic energy in his effort which allowed himself no quarter, no matter how arduous the job. John Joe seemed to shy away from people and in company he was embarrassed, awkward, even with those he knew well.

He shook Anamar's hand and followed her into the kitchen. His wife stood with her back to the open fire, arms folded across the bib of her apron. Una Cassidy thought she was smiling in welcome but her face showed no such greeting.

Anamar knew that apron well. Like the sheets on the bed and the shift her Grannie had worn under her dress, it was made from flour bags. Just as her Grannie Mac had taught her, she had carefully opened the seams of the bags. She had boiled and washed them, pounding and bleaching the closely woven cotton and hanging it out to bleach again in the sun's light until the print of the miller's name disappeared. She had cut and stitched the material and fashioned the kind of quality apron no money could buy. Even her mother had said she was pleased.

Una Cassidy's dark-brown hair was now mainly grey. She was nearly as tall as her husband but, like her mother, was of a much sturdier build. Her strong hands were reddened and becoming gnarled and painful with hard work and cold water. When she looked at someone, her dark eyes stared, as if there was a great deal to say which she had no intention of saying.

She hid her feelings from her husband and daughter, like she hid her body, behind that stout apron. Anamar knew she was welcome but saw no smiles and heard no words that would have told her so. It was exactly what she had expected but it saddened her all the same.

Her room in the loft was ready, the bed aired, the window cleaned outside and inside, as her mother had known she was coming. She pulled a chair across to the tiny window to look down on Lough Eske. This was the view she had carried with her on her travels. It had appeared unbidden in her mind's eye every day she had been away from it.

She saw the farm houses she knew amongst the bushes and woods of the low hills on the western side of the lake. Her Grannie Mac had told her that all seven noble trees of the sacred Irish grove - birch, alder, willow, oak, holly, hazel and apple, grew in their valley, and that the apple was the most noble tree of all. It was the tree of immortality.

It was the oak, however, which she revered as the sacred tree. It had given its Irish name, doire, or derry, to so many places in the province of Ulster. Ancient rites had been performed in its groves. Its wood was the most valuable of all trees. Its acorns could change the black coat of a horse to dapple grey. They could be used too in medicines so powerful they could only be prescribed with the greatest care.

The late afternoon sun glittered on the rippling water with that special brightness and shade which now, after her travels, she saw as Donegal's own special light. It was a view which, entirely on its own, would have brought her back.

Her time away from home had given Anamar an awareness of that special sense of place. In some locations she felt welcomed, accepted, not because of the people who might be there but by the place itself. In other locations, and for no reason of which she was aware, she might feel uncomfortable, ill-at-ease, perhaps even threatened.

It might be in a quiet corner of a village green or at a pavement table in a café on a town street. In the mountains she might sense it on a pass between high peaks, by a lake or a cascading stream or in a sheltered dell on a hillside. It could be in a room in a friend's house or sitting in a chair by a window. This sensation of being in the right or wrong setting was, for her, without any obvious evidence, unmistakable.

Now she realised that she had known this feeling since childhood. It was here, on this hillside above Lough Eske that she had felt it first, that sense of being totally at ease with her surroundings. As she ventured further away she had found more places which were welcoming, sympathetic, but had been surprised too, to find herself in other locations which were, unexpectedly, quite disquieting, perhaps even hostile.

On her own bed, in her own room, in one of her own most special places, she rested, and for a moment was at peace. There was so much to tell her parents. But would they listen? Could they let themselves hear what she had to say?

Earlier in the day, as she travelled by bus from Enniskillen to Ballyshannon and on by train to Donegal Town, a scene had come to mind. She was standing in the kitchen at home with her parents, speaking to them. But their eyes were blank, they were hearing nothing. The scene came to mind, clearer than ever, now that she was back. Before she slept she knew she still would have to speak.

In the morning Anamar sat between her parents. For nine months she had lived in Dublin, lodging with her father's sister Bridie and her husband Liam. Uncle Liam was a commercial traveller and had been able to find her a job in a book shop in Baggot Street. Although Anamar had not returned to Donegal during that time, she had written home every week without fail, never expecting a reply. Her letters had been in diary form, recounting what she had been doing and whom she had met, rather than recording her impressions of her new life. Even so, she had been sharing her life with her parents in a way she had never been able to do face to face, when she had been at home.

Occasionally her mother would reply, hoping she was fine, telling her that they were as well as could be expected, saying nothing.

After nine months she had gone to Lourdes with a parish pilgrimage and had decided to stay there for a time when the pilgrims returned. She had written to her employer in Dublin to give in her notice and had found employment almost immediately in a book shop in the commercial centre of Lourdes. The proprietor had been in the process of developing his stock of publications in English and needed someone to take a special interest in this section. The fact that she spoke English seemed to outweigh the fact that she was not yet fluent in French. He had asked her to start work the next day.

She continued to write home each week, describing the town of Lourdes, the pilgrimages, French customs, the food and farming. But there had been no replies from her mother.

As she sat with her parents in the farm kitchen and talked about her time in Dublin and Lourdes, she was aware that her words were only the traveller's tale that could be told to strangers. The real story would have to wait. Would they ever hear it at all?

Even more than that she wanted to tell them her Grannie Mac's story of the Seer of Belshade. But how could she explain that Grannie had told her that she, Anamar, might become the Seer, if she so wished? That she would dream dreams, be able to see the past in a person's eyes, foretell the future for good or ill but that these were as nothing compared with the greatest gift, the gift available to all. She would have the power to change the world.

The tongue-tied silence before the kitchen fire was suffocating them like a blow-down of smoke from the chimney. Anamar jumped up and went to the door as if to fill her lungs with fresh air. It gave her the courage to speak and she turned back to talk to them as Grannie Mac had talked to her, to speak as if she was the seanscealai.

Her father was wide-eyed, fearful. Her mother folded her arms across the bib of her apron. Neither spoke. This was beyond words.

The farm kitchen was almost silent. A stick in the fire hissed gently. A burning turf fell softly towards the back of the fire. A leg of her father's chair skraked on the tiled floor as he shifted uneasily. The wall clock ticked on the low beat that had been part of their lives for so long they had ceased to hear it.

Her mother stirred. She knew Anamar had dreamed dreams. The child had always been a dreamer, by day as well as night. She could believe that someone with the gift could see the past in another's eyes. It was easy too, to accept that such a person could foretell the future for good or ill. Such powers are rare but not unknown in Donegal.

Una had always known that her mother had the gift, although, if she used it at all, it was hidden in her stories. She had a strange feeling too, that had she herself tried, she might have been able to awaken such power in her own mind. There had been times when flashes of insight had made her sure she could do it, but fear of the unknown had made her hesitate and the revelations never came.

But the very idea that the power to change the world was available to all, that she could not believe. Where politicians and governments had failed, where sages, armies, dictators, priests, even the Pope himself had failed, only God could succeed. Only God could change the world.

Una said her piece and stopped as if there was nothing else that could be added. John Joe nodded his agreement. A lifetime of learning when to speak and when to stay silent was standing by him now.

Anamar sighed, suddenly more tired than ever she had been on the longest day of her travels.

'God does not change the world,' she said patiently. 'He leaves that to us.'

Her father's face was impassive. Her mother's lips tightened as if she was trying not to speak. Una hesitated. Then a voice she herself hardly recognised as her own came out with the words.

'Was this not a heresy? God is all powerful, God is the Almighty. The birds fly, the wind blows at his command. Drought and plenty are his to choose. Nations prosper or decline at one nod of his head. Every footstep is directed, every breath breathed or held, or stopped forever at his decree.'

Una had never spoken like this before but years of listening in church without hearing the words had still managed to lodge them in her mind. There was a long pause. The silence separated the three of them, the one from each of the others.

Anamar shook her head, not knowing how to continue. What she had said had horrified her mother but she knew it was only because her mother had misunderstood. She wanted to say, 'It's my own life I'm speaking about. I mean I can change my world, not change the world for everyone.'

But it was too late, too late now to back-track. Anything she said now would only make it worse. Now was not the time to explain. Bitter experience reminded her that it would be better to try again later, much later, to start from a different place, to find a way to have a discussion rather than an argument. She sighed, this chance had gone.

Una's face lost its colour. Her cheeks were drawn but not now in anger. She had the dreadful sense that her daughter, her only child, had lost her faith. How could it be otherwise? Anamar was doubting the very basis of their Holy Catholic faith.

'We will have to get the priest,' she said at last. 'It's the only way.'

Anamar's head went down and a sharp, audible sigh seemed to drain all the air from her body.

John Joe always knew what was expected of him by the look on his wife's face. He was relieved to have something to do, an errand that would take him out of the house and away from this struggle between two women he neither understood nor even seemed to know. He caught the pony in the wee field behind the house and had him harnessed between the shafts of the trap in minutes. The priest would be at the school that morning and it was only a couple of miles down the road. If he hurried he would catch him before he left.

The priest stopped his black Ford Prefect directly in front of the house.

'He's that proud of his grand carriage he'd park it in the kitchen if the door was bigger.' Anamar's mother's tone was sharp. She said it loudly as if she wanted the priest to hear. She might be facing a dire family situation but she could never abide show, not even by a man of the cloth.

Father Brogan was in his early forties. He was small, stockily-built, always neatly dressed, very confident of himself, regarded by some as authoritarian. He had been born and reared in the County Cavan and, although he had come to this part of Donegal five years before as parish priest, he knew that he was still regarded as a new-comer.

It was not that any of his parishioners would have made life difficult for him deliberately, that was not their way. However, he was aware that they had expectations of their priest which, without telling him what these were, he would be expected to live up to. There had been times he had needed all his self-possession and all the authority granted him by the church to ensure that he was accorded his proper place.

He came into the kitchen and smiled. Anamar drew a slow breath. This was another scene that had slipped into her mind when she was travelling back to Donegal. It was no surprise that it had changed so quickly from image to reality. But that it was inevitable caused her pain. She tried to smile too and failed.

For her own reasons Anamar's mother did not say that her daughter had dreamed dreams and could see the past in a person's eyes. Neither did she say that Anamar thought she could foretell the future for good or ill. She simply told the priest that her daughter did not believe that God had the power to change the world. Anamar shook her head and said nothing.

The priest was well aware that Anamar had been away from the area for quite a while. He knew too, that when young people left home, particularly for the big cities like Dublin and London, their faith could be undermined as regular devotions became irregular or lapsed entirely. He looked directly at her and frowned.

'What gives you the right …?' He paused, the words hanging in the air as if he felt them too harsh, perhaps realising that he had not given Anamar a chance to speak and knew that he was too late now to ask.

Words of reply began to form in Anamar's head but she stopped herself. She had read and prayed about such things, perhaps thought about them as much as he had.

It was so uncannily like the vision of this moment which had appeared in her mind on the way home. She had known then that she would not be able to explain, Now she could see no way to turn back. Annoyance changed to indignation at being made to feel that it was her thoughts that were sinful, negative, at odds with the world. She took a deep breath and thought of the good times here in the valley. The anger eased but she knew she had to distance herself from this hearth, to find some other way to let her thoughts be known.

It seemed a long way up the stairs to her room. The small haversack she had brought back from France was hanging behind the door. She put a few personal things into it, items she might need if she was away for some days. Back in the kitchen she shook her father's hand and put her other hand on her mother's shoulder. Her loose, dark blue coat, like a cape, was on its nail. She took it over her arm and left the house by the open door. They looked after her but no one followed to see her turn and wave.

They were on their knees, all three of them, a man who had only known life in this valley, a woman who had tholed marriage here for forty years as best she could, and a priest confronted for the first time in this way. Father Brogan felt no great self assurance now, nor any grand authority, temporal or spiritual. He tried to lead the man and woman in prayer to a God he accepted as his Lord but at this moment wondered if he knew.

Anamar did not go past the priest's car and down the lane to the road. She followed the track in front of the byre and across the hillside. Her grandmother's cottage, still unoccupied, was above, a big field away. She needed time on her own. Time to think, rather than to talk. Her instincts had already told her where she must go. Now she was on her way.

The Lough of the Jewel Mouth

At the high field the lane became a track on the hillside. Anamar followed it to the river and crossed the stepping stones on the upper side of the ford. Her first stride took her straight back to childhood. This was where she had played with Maureen and Eamon, the two youngest of the McGinley children, jumping from stone to stone, racing sticks in the water, building a harbour with rocks, damming a tributary stream to make a dam and a waterfall.

Maureen was her own age, so similar in looks, height and build, they might have been twins. Eamon was a year younger, dark and stocky, strong enough by the age of nine to help his father with the heavy jobs of the farm, full of restless energy, cheerful, good-natured, easy to talk to. 'The boy who always smiles', Miss Ryan, their teacher used to say when she was pleased with his work.

The McGinley's farm and land was on the other side of the river and the children had become Anamar's friends as soon as they were big enough to leap from stone to stone across the stepping stones.

Neither of her friends had uttered a word the day she told them that she was changing her name. From now on she was to be called Anamar. Eamon had smiled as usual but for once had said nothing. Although the others were aware of the wilful side of Anamar's nature, she herself was not. But here was the proof of it. And anyway, when they did have a fall-out, it was always two to one, the two girls against the one boy. Eamon did not seem to mind. He took it for granted that, should there be a disagreement, he would have to deal with both of them.

Before they reached their 'teens the river had become their passage to adventure. They followed it up the hillside to where it cascaded through rapids and over little waterfalls, rushing headlong down towards Lough Eske.

Maureen and Eamon's older brothers and sisters had all left home so there was no one to show them where to go, to take them to new places. These walks were their very own.

When the girls were twelve and Eamon eleven they had discovered its source, a small lake, linked to other lakes amongst the peaks near Croaghnageer. From there they could explore the high land and count the lakes and loughans. Master

Robson, their teacher, would have been secretly delighted had he known, for Geography was his passion. The shape and form of this part of Donegal had drawn him here to the small country school below the Blue Stack Mountains.

The children had their own name for this place in the mountains above their homes, they called it 'The Twelve Loughs'.

If the weather turned bad, the wind and rain sweeping in from the west or the mist slipping silently in behind them, the river was their life-line. They could use it as their escape route from the higher slopes, following it down to the ford and home.

Anamar felt her spirits rise as she remembered those good times. The McGinley's farm was just over the next rise but she needed one more step back into the past before she called to see her friends.

Above on the hillside, near the middle of a small field was a thorn bush. Years ago, when the field was first cleared, it had been left, a fairy thorn standing alone, left undisturbed by tradition and fear. The three friends thought of it as their very own tree and would often go to it, taking turns to stand within its branches. As they grew older, Eamon was not so sure but the girls remained certain. Inside the arms of the thorn you could make a wish, a wish which could not be told without the risk of losing it forever.

Anamar climbed the slope and slipped in amongst the twisted branches, resting her back on the trunk. She laid her hands gently on the arms of the thorn. Years of trying had taught her that the wish must not be for herself. That should have been easier now, much easier than in childhood. For a moment it was, and then it was not. It took a few moments for the confusion in her mind to settle. Then she gripped the branches of the bush and wished.

The McGinley's dog knew she was coming when she was still a hundred yards away and his barks brought Maureen and Eamon out to see who it was.

'I knew you were back,' said Maureen, once they had greeted each other. 'I saw the candle in your window last night. It had to be you.'

Neither Maureen nor Eamon asked where she had travelled, or whom she had met or how she had lived. As always, Anamar would tell them when she was ready.

'Where are you for?' asked Eamon. He had noticed the haversack slung from her shoulder and the coat over her arm and guessed that she was stopping with them for a few moments only.

They listened as Anamar told them of her conversation with her parents and the visit of the priest. She needed to tell them but when she had finished neither could find a word to say.

'I'm off to Lough Belshade for a day or two,' Anamar continued as if she expected no comment. 'When Father Brogan leaves, would you tell my mother not to worry? Maybe you'll be up to see me at the lake.' Although the invitation was less than direct she really needed them to come and to come that afternoon. She had no food with her, nor any of the things which she would need for a stay of a few days.

Like Anamar, Maureen and Eamon knew Belshade. Of all the lakes in the hills it was their favourite. It lay to the north of Lough Eske, in the very heart of the Blue Stack Mountains, hidden in a bowl-shaped depression behind a ridge of hills, surrounded by cliffs and steep slopes.

Visitors might come to Lough Eske and find a beauty that not many local people saw, although they looked at it day and daily. Tourists often said that it was the most beautiful lake in Ireland but then it was unlikely that any of them would have seen Belshade.

Lough Belshade was seldom visited except by a shepherd or the very hardiest of fly fishermen, heading for the water they called 'Fat Trout Lake' to keep its name a secret from other anglers. An occasional hill walker or naturalist might pass this way, or that rarest of rare birds, an intrepid rock climber seeking a pioneering route on the cliffs around the lake, fit to test his skill and daring.

The three friends had been to Belshade a number of times. It was a two-and-a-half hour walk from home so it was a full day's outing. Usually their visits had been in the summer holidays but once they had gone in the winter when there was ice on the bog and streaks of frozen snow on the peaks.

They knew the little beach at the north end of the lake. Near it was a cave formed by a great stone resting on smaller rocks. This was their favourite place of all. The wind from the south-west made little waves on the lake water washing gently on the beach. The cave was their shelter. They had covered the floor with dried grass and heather and used sods to block draughty holes and cracks. It was dry and cosy, a haven from the wildest wind and rain.

Eamon was the practical one.

'We know you're the great world traveller,' he said with a grin. 'But we'd better bring you a blanket and some food. It wouldn't do if you died of cold or hunger. Father Brogan might think it was something he'd said.'

Maureen was already making out in her head a list of the food that would be needed. Knowing Anamar, she might stay for more than a day or two. She began to fuss about what they should bring.

Anamar laughed for the first time since she had arrived back in Donegal. This was more like it. Now she was with true friends. They needed no explanations, no reasons, no excuses. They understood. Their help was available without request.

When it was time to go she walked for a hundred yards or more and turned to wave. They were still standing where she had left them, Eamon with his two arms above his head.

'See you later!' he yelled.

Maureen gave him a dig in the ribs with her elbow. Their mother hated the sound of them roaring at one another across the fields.

Anamar smiled and silently mouthed a reply. Her voice would not have carried the distance no matter how hard she had shouted. She smiled and held up her hands to them. Her friends had been part of the vision of her return. She had not realised then how much she was going to need them. Now she knew.

She turned away and headed for the mountains. Back home in Donegal the sensation of being on her own was so different from being alone when she had been away. It was so unexpected to feel it here. The shock of it almost made her turn back but it was too late now, she was already on her way.

The track took her around the hillside. Below, on the road that circled the lake, a car crawled behind a horse and cart, waiting to pass. She crossed the Corabber River on the stepping stones at another ford and headed for the Grey Farm.

The Corabber River's source was Lough Belshade and it dropped steeply down from the high ground to flow into the very head of Lough Eske. Connecting the two lakes made the river the link between Anamar's home in the valley and her destination in the hills.

The sun glittered on the surface of Lough Eske. It was surrounded on the slopes by farms and scrub land and rough grazing. The little houses were set amongst pines and a host of bushes, laurel, holly, gorse, rhododendron, hazel, blackthorn, willow. Above were the hills which bounded and sheltered the valley. On all her travels Anamar had seen nowhere more beautiful than the setting of Lough Eske below her.

There was no one around when she passed the Grey Farm and the good track climbed steeply towards a cleft cut by the river. She left the main path and walked around a shoulder of rock to see the Doonan Waterfall, hiding in the cleft. This was as far as the visitors came up the gorge. They would have needed to go very close to the edge to see the fall. It was hiding under the lip of a slippery bank, on a steep grassy slope. For those with nerve, peeping over, holding on to someone's hand for security, there it was, the whole flow of the Corabber River dropping over a rocky ledge, cascading down forty or fifty feet into a dark, deep pool in the heart of the ravine.

The visitors would have found the short walk up from the road a stiff climb but would have told each other that the Doonan Waterfall and the view of Lough Eske below were worth the exertion. They would have said that all the best views in Donegal had to be earned with a bit of effort.

Anamar knew that there was another view of the Doonan Waterfall which the tourists would have missed. Eamon had discovered it the first time they had come here. He had gone back down along the edge of the cliff and found a way into the base of the gorge. It was on a very steep and slippery slope but she and Maureen had been able to follow him with some difficulty. The reward had been to sit on a big rock at the edge of the pool and watch the white water falling into it from the cliffs above. It was another one of their secret places, as if only known to themselves and they had visited the pool every time they had trekked up to Belshade.

Those adventures now seemed so long ago. On this day she was alone, and although she was much more experienced in scrambling over rough steep ground, Anamar decided that it would be too dangerous to try on her own to follow Eamon's route to the pool in the depths of the gorge.

Higher up, the stony track gave way to a faint path on boggy land beside the river. The trick was to find a dry footing on every step. To a townie the bog would all look the same but to have been born in these parts left no excuse for finding the good path except in the very wettest of weather.

An hour later, where a tributary met the river, Anamar turned left to follow the main stream towards the crest. It was much steeper here and the water gushed down in its rocky bed in surging cascades. She had been here before but had never climbed the slope with such excitement. The speed of ascent left her breathless and she remembered what her friend in the Pyrenees would have said.

'Doucement! Doucement!' Hank would have called softly as they climbed a steep valley towards the high peaks, encouraging her to take it easy.

Anamar smiled to herself. Now she was home, would she get around to telling Maureen about Hank? She laughed aloud. Of course she would. What were friends for if you were not able to confide in them.

There was no path on the rocky terrain. She looked up and saw a view of cliffs behind the ridge. The cloud thickened as a skiffle of rain swept in and she pulled her coat on around her shoulders. She and her mother had made the coat using a pattern and a remnant of tweed bought from Magee's in the town. The material was closely woven, cut like a cape and a great comfort in bad weather. In a few strides she reached the crest and there it was, Lough Belshade, set in a rock basin, virtually surrounded by steep buttresses, its waters dark and choppy.

It might be a dull day now but the flow from the lake's mouth sparkled on the rocks as it fell towards the valley and Anamar knew this was the place which had given the lake its name.

However, before their first visit to Lough Belshade, Anamar and her friends had learned about the lake and the Blue Stack Mountains at school.

The National School which they attended had one large room which the two teachers shared, one at each end, facing each other. The Principal and his assistant may have lacked the privacy of a separate teaching space but each had a fireplace and a black-board and his and her own territory.

Geography, especially the Geography of the Hills of Donegal, was the love of Master Robson's life. School inspectors, a most formidable breed of former teachers, might have been brave enough, on the day, to hint that perhaps a little too much time was spent on this particular subject. But Master Robson would not be listening. He was certain that he owed it to his pupils to share with them his fascination for their own mountains. It was why he had come to Donegal. It was the reason he had stayed when many a time he had felt drawn back home across the North Channel of the Irish Sea.

Jamie Robson was a lowland Scot, short in stature but heavily built, as if designed for a life of hard physical labour. He had unruly black hair, streaked with grey and black eyebrows, each of which seemed to have a life of its own. To those who did not know him he seemed dour, unfriendly, self-absorbed. His few friends knew otherwise. They recognised his serious disposition, the intensity of his interests, the passion and energy of the man.

School discipline had never been a problem for Master Robson. He had a fierce tongue, used rarely, but to great effect when required. He possessed a violent temper and the threat of it had been sufficient. Few had ever seen it in full flow. It was his passion for the education of his pupils which made his teaching successful. Every boy and girl in the school knew that the Master would accept nothing but their best work.

His father was a Donegal man who had spent his winters working in Scotland, had married a Glasgow girl and settled in that city. His children had been born and reared there and he had never been able to persuade his wife to visit Ireland. His eldest son however, had decided that he wanted to teach in his father's country but, although he had qualified with commendation as a teacher in Scotland, to practice in Ireland required the possession of an Irish/English Bilingual Certificate. It might have been a stumbling block. However, with his father's help, he had scraped through oral and written tests at the second attempt.

Jamie Robson took the senior end of the school. He was a strict principal, not averse to applying the stick to the hand or the hind end of any boy who broke one of his spoken or unspoken rules. The girls he kept in order with his tongue and fearsome glare. Some said he had written Geography text-books used in colleges and that was easy to believe on the evidence of the wonderful maps which he drew on the black-board.

Each map was an artistic creation in coloured chalk. The rivers were thin blue lines, the sea and lakes hatched in blue. The forests were shaded in green, the mountains in brown. Red was for roads, towns and villages and the place names were carefully inscribed in white.

At the end of the school day, the pupil chosen to clean the board usually did so reluctantly, as if it was a shame to erase such a work of art.

One Monday morning the Master finished his map of the Lough Eske Valley and the Blue Stack Mountains and, as he stepped back, the class drew a collective quiet breath in almost silent admiration. It was as if the Master was paying them all a compliment by depicting their part of the country so beautifully. Master Robson would normally have been suspicious of such a display of appreciation but on this occasion he almost smiled.

For once the map was allowed to stay on the board after school, to allow everyone to make a fair copy. Next morning however, one of the boys had come in early and signed the map with the Master's nickname.

It was Master Robson's practice to go into the bar of the hotel in the town for a drink. His order was always the same. 'Whisky!' he would say, 'Proper whisky, Scotch whisky, wi' no 'e'.' So, out of his hearing, he had been christened, by a fellow patron, 'Whisky Jock.' The name had stuck, although no one had ever been known to call him this to his face.

In the bottom left-hand corner, the splendid map was signed in bold capitals, 'WHISKY JOCK'.

When his eye caught sight of the offending signature, Master Robson had grabbed the duster and scrubbed the map from the board. In one movement he spun around on his heels and flung the wooden-backed duster towards the back of the room. It scored a direct hit on Mick Hourrigan's head, sending chalk dust flying, pomading his hair like a Georgian dandy's wig

'Never think ye'll disguise your handiwork from me, laddie, nor that I'll forget ye for this.' For the rest of the day the class found themselves working harder than ever before on their least favourite lessons, long multiplication sums and detailed parsing of sentences.

By the middle of that week Anamar, Maureen and Eamon had begun to plan a walk. They had been hearing about Lough Belshade for years. Now they had a map which showed them exactly where it was. On Saturday they would leave as soon as they had finished their farm chores and head for it. Master Robson had said that it was the most beautiful lake of them all, surrounded by peaks, at the very heart of the Blue Stacks.

But it was not from Master Robson that Anamar had learned the secret of Lough Belshade's name.

Miss Ryan was Master Robson's assistant. She taught the junior classes and once Anamar had passed from her class into the Master's she found, that, far from losing touch with Miss Ryan, the teacher no longer regarded her as a pupil but as someone whose company she seemed to enjoy.

Deirdre Ryan came from Greystones in County Wicklow. She was tall, an imposing figure, somewhat angular in build, a handsome woman, always well-spoken, well-groomed, well-dressed. The school might be in the depths of County Donegal but Miss Ryan saw that as no reason to let her standards slip.

She was liked by children, but they kept their distance, familiarity was not encouraged. Most of the parents found her rather grand in her way and kept their distance too. Many were secretly pleased that their children were taught to read and write so well, that Miss Ryan insisted on good manners and cleanliness, that the early education of their offspring was in the hands of someone so dignified.

Anamar's mother would have said, 'Miss Hoity-Toity Ryan thinks she's a cut above the rest of us, keeps herself to herself, just the way a teacher should.'

Deirdre Ryan had a small two-storeyed house on the main road and most of her friends lived in or near Donegal Town. She owned a handsome dark green Riley sports car which betrayed the fact that she had an income to live on other than her teacher's salary. Deirdre loved driving and touring by car. On a Friday after school she would sometimes set off for a week-end in Dublin and every year she spent most of the long summer holidays abroad, usually in France and Italy.

Although her circle of friends was small, they had an active social life centred around tennis, bridge, music and the Drama Club in the town. Together they toured scenic parts of the country by car. Deirdre had a passionate interest in books. Her little house was lined with book shelves, carefully installed by a local carpenter in the very best mahogany.

She belonged to book clubs and received their monthly offers. She bought books by post from book shops in London and Dublin. If there were second-hand books at an auction of house-contents or a church sale, Miss Ryan would be there searching for literary treasures. And it was books which brought Anamar and Deirdre together as friends after they had been pupil and teacher.

While she was still in her class, Miss Ryan had seen Anamar's interest in reading and encouraged her, not only with books which would help with lessons, but with school stories, travel and nature books, history, general knowledge, poetry. She lent Anamar books from her own shelves, showed her the latest editions from the book club and when Anamar had passed out of Miss Ryan's classes, it was as if they were now free to become friends.

She became a frequent visitor to the house with the books. She still called her former teacher, Miss Ryan, and Deirdre was comfortable with that form of address. She enjoyed the young company and the conversations. They talked about films, drama on the wireless and the plays put on by local groups. They discussed the awful events of the war and the news, features and advertisements in the Donegal Democrat. Deirdre enjoyed telling Anamar about the fashions and the great social life to be had in Dublin and the art galleries, concerts, theatres and music halls.

They listened to records played on Deirdre's wind-up gramophone. Her friends would never have believed Anamar if she had told them that as well as the classical records and Irish music, Deirdre's collection included jazz, singers like Al Jolson, dance bands, crooners like Bing Crosby.

But most of all Anamar wanted to hear of Deirdre's travels abroad. Deirdre would fetch the photographs and post cards which she had arranged in albums, each snap or card carefully attached to the page with tiny black photo-corners and neatly labelled. Her traveller's tales would take them both to the very village in France she was talking about. They could almost hear the sounds of its market place and smell the cheese, wine and garlic on the stalls.

Anamar would sit on a cushion on the floor beside Deirdre's chair with her arms around her knees. In her mind's eye she was there too. It was far more evocative and exciting than the cinema, as if Deirdre had taken her to the very place.

France was Deirdre's favourite foreign country and one evening after she had been telling Anamar about the Loire Valley she shook a finger at her, mocking her own way of admonishing a pupil.

'If you're going to travel, m'girl,' she had said. 'We'd better start teaching you a foreign language.' From then on, each time Anamar visited her, they set aside a short time for what Deirdre called 'our French lesson'.

Without either making the slightest conscious effort Anamar's education was expanding, taking her into a new world beyond the valley of Lough Eske, beyond the shores of Ireland.

On the Friday evening of the week the map had appeared on the school blackboard, Anamar had cycled down to the main road to show Miss Ryan her sketch of the Blue Stacks and tell her of the walk they were planning to Lough Belshade. Deirdre Ryan had smiled. She would have loved to have gone with them but this had to be their walk, their own adventure. She had gone to the shelves in her bedroom where she kept her books on Ireland and returned with a big blue volume.

'Now there's a story in this book that you must read before you go,' she had said. 'I'm sure you remember me talking about Robert Lloyd Praeger. This is his famous book about Ireland, 'The Way That I Went'. In the chapter about Donegal he mentions Belshade and tells how the lake got its name, Bel Sead, the lough of the jewel mouth.'

Anamar had wrapped the big book in brown paper to keep it clean and padded it with newspaper before strapping it on the carrier of her bicycle for the journey home. In her own room, in her own bed, she had opened the untrimmed pages and found the right page. Praeger was careful to explain that he had taken the story from notes of a lecture given in the nineteenth century but based on a version in a much older book in Irish.

She must have finished the story before she had gone to sleep. Although the book was lying open beside her on the quilt as if it had slipped from her hands as she nodded off, the whole story was set in her mind. She would tell Maureen and Eamon about it, she decided, only when they reached the lake next day.

And here she was, years later, on her own journey, at the very place where she had told her friends the secret of Belshade's name.

The three of them had arrived then at the lake's mouth in the early afternoon, ready for the sandwiches they had brought as their picnic. It had been a warm day but not too hot. Even on the uphill walk, a light wind from the south had kept them cool. They had sat in a hollow sheltered from the breeze and watched the stream flow from the lake as they ate. Anamar had turned to face them both.

'Have you heard of Coerabar Boeth of the fairy mansions of Connacht?' she said and, like her Granny Mac, not expecting an answer, as if she was the seanscealai now. 'Well Coerabar Boeth was the very beautiful and wonderfully gifted daughter of Etal Enbuail. She had three times fifty maidens to attend her. Every year they were all transformed into three times fifty birds and the next year restored to their natural shapes.

'While they were transformed they lived high in the mountains, at a lake called Loch Crotta Claith. There, the birds were chained in couples by silver chains. Amongst them was the most beautiful bird in the world. She had a necklace of red Irish gold with three times fifty chains suspended from it, each chain ending in a ball of gold.'

Anamar had paused. She could see that this was not the kind of tale which Eamon liked. He was probably thinking that he had left all this fairy story nonsense behind him, years ago. But Maureen had been fascinated. She had always loved the stories from the Irish and this one had been new to her. Anamar had pointed to the stream which was the outflow from the lake, the mouth of Belshade. The water sparkled and flashed in the sunshine

'This is where the birds stayed. This is where they lived while they were transformed. And when the local people came to see them, they stood here where we are now, and marvelled. They could talk of nothing but the jewels at the mouth of Loch Crotta. From then on the name of the lake was changed. It became Lough Bel Sead, the Lake of the Jewel Mouth.'

Maureen had been enchanted. She had clapped almost silently with her finger nails. Eamon had started to smile and turned away quickly in case he might laugh and spoil the story.

And now Anamar was here again on the very spot but this time she was on her own. She felt lonely. She wanted company so that she could tell the story again. It would not have mattered if Eamon had been there, laughing. She longed to share this moment. She needed her friends.

The sky slowly brightened behind her. The lake glittered as a patch of sunlight flitted across the water. Anamar stood up and began to walk around the shore towards the beach at the furthest corner.

It took longer and was much more strenuous than she remembered. The ground was rough. There were peaty banks to cross where rivulets in flood had washed a channel through the turf. It was so very different from the way up to the lake. There the climb was steady, the cascades and waterfalls drawing her upwards rather than down with the water's flow. The crest of a little ridge hid the far end of the lake. She smiled to herself. They had always felt they were almost there when they had reached the mouth of the lake and it had always taken much longer than expected from there to the beach.

Anamar crossed the low end of the ridge which ran down from the cliffs to her right; and there it was, the little corner of the valley she had held in her mind's eye since she had left her home three hours before. On her left hand was the Lough. Straight ahead were the great rock buttresses below the Blue Stacks peaks. At the bottom of the nearest cliff was the rock face she and her friends called the Pink Wall and below it the tiny, gravel beach.

A short distance from the water's edge, at the top of a mound, a huge stone lay across rocks, forming a cave. Below its entrance was a tiny, sheltered dell. It was secluded, remote. Here, there was the feeling of isolation she needed. But this was the first time she had been to Belshade on her own. In the few months she had been away from home she had learned to live with loneliness. She had accepted the solitary life that came with having a room of her own in a foreign town, in a foreign country. She had even made a mountain journey in the Pyrenees alone.

But here, so close to home, there was a detachment from her friends and family that brought a stomach-turning surge of fear. She would have to accept loneliness as a companion if she was to stay here for even one night.

Anamar busied herself to take her mind off depressing thoughts. Near-by a little stream emerged from a deep gully and tumbled down into the lough. She knew that water. It was good. She peeped inside the cave and found it as dry and sheltered as ever. She sat down on a stone outside, suddenly so tired, not in her legs as she might have expected, but in her mind. The physical effort of walking up to the lake was no more than she was used to, but after the conversation with her mother and the priest the effort of getting to the lake had drained the little energy of spirit that remained.

With an effort she stirred herself and felt hungry. Having brought no food with her, hunger seemed pointless and the pangs eased. She crouched beside the stream, sipping water from her cupped hands, and found herself smiling. Every time she drank from a stream like this, she remembered one of her favourite bible stories. It told how Gideon had chosen his warriors before he faced the Midianites. 'Would he have picked me?' she wondered. 'I always crouch and lap from my hands rather than drink directly from the stream.' Her smile broadened. 'But would he have chosen a woman?' She laughed at the very idea of it. 'Would only men have been selected by Gideon, and maybe God too, for their most important work?'

The little diversion cheered her up and she gathered a great armful of dry grass and heather to add to that already in the cave.

Towards mid-afternoon Maureen and Eamon came up the valley and crossed the ridge which hid the lake. Once over the rise Eamon was walking so fast Maureen though he was running over the rough ground. She took it much more easily. There were rocks and weathered turf banks to cross and there was no sense rushing when they were almost there.

Eamon saw Anamar sitting at the water's edge, so still she might have been a part of the landscape. Glimmers of sunshine were breaking through the cloud. The breeze was from the west. Its soft air rippled the water and ruffled Anamar's hair. She was watching the light glittering on the surface of the lake so intently she had neither seen nor heard their approach.

Eamon stopped to wait for Maureen as if he was too shy to go any further on his own. Anamar turned her head and saw her friends approaching. She waited where she was and let them come to her.

'We thought that even you couldn't live on fresh air alone so we've brought you food,' said Maureen, by way of greeting.

'And a few other things too,' said Eamon not wanting to be left out. He swung from his back a light creel made from willow wands to carry turf. It was filled with every item they could think of which Anamar would need if she was to stay here for a few days.

They unpacked a woollen blanket and a small towel wrapped around a piece of soap, a tooth brush and a tin of tooth paste. There was a cardboard box of food, two candles, a box of matches, three blue and white ringed delph mugs and three tin plates. A folded tea cloth made from a flour bag contained a sharp knife, a fork and two spoons.

At the bottom of the creel, below a layer of newspaper, there was a cooking pot and a frying pan. They were wedged in with a Primus stove wrapped in paper, as were two glass bottles, a small one of methylated spirit to light the stove and a much larger one of paraffin oil as fuel.

Maureen arranged the items on a bank so that Anamar could see the full extent of her stores. Eamon was already opening the food box. He was hungry. There was a slab of their own butter wrapped in grease-proof paper, a dozen eggs, individually wrapped in newspaper, a brown paper bag of vegetables, a large pot of home-made rhubarb jam and a jar of their father's honey. At the bottom of the box was a slab of cheese and a parcel of bacon rashers, a small tin of tea, soda and wheaten bread and a bag of flour protecting the eggs and the glass jars.

Anamar was radiant with pleasure. Her friends understood. They had been thinking of her, determined to help. She had never been more pleased to have company in her whole life. The three of them sat in the dell outside the cave while the water boiled on the Primus stove. Eamon made a sour face when he tasted the tea.

'We didn't bring sugar because you don't take it and we had nothing to carry the milk in, so this tea tastes like poison.'

'Just as well I like tea on its own,' said Anamar laughing. 'It's wonderful what you learn on your travels. This is the way they take tea in France. You'll have to try it sometime or you'll be a country boy all your life.'

'I'll make you something,' said Eamon. 'That you won't have tasted on your travels.'

The stove was already turned down to a low flame and he melted some butter in the frying pan. He topped and tailed four fat scallions from his garden at home and chopped them into the sizzling butter. With the speed of an expert cook, he broke four eggs into the pan, stirred them with the scallions and let them cook very gently.

Maureen sighed with an air of feigned resignation.

'This is his big moment,' she said. 'Mother taught him to make what she calls 'scumbled eggs'. The scallions are his own touch and now he thinks he's a great cook. He's probably invented some fancy name for it.'

The girls laughed at Eamon's embarrassment and the delicious, appetising smell told them the eggs were ready. For the first time in a long while, Anamar was looking forward to the food. When she was a child, meals at home had been simple but she had always been well-fed, even during the war when some foods were rationed. During her travels in France food had often been scarce but there had been times when she had had the chance to appreciate good cooking. Now she was looking forward to something special.

Eamon split and buttered three big farls of soda bread. He spooned the scumbled egg on to the six pieces in exactly equal portions with a precision which only an eight-year old could have bettered.

'I'll never be able to manage two of them,' said Anamar, but she did.

The three of them sat on a bank, each with a mug of tea wedged beside them on the ground and a tin plate on their knees. They passed the knife around and cut the bread into manageable strips.

When she had finished, she found herself talking excitedly. Usually she was the quiet one, listening while Maureen chattered and Eamon tried to outdo her.

When she had left home to live in Dublin, Anamar and Maureen had written to each other. A letter from Anamar had explained that she was going to Lourdes with a parish group which included some ill and disabled people. From then on Anamar's letters from France had been very brief, as if she had much to say but had no intention of committing it to paper.

Now she was telling them about the pilgrimage to Lourdes, the journey out in an old 'bus which broke down three times on the drive through France. She described the church services and the candle-lit processions at night. She talked about the work the helpers did to bring the ill and disabled to the baths and to visit the grotto.

When it was time for the parish group to go home, Anamar had begun to wonder about the real reasons which brought so many people from so many countries to Lourdes over the years. The ill and the disabled might have come seeking a miracle but was there a healing they sought which was even more important than a physical cure? She had decided to stay on for a while and had found a job in a book shop in the town.

'One day I was serving behind the counter,' she began to tell them. 'When an American came into the shop to see if we had any maps of the Pyrenees Mountains …' She stopped abruptly, amazed at how much she was talking.

'But that's a long story,' she said. 'We'd better leave it to your next visit.'

Maureen and Eamon knew they would hear no more for the present. This was the Anamar they had always known, ready to let them chatter, in control of what she herself said, more comfortable as the listener, the observer.

'We'll be back the day after to-morrow,' said Eamon. 'Is there anything else you want us to bring?'

Anamar told them not to be concerned about her.

'Don't worry,' said Maureen. You can be certain of one thing. We'll be back. I can't wait to hear about this American of yours.'

It was early evening when they left, the empty creel swinging from the leather shoulder straps on Eamon's back as he turned to wave. And when they crossed the ridge which led to the valley below, Anamar felt totally on her own.

She would live with the loneliness. She wrapped her coat like a cloak around her and hardly moved as the evening slipped stealthily across the lake towards the cave.

While there was still a little light, she brought everything inside the cave. Maureen had included four blanket pins, like huge safety pins. Anamar folded the blanket in three, length-wise and used the pins at the bottom and on one side to make it into a bag.

She took off her outer clothes and slipped into the blanket bag resting on a bed of grass and heather, two thicknesses of the material below and one above. She rolled her cardigan into the shape of a pillow and pulled her coat over the bag.

Before she slept, she had intended to go over the events of the day in her mind, but it was too late. She was asleep as soon as her head touched her pillow.

The Cave at the Lake

When she awoke next morning, Anamar was immediately aware of where she was. Often on her travels she would stir from a deep sleep knowing she was in a strange place but not sure precisely where she was staying. Now the cave was a haven. She was here, beside Belshade. It felt as if she was in the safest of places. A place where she would be able to think without fear, without worry about other people's rules and taboos.

The sun was shining but the lake was as cold as a glacier stream in the Pyrenees. Anamar knew what it was like to wash in a stream fed by the snow melt from high peaks but it was still a surprise to feel the same stinging chill in the mountain water of her own county in summer.

She had left her clothes in a neat pile on a rock and stood ankle deep, splashing herself all over, shoulders first and face last. In seconds it was finished and she hopped out to scrub herself dry with the little towel. The soap sat on a stone, unused, unneeded. The intention had been to wade out for a total immersion but this quick dip, her mother would have called it 'a lick and a promise', would have to do for the present.

Walking back to the cave, her whole body surged with energy, she laughed out loud at the idea of leaving home to come here for a few days without food, or a blanket to keep warm at night or even soap and a towel for a daily wash. She really would have to thank Maureen and Eamon properly. It was not enough to feel grateful, she would have to say something.

Breakfast was a split farl of wheaten bread and a mug of tea. Anamar had not looked at her watch since she had risen and was surprised to find that it was just turned eight o'clock. It seemed much later. The rhythm of the day gently imposed itself without the slightest effort on her part. She saw no one and expected to see no one. Except for a few moments at meal-times when Maureen and Eamon were very much in her thoughts, she missed no one.

She had wondered, on the way up, how she would fill the long hours alone. Now it was a surprise to find how quickly the time was passing. She explored her corner of the valley, walking up to the very base of the cliffs, following the little stream up the steep slope. The rushing water had found a narrow cleft between the rocks and one rowan tree, its roots in a crack in the stone, had managed to survive the harsh winters and the attentions of the few sheep that grazed these slopes.

The lake's beaches were tiny and she found bright stones just below the water line like a treasure of semi-precious gems. Walking from one to another she noticed that the finest sand was towards the southern end of the most southerly beach and at the northern end of the most northerly beach were the largest nuggets of gravel and all the pebbles which gleamed the brightest.

The sky had clouded over during the morning but in the afternoon it became bright and warm as if the sun was almost ready to break through. Anamar went around the head of the lake and climbed on to a grassy promontory of land. She made herself comfortable, sitting back against a bank, surrounded on three sides by Belshade, and let her thoughts race through what had happened since she had arrived back in Donegal.

It was confusing, disturbing. But, although she sensed that she had reacted too hastily to her mother and the priest, at the heart of it all, she was right to have come here. She would have had to come here anyway. It had been in her mind since she had left France. What had happened at home had given her the reason she needed to do so, so soon after her return.

In the evening, when it was time to eat, she decided to cook something she had missed during her travels. Her mother would have said, 'You can't make poundies without your own spuds, scallions and butter'. Anamar remembered a time in Dublin when a friend had smilingly told her that no one would know what she was talking about if she mentioned 'poundies'. The proper word was 'champ'.

Anamar boiled and mashed two big potatoes with two of Eamon's scallions, chopped small. She spooned the mixture on to an enamel plate, made a hole on the top for the butter and stuck a chunk of cheese into the side of the mound. The champ looked appetising with its flecks of green scallions and the golden sauce of the melted butter. The taste was delicious. It was not only a filling meal, its familiarity was a comfort to her as well.

'All I need now is a glass of butter-milk' she said to herself. 'I wonder if they'll bring some to-morrow?'

Next day was bright and sunny but there was a cool breeze. Anamar spent most of the morning wrapped in her coat, sitting in a small, sheltered depression, high above the lake on the north-east side. The rippled water seemed a long way below. To her right the cliffs shone in shades of light grey, almost white in places, with the big pink wall at their foot.

Not for the first time since she had left for the lake, she was thinking of her mother, hearing what her mother might say, aware of the exact words she would use in any given circumstance. When she had been away from home before this had never happened. Now it was as if her mother was closer to her in some way, even though they had parted with such lack of understanding between them.

Would her mother talk to anyone about their conversation and the visit of the priest? She was almost certain to tell her sister Maeve, who lived on the other side of the lake. 'Maeve and I have no secrets' her mother would say. 'And why would we? Two women and only our sorrows to share'.

As she had left home on her travels, Anamar had thought that she and her mother would never be able to talk about anything other than cooking or dress-making or shopping in the town. Before she returned she had felt that this would change. Her mother would understand. And then on her first day home she had rushed head-long into telling them her thoughts, in spite of knowing that it would be too much, too soon.

She sat as still as a stone on the open mountain and suddenly shivered with cold. Anxious, unsettling thoughts for her mother came to mind. At this moment, it seemed of the greatest importance that they would be able to talk next time they met. But would they understand each other? She felt a cold which was the chill of sadness.

Too much serious thinking was making her depressed and she found herself looking forward to the coming of her friends. Maureen and Eamon were the youngest in their family. There were three older bothers and a sister born when their parents were young. After a gap of twelve years, first Maureen, then Eamon had arrived. Their brothers and sister had long since left home. Eamon shared the work with his father and would eventually take over the farm. Maureen and her mother ran the house, cooked and baked, looked after the hens and made the butter and butter-milk.

In a valley where most young people left to make their way in the world elsewhere, Eamon and Maureen's parents anxiously hoped that their two youngest would stay.

Anamar knew almost exactly when Maureen and Eamon would come. They would have risen early to have their chores completed well before noon. It would be hard for them to get away before eleven o'clock but if they left then, they would be with her by half past one. She walked across to the rise to meet them and watched them climb the valley.

But there were four figures in single file wending their way upwards. Maureen was apologetic when they met on the ridge beside the lake's mouth.

'When they heard you were back, they insisted on coming,' she said, embarrassed, but Anamar seemed not to mind. She had known Rose and Maggie since school days.

They were taking turns to carry a haversack and had brought a big Thermos flask of soup, parcels of sandwiches and a bag of scones.

They sat outside the cave and picnicked. Eamon poured out the soup into the four mugs and the top of the Thermos. He placed himself close to the food as the girls talked excitedly. When the questions about what they had all be doing in the past two years had been asked and answered, Maureen was uneasy. Now that the others were here, would Anamar talk about the American she had met in the book shop in Lourdes? She had told Maggie and Rose already about Anamar's trip to Lourdes but had not dared to mention that meeting.

Anamar looked her straight in the eye and winked.

'I suppose you're itching to hear about the American I met,' she said.

'You didn't tell us about the Yankee!' said Rose, shaking a finger at Maureen. 'We nearly didn't come because of the long, old trek and those wild bogs below and then we would have missed the best bit.'

'No!' said Anamar. 'It wouldn't do to call him a Yankee, he's from the Deep South.' She settled back and began to tell them about Hank and the chance meeting at the book shop in Lourdes.

Hank had been an officer in the American Army and had fought in France in the war that had ended in 1945, just three years before. He had been wounded during a battle for a beach-head in the South of France and discharged as soon as the war ended.

Eamon was not sure he wanted to hear anything more about this American war hero. For all of his teenage years he had secretly admired Anamar. But the friendship was between the three of them. Maureen was always there. He had never been alone with Anamar. He had only ever spoken to her on her own to give her a message or pass the time of day. Maureen would have laughed if he had told her.

'Anamar is a woman, like me', she would have said. 'You're a whole year younger and males are younger than females at any age under twenty-five. You're still only a bit of a boy.' But to Eamon, Anamar was his girl-friend, whether she knew it or not and the time she had been away had been hard in ways he could never have discussed with anyone. He lit the Primus stove and put some water on to boil for tea.

Anamar was telling the girls that Hank was a mountaineer and was passing through Lourdes on his way to climb in the Pyrenees. He had come into the book shop, where she worked, to try to buy a map. Good maps were scarce but the owner of the shop had somehow managed to save some pre-war stock. As he talked, Anamar realised that this was a very unhappy man, deeply depressed. He had loved mountains since boyhood but was in the Pyrenees without joy, as if it was the only place left to go.

Eamon washed the mugs and the top of the flask and poured the tea. He went over to the cave where he had left his creel of food and fetched the milk. For this trip he had found a container, two in fact, one for milk and the other for butter-milk. They were glass lemonade bottles with a white ceramic stopper which, when a wire loop was depressed, fitted tightly into the neck of the bottle with a red rubber collar. He had brought too, a paper twist of sugar and a spoon. The others might have given up taking sugar in tea during the war when it was in short supply, but he could not take tea without.

The girls had hoped that Anamar would tell them a romantic story of love-at-first-sight with an exciting American. But this was a sad tale and in the telling of it Anamar's head went down and they thought she might cry.

'I was worried about Hank,' she said. 'He had come here to climb in his favourite mountains but he was so unhappy, so low in his spirits. I felt he was so depressed there might be something seriously wrong.'

Another customer had asked her a question and when she had turned back to speak to Hank, he had gone. She had rushed out into the street after him.

'You'll never believe it,' she said. 'But I told him I'd never walked in the mountains here and that I had the next day off. I asked him to show me the Pyrenees?'

Rose whistled softly through her teeth.

'That's not like the wee goody-two-shoes we waved good-bye to when you first left Lough Eske. What did he say?'

'What could he say?' Anamar was laughing. 'He said O.K. If you're sure that's what you want. He didn't sound too enthusiastic but I just put that down to his southern drawl.'

They all laughed. Anamar told them that she and Hank had gone walking in the hills near the town and had travelled on his motor-bike to do a full day's walk amongst the high peaks.

Then he had offered to take her to a mountain called Vignemale, one of the highest peaks in the Pyrenees, to see if they could climb it together.

The others settled themselves to listen and Anamar began her story.

The book shop was closed on a Sunday and she had Mondays off as well, so she had arranged to meet Hank outside the shop the following Sunday morning. When she arrived he was waiting, sitting astride his dark green motor bike with its shining chrome exhaust and handlebars. On either side of the pillion seat there was a sturdy pannier bag, full to bulging. She learned later that it was a 350cc.

Matchless and had been a British Army dispatch-rider's bike, sold as war-surplus equipment. An enthusiast had reconditioned the whole machine so successfully it looked like new and Hank had bought it in England for £85.

It was raining. Hank was wrapped in a great coat and wearing a German soldier's cap with ear flaps which buttoned under the chin.

'Let's go,' he muttered without as much as saying 'Hello'. We've a ways to ride first.'

They left Lourdes, heading straight for the mountains on a surfaced road. Anamar was perched behind Hank and the motor bike engine ran with a deep-throated rumble as if it could go on for ever. Although she could not see his face, Anamar fancied Hank was in better humour now they were on the way.

But it was all right for him, he had a large, shaped saddle to sit on. Her pillion seat was so uncomfortable, it felt like she was perched on a padded block of wood about the size of a building brick.

An hour later the road's surface was poor but the bike roared steadily up through a gorge. At the village of Gavarnie they turned right into the deep valley of the River Gave, heading into the heart of the range. The track was rough and stony, at times perched above the river or hacked out of the hillside, in places a narrow ledge blasted out of the side of the cliff.

Hank stopped for a moment to go down to the trees and came back trimming a long stick. He sharpened it to a point at one end and smoothed the surface with his knife. When Anamar held it near the top it reached as high as her shoulder.

'This is your third leg,' he said. 'You'll need it when we hit the snow,'

Half an hour later he parked the motor bike under an overhanging rock and the rain stopped.

'This is it,' he said. 'Riding time is over.' His rucksack was strapped to a carrier behind the pillion seat and he transferred to it the contents of the two pannier bags, making it look almost too big to carry. His wet great coat folded just small enough to fit into one of the panniers but the soldier's peak cap he strapped to the outside of the rucksack to dry.

They shared some bread and cheese and Anamar tried to ignore the uncomfortable feeling of not having a conversation as they ate. They had barely finished when Hank swung the big pack on to his shoulders and set off as if he was on his own.

Anamar followed, trying to use her long stick like a shepherd's staff. She had rolled her wet mackintosh and tied it across one shoulder. During the war she had seen it on News Reels, it was called, a Russian roll. She was wearing slacks and her sensible, rubber-soled, brown lace-up shoes with a high upper which made them look like half boots.

Hank was dressed like a proper mountaineer with knee breeches and climbing boots. Was he pretending not to be with her? 'If he is,' she thought. 'He needn't bother, for we're the only people in the whole of this valley'.

After half an hour's steady walking Hank stopped at a lake and allowed her to catch up. He reached the map to her and put his finger on a spot without a word. This must be where they were, the Lac d'Ossoue.

It was a place of mountain grandeur such as she had never seen before but it was intimidating, too. Anamar was glad that Hank seemed familiar with this terrain.

The Lac d'Ossoue was smaller than Lough Belshade and, whereas Belshade was in a bowl, surrounded by hills, in the very heart of the Blue Stacks, Ossau was set at the lower end of a broad, rock-strewn meadow below a gorge which reached up into the mountain fastness of the Pyrenees.

The steep slopes on either side were patched with snow, split by scree inclines. Behind, the valley fell away towards the lower reaches. Above was a sharp skyline of jagged summits with one great peak surmounting all. Its serried tops were black rock against a pale blue sky. Below the upper slopes, it was guarded by a glacier, gleaming white, sweeping up from a tongue of snow at the foot of a cliff to an ice bowl below the highest rocks.

Hank pointed and said the one word,

'Vignemale!' like a soldier's command, without betraying what he was thinking.

Although they were now amongst his beloved mountains, although this was his most favoured peak of all, he was still dejected. His head was down. Anamar thought she had seen the wet streak of a tear on his cheek when he looked towards her. She tried to encourage him to talk but every time she spoke he seemed to turn away at the sound of a voice.

A wild screech from a jumble of boulders nearby startled Anamar. When Hank turned and saw the look on her face, he began to laugh but it was a sound without mirth.

'Don't worry,' he said dryly. 'It's not the Irish banshee wailing for a death. It's a marmot. Look!'

He pointed towards the rocks and Anamar saw a light-brown furry creature, bigger than a hare sitting up on a rock, watching them. It let out another screech and she saw six or eight more marmots scurrying for safety behind the boulders.

At the head of the plain they crossed the river and climbed on a steep, narrow path which zig-zagged up the slope towards the top of a rocky bluff. To their right was a cliff which guarded the upper part of the valley. The river fell over its edge in a stunning waterfall, perhaps a hundred and fifty feet high. Its gushing sound was a low roar which filled the space between. Every footstep on the track needed care. Anamar wanted to stop to look but Hank was surging upwards, his huge rucksack swaying gently in rhythm with every step.

When they were much higher, Hank suddenly paused on one of the sharp bends and Anamar could see why they had to climb to earn the view. They were now high enough to see the full fall of the water right down to its plunge into a pool below. The left hand edge of the cascade caught the sun and spun, in gleaming, running threads, all the rainbow colours of the spectrum of light.

Neither said a word, but Hank's stare was as long and as full of wonderment as Anamar's.

Her rubber soled shoes gripped well on a ledge of dry rock higher up. A trickle of water from a spring fell in a miniature waterfall on the path. Hank filled two metal water bottles, drank from one and handed the other to Anamar.

'Fill it up when you've had a drink and clip it on to your belt,' he said. 'On a warm day like this we need to keep drinking.'

They reached the top of the rocky bluff and the next level of the valley opened out before them. The river was now under a great depth of snow and tongues of snow reached up the slopes on either side. Between these icy banks there were scree slopes, so steeply angled it seemed that any movement might make them slide and cause tons of rocks to come tumbling down.

Anamar used her long stick as a third leg, carefully crossing patches of snow and scree, keeping on Hank's heels, stepping in his footprints. She heard the rushing of water below her feet as they crossed a bank of snow and realised that a stream was flowing underneath the frozen surface. She edged forward nervously but when Hank strode on, without a pause, she had to follow. Once over, she was elated. 'This is real mountaineering,' she thought, not daring to say anything.

Hank descended the scree for a little way and turned to point to a large hole in the snow, just below the line of their footsteps, where the whole bank had collapsed into the river below. He showed her the map.

'It's always here,' he said, pointing to a name on the map. 'It's called Le Pont de Neige, The Snow Bridge.'

He almost smiled when he saw the incredulous look on Anamar's face. She shook her head in disbelief that such a fragile, apparently impermanent feature could be actually marked on a map.

Her spirits had been rising with the climb In spite of Hank's mood of depression. Now she had nearly caused him to smile. Things were looking up.

All around were patches of bright snow, unmarked by others' footsteps. Much later, and very much higher, they stopped again. Below their feet, the valley dropped abruptly down to its lower reaches, now caught in the sunlight, seemingly miles away. Anamar could look up and see the very highest peaks that had been hidden behind the ridge since they had left the lake.

Her feet were sore, her legs ached, she was breathless, but this was living. She was ecstatic.

Hank looked over and, in spite of himself, he must have been affected by her joy.

'Vignemale!' he said again pointing up to the most magnificent summit, 'Climbed it in the summer of '39 just before the war. The fairest peak of them all.'

There was no hint of boasting. It was as if the mountain had given him back the power of speech. They sat in the shelter of a rocky outcrop, looking out over their world and shared their food.

'This is where we camp,' he said.

Now that they had reached their objective for that day, Hank began to talk.

'It's not a hard climb but Vignemale is one of the classic peaks. It has a proud place in the mountaineering history of the Pyrenees. There's even an Irish connection.'

The words came with a rush, as if they had been pent up inside his head. He began to speak as if he might not be able to stop. There was even a hint of enthusiasm in his voice as he told her of Count Henri Russell, one of the great mountaineering pioneers of the Pyrenees, over one hundred years before. Henri's father had been born in County Down in Northern Ireland and Henri had made thirty-three ascents of Vignemale.

Such had been his love for the peak that the people of the valleys below had given him a deed of ownership for Vignemale. It was for a ninety-nine year period, at the peppercorn rent of one franc per year. Henri had become the proud possessor of the mountain he adored.

Anamar was captivated by Hank's fascination for these Pyrenean peaks and intrigued too. His mood of melancholy was lifting.

She went off on her own to a rocky outcrop which gave her a view of the peaks on the other side of the valley. Although she and Hank had shared so little conversation, she felt that she knew him much better than she should have a right to expect after such a short acquaintance. It was obvious that she trusted him. Otherwise how could she have come here, alone with him, prepared to camp the night in this wild place?

Her instincts had answered the question. Such was his preoccupation with his own mental turmoil, she was safe with him amongst the mountains that he loved.

When she returned, he had pitched the tent. It was tiny, barely high enough for them to sit upright but it looked strong enough to withstand the roughest of weather. It was set in a grassy dell, sheltered by boulders and rocky outcrops, in a little niche high on the shoulder of a great mountain ridge. As evening approached, swirls of white mist drifted up the valley, blocking the view for a few moments, then clearing rapidly to restore the magnificent panorama around them.

Hank made tea on a small stove, he said he usually preferred coffee but tea was a much better drink at altitude. Their evening meal was simple. There was bread, fruit, cheese, slices of cured ham and a jar of honey. As they helped themselves, Hank began to talk again as if there was much more he needed to tell Anamar about himself.

His quiet, slow, drawn-out manner of speech was so different from the facile, ready Irish way of speaking English she was used to at home. He told her of his home in Lafayette, Louisiana and about the beginning of his interest in climbing. He had gone with some friends to the San Juan Range of the Rocky Mountains for his first big climb and they had scaled a pinnacle of rock called Lizard's Head. It had been an awesome experience.

His initiation into the vertical, gravity defying world of the big peaks had been exciting beyond his dreams, frightening, spellbinding. Climbing mountains had become the focus of his life. In the summer months before the war began in September, 1939, he had come to Europe with a group of friends to climb in the Alps and the Pyrenees. They had found the Alps a magnificent challenge but Hank had felt a special affinity with the Pyrenees and he had stayed there for an extra month after the others had gone home.

At the age of twenty he had joined the United States Army. A few weeks after he had passed out of West Point Military Academy, commissioned as an officer, the Japanese had bombed the U.S. naval base at Pearl Harbour in December 1941. Hank had found himself on a war footing as the United States entered the conflict on the side of the Allies.

Anamar paused to collect her thoughts. Eamon had hardly moved since she had started to speak and she had never known the girls to be so quiet for so long.

'Go on, woman,' said Rose. 'You can't stop now.' Anamar continued slowly as if she wished her friends to hear every word.

After she and Hank had eaten, she had gone back to her view-point on the rocky outcrop. The mist returned in patches, sweeping up in great billows, spilling out of the head of the valley, drifting in white clouds, above, below, all around their camp. The sun was behind her and flickered through the wisps of white vapour.

Suddenly a figure appeared on the low cloud, a shadowy figure but plain to see. Within seconds the apparition increased in size until it was huge, towering over her, dominating the whole mountain. Then, as quickly as it had come, it began to retreat and she saw its head encircled with a halo of multi-coloured light.

She called to Hank, her voice trembling. He must have heard the urgency and he came at a run. She pointed at the figure on the cloud and it raised an arm as if in greeting. Now there were two figures, side by side, both with perfect rainbow halos.

Hank took hold of Anamar's arm.

'It's O.K,' he said reassuringly. 'Mountaineers see this as a good omen. It's called the Brocken Spectre. The sun is low and it's throwing our shadows on the mist.'

Anamar let her breath out in a long sigh. Hank let go of her arm. He told her he had never seen the Spectre so clearly or so close. As they walked back to the tent Anamar accepted it as a good omen and hoped it was not just for the next day's climb.

Hank's sleeping bag was in two parts, one fitting inside the other for very cold conditions. He used the outer bag and gave her the inner. When she followed him into the tent a few minutes later, he seemed to be fast asleep. The inner bag was so comfortable she slept too, almost as soon as she had laid her head on a make-shift pillow formed by her coat on top of her little half boots.

It was still dark when she was wakened by Hank's hand on her shoulder. He had made tea and they drank a mug each before leaving. The climb of Vignemale was a breathtaking experience. They set out before dawn and, at first light, reached three caves which Henri Russell had caused to be cut into the mountain.

Hank told her that Russell had lived in the caves for days at a time. She laughed when she heard that he had invited his friends to dine with him at this place which he called Bellevue. His guests, of course, would first have had to climb to this point high on the mountain, but then their reward was more than the view. Count Henri's chef would have provided an excellent dinner with superb food and fine wines.

Hank led the way on the next stretch. He tied on to one end of his climbing rope and attached her to the other. On the frozen snow he cut steps at the base of the glacier where the angle was steep. There was ice below the snow and he warned her to tread warily. Slowly and steadily they climbed on a long sweep of steps kicked in the snow up to the ice bowl below the peak.

They stopped to drink from their water bottles and to look at a huge split in the ice where the glacier met the cliff opposite the summit. Hank called it the Bergschrund. It formed a spectacular ice cave, glowing green and blue in the depths behind long icicles. When they reached the steep rock which led to the summit, Hank climbed first and drew the rope in as she followed.

And there they were, on the very topmost ledge, as high as they could go, a tiny space between jagged rocks, a true peak, a place which must have changed little since Russell had rested here, and all the world below.

The mist moved in again from the valley and covered everything except the highest summits. The cloud looked solid enough to walk on and hidden below it were the valleys where people lived and worked and played. A world from which they were now apart in space and time.

Hank smiled when they reached the top. It was a wan smile but a real smile none the less. He had been here before but Anamar knew that this time, some of his satisfaction was for her achievement.

They ate a little bread and cheese and drank from their bottles. Anamar would have expected herself to be talking excitedly about the whole experience, but she was overcome. She had climbed a big mountain. No matter what happened henceforth in her life, no one could ever take this away from her. It was her own to keep. It would help in the bad times to come, giving strength to her spirit, when it was sorely needed.

Such was her elation, Anamar found the descent from the summit rock and the glacier much easier than the ascent. When they stepped off the snow at last she looked down at her little brown boots. They were sodden. She took off her socks, wrung them out, tied them to her Russian roll to dry and put her boots back on her bare feet.

On the way down Hank collected the tent and camping gear. As she waited for him, Anamar saw a creature move amongst the rocks about fifty yards away. She thought at first it might be another marmot but the shape and movement were quite different. Then the creature came out into the open and she saw it was cat-like, much bigger than a domestic cat, but with the same feline grace. It was still there when Hank arrived back with the gear. It was the first time he had seen such a creature in the Pyrenees and he had no idea what it was called. It almost made him smile again.

'I guess this is your Irish way,' he said. 'Take you into the hills a couple of times and you're now the wild-life expert.'

And that was it, the end of Hank's speech on the way down the valley, as if he had exhausted his entire conversation. But Anamar was in jubilant mood. She had climbed a Pyrenean peak and they were down from the mountain safely. Although Hank was silent, she felt that he had appreciated her own feelings of exhilaration and delight.

The motor-bike ran easily down the rough road to Gavarnie. Hank stopped at the bridge to show her the statue of Count Henri Russell set into the cliff wall *beside the bridge.*

'The most inspirational mountaineer of them all,' he said and Anamar wondered if she and Henri were helping Hank to see flickers of a light which might brighten the gloom of his depression. The omen of the Brocken Spectre had proved itself on Vignemale. Could it presage a happier time to come in Hank's life?

They stopped again for coffee at a bar on the way to Lourdes and Hank continued his own story. It was as if, having gone so far, he had to tell Anamar a little more.

Soon after the Allies' invasion of Normandy on D-Day in 1944, he had been involved in a major Allied landing on the south coast of France, to try to divert the German forces from the north. It was the first time his unit had been in battle.

Suddenly Anamar stopped. All at once she felt exhausted, so tired she could hardly stir.

Maureen, Rose and Maggie had been sitting, spellbound, listening to Anamar's voice without a sound. In spite of himself, Eamon was fascinated by this American serviceman's story. He could remember sitting close to the wireless to hear that Hitler's army had invaded Poland. The whole family had crowded around the set in silence to hear the news that Britain and France had declared war on Germany. Later, from the supposed safety of neutral Donegal, he had followed the events of the war, trying to make sense of local rumours and news reports.

He had been eight years of age when it had started, too young to feel fear, or appreciate the horror of war. But each news bulletin on the wireless had brought details of the war machines, the planes, tanks and battleships, the huge guns, and later the flying bombs. On the rare occasions when he had been taken to the picture house in Ballyshannon, the Pathé News was his favourite programme. The vivid pictures and roar of battle had brought the war right into the cinema. It had been exciting, frightening, at times horrific. It had been almost real.

But Eamon hardly dared to think about this new friend of Anamar's. On only their second meeting Hank seemed far closer to Anamar than he had been able to manage in all the years they had been friends.

Neither Rose nor Maggie were known for their patience, but they waited without a word to hear about the romance. Would it be like one of those war-time love affairs where the handsome soldier and the lonely girl are instantly attracted to each other? There were so many questions. What did he look like? Was he tall and strong? Did his family have money? But this was Anamar talking and they knew they would have to wait until she was ready.

Maureen was concerned for Anamar. She was sure that her friend was feeling the pain of some awful event in Hank's story.

Anamar shook herself.

'You've heard enough of my story for one day,' she said. 'I'm dying to hear what you've been up to.'

Maureen and Eamon unpacked the creel. Instead of a second blanket Maureen had brought a patch-work quilt. It was the first quilt she had made when her mother had taught her the traditional way, using scraps of cloth. They had brought too, a remnant of cloth to hang across the mouth of the cave and another box of food.

Anamar laughed to see herself so well stocked. She pointed to the red patch in the very middle of the quilt and Maureen smiled. They both knew a quilt had to have a red patch at its centre to represent the glowing hearth of a good home. This one would have to do for her fire.

'And finding the deliberate mistake will keep you from thinking long on a bad evening,' said Maureen, laughing. A hand-made quilt always had to have a deliberate mistake. Only God created things in perfection.

Anamar hugged them all, whispering her thanks. When it was his turn, Eamon blushed and the girls began to tease him.

'That Yankee's fairly wiped your eye,' said Maggie. 'I'll bet you can't even jitterbug.'

'He's not a Yankee,' said Eamon crossly. 'Yankees are from the Northern States. Did you not hear Anamar say he was from the deep South.' But it would have taken more than a little error of location to turn Maggie.

'Yankee or not,' she said cheerfully. 'You'll have to start taking the rest of us under your notice for a change. But don't worry your wee self. I'll teach you how to chew gum and jive and tell a girl she's great. And all at the same time!'

Eamon busied himself by taking the food and stores over to the cave. Two against one was bad enough but four to one was impossible.

When it was time for her friends to go, Anamar seemed to have recovered her good spirits completely. She walked with them back to the mouth of the lake.

'What about building a cairn of stones here?' said Eamon. 'It might be a help on a misty day.' The idea pleased Anamar so much Eamon was delighted with himself. The five of them carried stones from the river to the top of a small mound. They built the cairn about knee height, larger rocks for the bottom of the pile, smaller ones for the top.

There was something very satisfying, working with stones. When they were young, Anamar, Maureen and Eamon had played with stones in the river between their homes. They had built dams and harbours and fortifications with pebbles and rocks. Later, they had all helped repairing stone walls around the farm fields, blocking gaps in ditches, clearing out streams which were flooding after heavy rain.

But this was the most satisfying job of all. It was a symbol of the way to the cave. It would be the Belshade Cairn.

As her friends were about to leave, Anamar stopped them for a moment.

'Maybe someday I'll be able to tell you what happened to Hank.' She spoke carefully, 'But before we returned to Lourdes on the day we climbed Vignemale, he told me he had come back to the Pyrenees, the place he loved best, to take his own life amongst the mountains.'

Anamar watched her friends descend the steep valley. The girls stopped to turn and wave but Eamon looked around so often he had to keep walking at the same time or be left behind. In the middle of a bog he slipped off a tussock of grass as he looked back and almost fell. Although they were too far away to be heard, Anamar knew the girls were laughing. Eamon would be so embarrassed. They would tease him the whole way home.

She had enjoyed the company and although it felt so good to be on her own again, she hoped they would come back soon.

It began to rain on the way back to the cave and quickly became a wet evening, more like November than the height of summer. She fixed a low stone seat in the mouth of the cave, padded it with a folded blanket, and sat there watching the big drops driven on the wind, gusting across the water, peppering the surface of the lake.

There was no hurry to make the meal. Two potatoes, parboiled, sliced and fried with an egg and a rasher seemed just right for the evening that was in it. When it was time to make the bed, that extra blanket Maureen and Eamon had brought would be appreciated, as would the remnant of cloth to hang across the mouth of the cave.

For two days there was heavy rain. The streams gushed, the bogs overflowed in little rivulets between the peat banks. To someone inside a house down at Lough Eske it might have seemed the heavens had opened, that it had poured the day long, but Anamar was closer to the elements. The showers came in great squalls from the south-west sweeping around the bulk of Mullaghnadreesruhan and across the lake.

There would be a lull, long enough to fetch water or stroll down to the shore of Belshade. She had set the stove and the food on a flat rock in the cave opening and had to be careful not to knock anything over as she climbed out, facing outwards, into the little dell below.

The nights were chilly. It was the dampness in the wind. The very air was moist and cold. The blanket made up into a cosy bag with the blanket pins. She was glad that, when the weather had been fine, she had padded the floor of the cave with a deep layer of dried grass and the finest shoots of heather. The rain might make it a miserable day outside but inside the cave, her nest was warm and dry.

The rain eased on the second evening. The clouds were swept away before dark and the next day dawned fresh and clear, as if washed so by the downpour. Anamar was sure that she would have visitors.

When they came, Maureen was the first to show over the rise at the new Belshade cairn. There was no sign of Eamon. His father had gone to buy sheep from a farmer on the far side of Lough Eske and needed him for the return journey. But his mother was there, one of a party of five. They were led by Maureen with a canvas bag slung over her shoulder, followed by three women carrying shopping bags and a boy with a haversack.

Ellie McGinley had been curious when she heard her two youngest talk almost non-stop about Anamar and her cave at Lough Belshade. She had already heard from Una Greenan about her daughter's return and the priest's visit. But when Maureen told her that Anamar had been to Lourdes, she had made up her mind to come on this outing. For years she had thought about going there on pilgrimage and here was a chance of first-hand information.

A neighbour, Lena O'Driscoll, and her married sister Mary, had insisted on coming too. They had always liked Anamar and, although neither would have said as much, they were intrigued to hear about the confrontation with Father Brogan. Not that either had anything against priests. It was just that the young Father seemed a bit too full of himself at times. He sometimes gave the impression that women needed to be told what to think, whereas a man might be expected to have a view of his own.

The fifth member of the group had joined them at the last minute. James Cassidy was a serious sixteen-year old, small, dark, inquisitive, a distant relation of the McGinley's who had arrived at the farm the previous day. James was on holiday from his college in Dublin and his mother had been delighted when Ellie had agreed to have him at the farm at Lough Eske. Ellie had given him no choice on this particular day, however. He had been told to be ready to leave for the hills at half-past nine sharp.

Anamar met the party half way to the cave. The women were all well used to walking but the steep slope up to the cairn at the mouth of the lake had left them breathless. They flopped down on the heather near the cave and James continued on his own, exploring the nearby jumble of big boulders and wandering down to the beach.

'You know me, always ready for an outing.' Lena was addressing Ellie but the remarks were meant for all to hear. 'But your great daughter never told us we'd have to climb the highest mountain in the county to get here.'

Ellie smiled, Lena was obviously enjoying herself and if she did, Mary would too. 'Even for sisters,' she thought, 'that pair's very close.' She had never dared to say it to anyone but in her own mind she called them 'The Siamese Twins'.

'Am I glad I changed into the sensible shoes,' said Mary. 'I had on the sling backs, thinking we were for picnicking at some wee beauty spot the tourists visit, ten minutes from the road. Luckily I changed my mind.'

The water came to the boil on the Primus Stove and Anamar made tea. Out of the bags came the picnic, the sandwiches in neat grease-proof paper packets, a bag of almond buns, a cream sponge cake in a tin box, a dozen marshmallow biscuits. James appeared in their midst, summoned by the food.

Everyone was at ease at Belshade. They sat in bright sunshine in the dell in front of the cave. A breeze across the water meant that it was pleasantly warm, not hot. The women were on a rare day out and, as James did not really count, it was an outing on their own. This was not the same as a trip to the sea-side at Bundoran. There was no one else here except themselves. They had come on foot to meet Anamar in her own domain. Ellie had a feeling that this was a special journey, that, somehow, they had earned this moment of peace.

The talk was of the great adventure of the trek over the bogs and up the hill, of the fine spot Anamar had found for herself, of the local gossip she would have missed when she was away in France.

'Tell us about Lourdes,' said Ellie suddenly. 'I've always wanted to go there. How did the pilgrimages start?'

Anamar was surprised to feel so elated by Ellie's request, as if she had been hoping someone would ask her about her time in France. They had all heard of the young French girl called Bernadette who had seen an apparition of Our Lady but Anamar had been to Lourdes and not just for a quick visit. Even James paused for a moment, half-way through his fifth sandwich, to hear the story.

There was hardly a sound as Anamar told them how Bernadette had seen a vision of a girl in white in a cave near her home. Bernadette had called the girl, 'Aquero' which simply meant 'that one' in the local dialect. She had gone back to the cave many times and on each occasion the vision had appeared. Very few people had believed her at first and her mother had been so upset on one occasion that Bernadette and her sister had been forbidden to visit the cave for a day or two.

Local people had begun to accompany Bernadette on her visits to the grotto. After a few days, over a thousand had gathered around the cave to watch when she made her daily visitation. They were looking for a sign. A priest had demanded that Bernadette ask Aquero to cause the rose bush above the cave to flower, as a miraculous sign. Aquero had merely smiled.

On the way home Bernadette had embraced a sick girl who removed the bandages from her eyes and found she could see. The crowd now had its miracle. The rumour was that Bernadette had restored a young girl's sight. But the young girl in question had not been blind. The bandage was to keep the bright sunshine from hurting her eyes.

Then, fifteen days after she had first appeared to Bernadette, Aquero had told her in the local dialect that she was the Immaculate Conception. And this was how the great pilgrimage had been born. Six years later, twenty thousand pilgrims had attended when a small statue was erected in the grotto and two years after that, forty thousand were present for the first Mass to be celebrated there.

Ellie and her friends were aware that Lourdes had become one of the most popular places of pilgrimage in the Christian world. They knew about the crowds around the Grotto filling bottles to take the water home and the ill and the maimed attending in wheelchairs and on stretchers. But none of them had ever heard the story of Bernadette and her vision of Our Lady of the Grotto. They were fascinated.

Except for an odd mumble about the food, James had yet to speak.

'In 1945,' he said, as if he knew more about Lourdes than any of them. 'There was a special pilgrimage for people who had been prisoners or deported to forced-labour camps during the war. Thousands of them came to the grotto.'

Mary and Lena looked at him as if amazed that he had the power of speech. James smiled smugly and sat back against a rock to concentrate on another big slice of sponge cake.

'There are always claims that people who had been ill or disabled have been healed miraculously,' said Anamar. 'But the Church takes a strong line about cures. In the ninety years of the pilgrimage and although there have been thousands of claimed cures, so far only forty-one have been recognised as miraculous.

'I thought people only went to Lourdes to drink the holy water or wash in it to cure whatever ailed them.' Lena was not trying to be argumentative.

'You're right, of course,' said Anamar. 'That's why so many of them go. But I think they find it different when they're there. Maybe it's their faith which makes Lourdes what it is.'

'She doesn't believe in the miracle cures,' said James. 'Neither do I. They only put that out to get the faithful to go.'

'Don't be cheeky.' Ellie was annoyed with her young guest. He had always been a quiet lad but, now he was at college, he was becoming a bit too smart for his own good.

Anamar smiled. She had said enough. She knew Ellie would not misreport her when next she met her mother. Mary was hoping the serious chat had come to an end.

'I hear you clicked an American when you were there. So it wasn't all holy water and candle-lit processions to the Grotto.'

The five women all laughed and James knew it was time for him to wander off again. He took some buns in his pocket, just in case he might be hungry, and decided to explore a bit further. Maureen unpacked some food for Anamar which James had carried up in his haversack. There was a bottle of Paraffin too, wrapped in a copy of the Donegal Democrat and tied tightly with string.

She showed Lena and Mary the cave and Ellie put her arm around Anamar's shoulders as they walked down to the beach.

'You shook your mother the other day,' she said. 'She just didn't expect you to come out with something like that.'

'I know,' said Anamar. 'But I had to tell her what I felt.'

'You must remember,' Ellie held Anamar tightly. 'You've been away and have had time to think outside the parish walls. We hardly have time to bless ourselves, never mind think, except on days like to-day and they're as rare as hens' teeth.'

Thin skeins of white vapour, like wisps of low cloud, drifted in across the hills at the far side of the lake. Ellie and Anamar watched them weave together as they reached the water. They turned to walk back to the cave and were surrounded by mist, even as they reached it.

Suddenly all the landmarks disappeared from view, the peaks and cliffs, the lake, even nearby boulders. It was as if a great white cloud had descended and was lying its full length across the mountain.

The other three joined them outside the cave and they shouted for James as they would have called the hens in for feed. There was no reply but he had heard them just as he was beginning to panic. He decided not to reply but to let the calling continue and surprise them as he appeared out of the mist. He came into view when he was less than ten yards away. He smiled, pretending that he had known exactly where the cave was located.

When it was time to go, the mist still enveloped the whole mountainside. Anamar went with them around the lake to its mouth and the Belshade Cairn. She led them down the steep valley to the stream junction where they had to turn right to follow the river towards Lough Eske.

They stopped to rest and the mist cleared in seconds.

'You should have another cairn here,' said James with the air of an expert.

'The cloud might have been down right to the road.'

Anamar laughed. It was as if James, of all people, had been able to read her mind.

'You're just right,' she said. 'We do need a cairn here, and there's no time like the present.'

James jumped down and began to heave rocks from the stream on to the bank. The others carried them to the top of a small mound and found more nearby. In twenty minutes the cairn was finished.

'We'd better call this one after the river,' said Anamar and James went through a little charade, standing beside the cairn and declaiming in a very correct voice, 'I hereby name this pile of stones,' and he paused, having forgotten the river's name. Anamar leant forward and whispered a word in his ear. He continued as if he had known it all the time, 'The Corabber Cairn.'

Ellie hugged Anamar and they all shook hands. When it was time for them to go, Anamar watched until they were well on their way. As she climbed back up towards Belshade, she wondered what they might be thinking as they crossed the bog beside the river and descended the steep path. There was no need to rush back and she took it slowly up to the low ridge and across to the cave. She was aware that this had been a very special visit but then every one of her previous visits had been special, each in its own way.

The members of the little group made their way down towards the road. James strode ahead, finding the best route through the bog and down to the path. It had been a far more interesting walk than he had imagined it might be, when he had set off that morning with only four women as companions.

Maureen was elated. Her mother and her friends had not complained once about the hard going on the way up. She knew they had enjoyed the visit to Belshade.

As she walked on her own, Lena smiled to herself. She knew Maureen and Anamar were close and without being able to put her finger on the reason, it made her feel happy.

Lena looked at Mary, leaping from tuft to tuft across the bog.

'It's as well we were all brought up like mountain goats,' she said loudly, for all to hear.

'Speak for yourself,' said Mary. 'I just happen to be born nimble. And the next time you're off across the hills and bogs forget to include me in your gallivanting.'

But Lena knew that Mary was joking. She herself would not have traded the day even for an excursion to Bundoran on the twelfth of August, and she was sure that they all felt the same way.

The Three Priests

Over the next few weeks Anamar's life took on a daily pattern. In the morning she washed in the lake, rain or shine. There were few enough clothes for her to look after, Maureen had brought some underclothes, socks and a second blouse and this was the time to do the washing. It could be spread out on heather clumps, the way a tinker woman would do around her camp, and it dried in no time.

Cooking was no chore at all for there was only herself to cater for. The Primus had begun to splutter but Eamon had left a packet of prickers, a spare washer for the pump and a small spanner to fit the nut on the nipple, in case it needed to be removed for cleaning. An hour spent servicing the stove had it working perfectly. It was a most satisfying feeling to have it going so well again.

Each morning and afternoon there was time to roam the hills around the lake. Eamon had brought her the map they had made from Master Robson's drawing on the blackboard. She could put names to places now, Altagarranduff to the south, Binmore in the north-west and Mullaghnadreesruhan standing over Belshade. Croaghgorm, the Blue Stack itself, at two thousand two hundred feet, the biggest of them all, was behind Mullaghnadreesruhan, like the highest defences of a great castle. As she explored, she found small sheltered depressions, grassy ledges below boulders or high amongst the rocks where she could sit and watch the day.

From one of these, high on the hill, the sheer cliffs dropped down beneath her feet to the edge of the lough. From such a perch, the shelter stone might be hard to see but she could pick out the little sandy beaches at the north end of Belshade. In one direction were ridges and mountain ranges rolling back into the far distance. Looking the other way, the lower hills rolled down to the forests and farms around Lough Eske and beyond that to the lake-land of Fermanagh.

To the south-west was the great inlet of Donegal Bay and, in her mind's eye, Anamar, the spirit of the sea, could see the white rim of surf around its coast.

It was useful too, to have a good view west. More than likely that was where the worst of the weather would come from. Even on a good day, it needed to be watched. It would never do to be caught out, up here on her own, so far from the cave, in mist or driving rain.

The days were neatly punctuated by the arrival of visitors. Maureen and Eamon usually came on a Wednesday. At the weekends, either on the Saturday or Sunday or both, small groups of people would appear at the crest of the rise, near the mouth of the lake.

The first was a family party, relations of Anamar's school friend, Maggie. They lived in Donegal Town and had a car which had been parked at the head of Lough Eske. The father had appeared first with his twelve year-old son. Anamar saw them on the rise near the cairn, looking across towards the cave, as if they had been told where it was but were not sure that they could find it amongst the jumble of rocks on the mountainside.

They saw her as she walked across and came quickly to meet her. It was only when they met that she realised they were not alone. Three more figures appeared on the crest, who proved to be the mother, her sister and the ten-year-old daughter.

'Maggie was telling us about you,' said the mother, when she had recovered her breath. 'She says you live up here like a hermit.'

Anamar was smiling broadly, not just at the idea of herself being a recluse, but at the thought of the man and his big son striding up the hill, without a thought for the women following as best they could, towing the youngest child between them. But Anamar knew it was not only in Ireland that men felt the need to lead the way. In the hills of France the men had to be the trail blazers too. There was a difference however. There, the women mountaineers sometimes competed with the men, and in a mixed group the pace could become faster and faster until everyone was exhausted.

Once the family group had settled near the cave, they wanted to hear about Lourdes and Anamar found herself telling the story again as she had told it to Ellie and her friends. Before she had left for France, Anamar had been aware of how highly regarded the Pilgrimage was in Catholic countries like Ireland. Now she was seeing the attraction it could have for someone who had heard of the cult but had never been there.

She spoke about some of the people she had met in Lourdes, the spiritual feeling she had sensed, the serenity of the place and the feeling she had of a renewal of faith for many who made the pilgrimage.

She told them about the wonderful candle-lit processions to the Grotto at night and the shops and stalls in the streets nearby. When she mentioned the stunning view of the Pyrenees mountains, she thought she saw the two women exchange a knowing glance. No doubt they had heard about Hank from Maggie, but it was not a subject they intended to raise, not in this company. Patience would be rewarded in its own good time. Eventually Maggie would be able to tell them the full story.

As they were leaving, the son spoke, ready to stride off in the lead,

'I'll go ahead and look for the heap of stones.' He turned to Anamar. 'I found both piles on the way up. Maggie told us about them. They're a great idea for the bad weather.'

Father set off in hot pursuit and the two women took their leave of Anamar in much more leisurely fashion, resigned to following at a distance, with the younger child.

'Tail-end Charlies again,' said the mother to Anamar with a smile. 'It's well for you, perched up here on your own and not a one to bother you.'

They had left some farls of griddle wheaten bread and half a dozen eggs. As she stored them away inside the cave, Anamar found the copy of the Donegal Democrat which had been wrapped around the bottle of paraffin brought up by the last group. She smoothed out the pages and put them in order and found herself reading the front page.

It was the first time she had read a word since she had arrived and the first time she had seen the Democrat since she had left home for Dublin. She carried it off to one of her sheltered nooks and read it from front to back, advertisements, announcements, news, sports' reports, the weekly story, 'Children's Corner', political statements, the 'Mainly for Women' column. Anamar devoured every word.

There was a sale at a gentleman's outfitters in the town. Every item was priced, trousers 11 shillings and 11 pence, Botany wool socks 2 shillings and 11 pence. She could hear her mother insisting to her father that they go to the town to get him kitted out for the winter and it only six months away.

Farmers' loans were on offer at 4% per annum There was a talent competition in Ballyshannon with a £5 prize. A political party had paid for space to set out its agricultural policy on tillage, fertiliser, pigs, bacon and veterinary services. She could hear her father muttering as he read it, 'They'll promise everything to get your vote but once they're in, they'll do nothing.'

The Abbey, 'Ballyshannon's Luxury Cinema', was apologising to patrons unable to gain entrance on the previous Sunday evening. 'We can only suggest that you come early and secure your seat' was the management's tongue-in cheek advice. The films were advertised in a prominent position on the front page. 'Sue City Sue' was billed as a 'blazing tune-filled saga'. 'Steppin' In Society' promised to be 'hilarious comedy'.

On an inside page, the serial story was 'another exciting episode of The O'Driscoll of Dara, The outlaw of the mountains'.

Anamar was only now realising just how much she had missed reading.

Her visitors always came by the same route. Anamar usually saw them as tiny moving figures on the skyline of the crest of the rise at the Belshade Cairn. There was plenty of time to leave whatever she was doing to go to meet them, as they made their way to her end of the lake. But early one afternoon three figures appeared from the opposite direction.

She saw them on a high ridge, hundreds of feet above, silhouetted against the sky, as if they had just climbed Binmore from the far side. They descended rapidly towards her and she could see that they were young men dressed like mountain walkers in tweed trousers and hiking boots, each wearing a little knitted tea-cosy hat. Anamar made herself comfortable on a grassy bank, with her back against a stone, and waited for their arrival.

Two were tall, angular, long-legged men who strode across to her with great bounding strides. They reached her first, but stopped short of where she sat and looked as if they were unsure what to say in greeting other than 'Hello'.

Their companion arrived on their heels, almost running to keep up. He was shorter and burlier, younger than his friends, his black hair sticking out from under his woolly hat, cheeks red with the wind and the effort. In spite of being out of breath, he was the one who came forward and spoke for the three of them.

'You must be the famous Anamar,' he said, his eyes twinkling, unaware that she might be embarrassed being so addressed by a stranger. 'Father Brogan was telling us about you.'

For once in her life Anamar was short of a word. This visit was unexpected, particularly because of the direction from which they had come, but even more so because it seemed that Father Brogan had been involved.

'He said we should come to talk to you.' The young man was still smiling, making it difficult for Anamar to decide if he was teasing. His two friends were nodding shyly in agreement, apparently pleased that he was doing the talking.

They introduced themselves. The talkative one was Eoin. He presented his friends as Patrick and Jack and they shook hands with Anamar, formally and diffidently, but as if they had been looking forward to meeting her. Patrick said he was a nephew of Father Brogan, who had invited the three of them to stay with him when he heard they were coming to Donegal for a few days' walking.

That morning, Father Brogan had taken them in his car through Glenties to the northern side of the Blue Stacks. This meant that they could walk across the mountains to Belshade and then come back down to Lough Eske without having to retrace their steps.

They had no map and when Anamar let them see hers, Patrick and Jack were like boys with a new toy. They traced their route over the hills, putting names to peaks and valleys. That suited Anamar. In spite of Eoin being so friendly, she felt shy in the company of these strangers. She guessed they were college men, perhaps members of the college walking club, but they were cautious too. Even Eoin, for all his good-natured chat, was as wary of her as she was of them.

Then Eoin explained that he was the new curate in a parish in Dublin. He said that Patrick and Jack were from County Clare and had known each other since their school-days. Although they had been one year ahead of him at Maynooth, an interest in walking had brought them together. The other two were also serving as curates, Jack in a village in County Fermanagh and Patrick in Sligo Town.

It answered many of the questions in Anamar's mind. She lit the paraffin stove and put on a pot of water. They sat near the cave but none of the men asked to see inside, as all her other visitors had done. When the water boiled, she made the tea and they produced a large packet of sandwiches. Anamar had already eaten and she sat at her ease, back against her rock, sipping her tea, waiting for them to speak.

Eoin ate a sandwich quickly and, as if he could contain himself no longer, asked straight out about her feeling that everyone had the power to change the world.

Anamar smiled, not in the least put out by such a question. She felt comfortable here in her own domain and as well disposed towards these three visitors as she had been towards everyone else who had come to see her. But she had no intentions of discussing her thoughts.

Instead, she talked about Lourdes and the wonderful walking in the Pyrenees. When Eoin tried to bring her back to his question Anamar would say something about the sense of spirituality she had found amongst the pilgrims at the Grotto of Our Lady.

Patrick frowned and Jack looked earnestly at Eoin. They were embarrassed. Both seemed to understand Anamar's reluctance to become involved in Eoin's discussion. They began to ask her questions about the Pyrenees. Patrick said that they had been thinking of a walking holiday in France: Then Jack showed Anamar his rucksack.

'I got it in the market in Enniskillen,' he said. 'There's a stall there selling ex-army equipment very cheaply. It's called a Commando Rucksack because it was used by the British Marines during the war. I'm going to get one for Patrick when I go back to the parish.' He stopped and looked at his friends, as if surprised that his enthusiasm had run away with him.

'If we can get away next summer for that walking holiday,' said Patrick seriously. 'It looks as if it'll have to be the Pyrenees.'

'Good thinking, Packie,' said Eoin quickly. 'We could go to Lourdes first ...' he stopped, conscious that the others might think he was using Lourdes as an excuse to go to the mountains.

Anamar laughed.

'And when you do, you can say your prayers on the peaks as well as at the Grotto. If you reach the tops you'll be a long way up. Much closer to God.'

Patrick and Jack smiled for the first time since they had arrived. Eoin giggled, relieved that he had not been taken up the wrong way.

'Are you never lonely here?' he said and immediately regretted asking the question of a girl confronted by three men. 'I mean, is there not something you miss being up here on your own?'

It was Anamar's turn to giggle, not in the least put out by the query. She went into the cave and brought out the copy of the Donegal Democrat.

'I'd forgotten how much I enjoyed reading,' she said, patting the paper. 'The whole life of the country is here. Potatoes for sale at 1 shilling and 3 pence a stone. Midwives wanted by the County Council at £100 per annum, increasing by £5 per annum to £130, with a uniform allowance of £5 extra. 'The Jolson Story' on at the Abbey Cinema. Buckfast Tonic Wine for depression and exhaustion, made by the monks of Buckfast Abbey.' They were all laughing but now it was time for them to go.

As they left, Jack turned and opened a side pocket in his rucksack.

'I've a book here you might like to read,' he said shyly. 'I'm not sure I understand any of it myself but you can have it, if you like.' He reached her a thin Penguin paperback. It was 'Collected Poems' by T. S. Eliot. 'I got it in a bookshop in Enniskillen, I'm not sure I'm even supposed to have a copy.'

Anamar could hardly believe her eyes. Eliot was one of Deirdre Ryan's favourite poets and she had enjoyed reading verses to Anamar like 'The Journey of the Magi'.

She took the book and held it to her as she shook hands with the three men. They had arrived in haste but now, as they turned again to go, they were leaving as if reluctantly. Not one of them could have given a reason, nor would they have dared to discuss it, but they all felt the better for having made this journey. They parted unwillingly from Belshade and this young woman who had brightened their day.

Next day Eamon and Maureen came over the rise and Anamar was so engrossed in the book of Eliot's poems that she was unaware that they were so close. She had found a little flower pressed amongst the pages. It was a birdsfoot trefoil with three hooked yellow flowers at the end of the stem like a bird's claw.

The book had opened with the flower at 'The Love Song of J. Alfred Prufrock' and reading it slowly she came to the lines,

'I grow old ... I grow old ...
I shall wear the bottoms of my trousers rolled.
Shall I part my hair behind? Do I dare to eat a peach?'

Deirdre Ryan and she had always laughed when they took it in turns to speak the words aloud in an upper-class English accent. Mr Eliot might have been an American but his words sounded as if they were meant to be read in the accent of his adopted country. He was such a serious poet, it was a relief to come on this cheerful verse so unexpectedly. It set them giggling.

Anamar was still smiling broadly when she heard Eamon shout a greeting. He and Maureen were only fifty yards away and Anamar jumped to her feet to run towards them.

'What do you think of that?' she said, holding up the book. 'I had gentlemen callers yesterday and one of them gave me a present.' She handed the little volume to Maureen. 'And I've had some fun too with that Donegal Democrat you brought to me, wrapped around the paraffin bottle. It's a terrible smell but a great read.'

Eamon was pleased to see Anamar so light-hearted. He had been wondering how anyone could stay here alone. What would she do when she felt low and with no one to cheer her up?

'Oh we know all about your clerical visitors.' Maureen could see Anamar's happiness growing each time they came here. 'There was a parish social in the hall last night and the three of them could talk of nothing else. That Eoin McCartan one was imitating your saintly smile and the serene way you walk. He should be up on the stage instead of the pulpit.'

Anamar began to laugh. She could imagine the antics of Eoin. Every time he had opened his mouth to speak, whether serious or flippant, she had wanted to giggle.

'And you'd have been surprised to hear how talkative the two quiet Fathers became.' Maureen could not resist teasing her friend. Too much of their conversation since Anamar's return had been far too serious. 'Father Jack is mad now to go to the Pyrenees. And to hear Father Patrick, you'd think that our Anamar was already a legend in her lifetime.'

Eamon managed to smile as the others laughed. He was worried about Anamar, up here in the wilds of the mountain. So far, all her visitors had been pleasant, but she was a girl, here all alone. If she needed help, the nearest farm house was well over an hour's walk away.

'Have you not been here long enough?' he said. 'Are you not thinking of coming home for a while?'

Anamar was startled. She looked at Eamon as if she had been unaware of time since she had come here.

'Right enough, I must keep a check on the days I've been here, but the time just slips away.' She was speaking to herself rather than to her friends.

They ate lunch and climbed the steep slope towards the ridge. After each visit, Maureen had gone to see Anamar's mother to say that all was well at Belshade. She had explained that Anamar just needed some time on her own. Having talked to the mother, it seemed sensible to tell the daughter what she had done.

When they sat down for a rest near the top Anamar began to speak to them again about her Pyrenean adventures. It was the story of the first time she had gone with Hank to walk in the mountains. Maureen was fascinated, not just about the walks. She knew Anamar had never had a steady boyfriend before she had left home, but she was already guessing that this relationship with Hank was more friend than boyfriend. Eamon was keen to hear about the mountains, but every mention of Hank annoyed him.

Anamar told them about watching Hank climbing on a huge rock face on one of the biggest of the mountains. He took her on his motor-bike to a valley to the west of Lourdes. They left the bike and climbed over a grassy ridge into the heart of the Pyrenees. A massive mountain, detached from the main range, dominated the whole terrain. Hank told her that it was called the Pic du Midi D'Ossau. Beside it, and separated from it by a narrow chasm, was a smaller peak which he called Le Petit Pic, the small peak.

Anamar sat in the sunshine and stared as Hank climbed hundreds of feet of what looked like sheer, smooth, hold-less rock. On the face, he was a tiny figure finding his way like an insect on a boulder. For a few moments he would ascend slowly and gracefully, then an agile series of steps and a long reach with one arm would take him to a higher level. On the walk to the peak he had been dull and despondent, plodding dourly up the slope, but now on the rock he moved with ease.

There were moments when she could watch no longer. It seemed that he must fall, as if he was daring the mountain and the Law of Gravity to do their worst. But with her eyes averted, Anamar knew that this was not the way Hank would die. When she looked back, there he was, another fifty feet higher, still clinging to the rock.

Maureen's pulse was racing. She felt as if she might have been there too and seen it all with Anamar.

'I would have been petrified,' she said, shivering, feeling a chill in the air, although the sun was shining here in Donegal. 'What would you have done if he'd fallen down the cliff?'

Anamar knew there was no need to reply. Maureen was living her fears for her. They were closer than either had ever realised.

'Was he showing off in front of you?' Eamon asked the question and as soon as he did, regretted it. The girls were sure to think he was jealous. He changed the subject so that Anamar would not have to answer. 'Was this what made you want to try the climbing, I mean on somewhere easier? Wasn't this the day he offered to take you up the big mountain?'

Anamar nodded and Maureen leaned forward and looked at her. She spoke so softly Eamon had to strain to hear.

'You were saying he had been very depressed. Was he trying to kill himself? Did he care whether he slipped or not?'

Anamar knew she had to respond this time.

'I can't be certain,' she said thoughtfully. 'I was sure he intended to take his own life, but not on this day. Not with me there. In some way he was sharing the mountain with me, trying to make me part of the climb.'

She went on to tell them that, after a few minutes, Hank had climbed to his right to reach a rocky ridge. This allowed him to descend quite quickly, right back to where she was sitting.

Eamon was about to ask why Hank had not continued to the summit of the mountain, but Maureen put a hand on his arm. She knew that Anamar had more to say.

'He was a different man as he came back to me,' Anamar said seriously. 'His face was flushed with the sun. He was walking just as quickly as ever but with a more relaxed stride, not as tense and nervy as before. We were able to talk. That was when I told him I'd love to climb a Pyrenean mountain, if there was one he thought I could manage.'

'O.K,' was all he had to say. 'Next time we'll make it Vignemale.'

But by the time they had parted that evening in Lourdes, however, Hank had slipped back again into deep dejection. It had been left to Anamar to suggest the day and time, and when she did, he seemed reluctant to commit himself. Anamar had insisted, however, as Maureen knew she would have done, she knew that determined streak in her friend from years of experience.

Anamar lay back against the heather and spoke as if she were talking to herself rather than to them.

'Although he was miserable each time we met, his spirits would rise during the trip, a little higher every time. But, at the end of the day when we were leaving the mountains, he would be as low as ever.'

Maureen knew now that although Hank was a deeply unhappy man, the relationship had not brought Anamar down. It even seemed as if it had made her stronger in herself.

Eamon had heard enough of Hank, even though he had been fascinated by the description of the climb.

'Tell her what we were talking about,' he said to Maureen. 'Go on! Tell her!'

'He's too shy to ask you himself.' It was obvious that Maureen had agreed to do the talking. 'We were wondering if we could come up to stay the night with you, sometime soon, say this time next week.'

'What a great idea! I was beginning to think you'd never suggest it.' Anamar was delighted at the thought of company for an evening. 'Come early and we'll climb the Blue Stack and have a wee party in the evening.'

The Enchanted Mountains

Anamar gathered more dry grass and heather for the cave, enough to make two more sleeping places. She pulled only the tops of the heather, the flowers, the fine stems. The main stems were gnarled, hard, twisted. Lying on them, the first night she had slept here, had been torture, until she had knelt in the darkness, combing through the bed with her fingers, searching out every last stalk of rough twig.

On the day that they were due, she headed across to the Belshade Cairn early and made her way down to the Corabber Cairn at the river junction. There was plenty of time, they had their chores to do before they could leave home. They would be heavily laden, she was sure of that, and she wanted to help them carry their stuff up the steepest part of the hill.

When they came into view, they were walking slowly on the little track through the bog that flanked the river. Anamar had placed herself on the mound beside the cairn, sitting quite still, watching them come towards her. Maureen was in front, eyes down, picking each footstep to avoid the wet patches. Eamon walked a few yards behind. The great load he had in the creel on his back was piled up as high as the top of his head.

The only sound was the rush of water in the river. As she neared the river junction, Maureen looked up to the cairn and was startled to see Anamar perched beside it, looking so calm and unruffled she might have been spirited down from Belshade, without having had to walk a step of the way.

'My turn to give you a fright,' said Anamar. 'I knew you'd bring everything except the butter churn, so I though I'd better come down and help with the carrying.'

She and Maureen made a bundle wrapped in a blanket and tied it with string. Eamon was reluctant to part with any of his load but the girls insisted. Anamar attached her leather belt to the package so she could carry it slung over her shoulder. Now Eamon led the way and the girls walked behind, talking the whole way up the slope and across to the cave.

Anamar showed them the sleeping arrangements. The heather beds were in a fan shape, pointing outwards, heads near the inner wall of the cave, feet towards the entrance. She and Maureen would lie together to one side, with Eamon under the lowest part of the roof.

They had brought two blankets. The girls decided that Eamon could have both of them and they would share Anamar's blanket and the quilt. At mid-day they made tea and left to climb the Blue Stack. It was further away and higher than it looked. Master Robson's map had it's summit at 2,219 feet. There was no track and they followed a stream, struggling upwards through knee-high heather and on rough scree, the view improving with every step.

They kept together and the girls joined hands as they reached the top, For Anamar, it was as great a thrill as any of the Pyrenean climbs she had shared with Hank. And it was the first time any of them had seen the view to the north. No one spoke. There were hills behind hills, falling back, ridge after ridge, into the far distance. It seemed as if the whole of north Donegal was laid out as one huge range of mountains.

The breeze was from the north-west and they flopped down in the heather on the sheltered south side over-looking their own part of the county. Up here, on the top of the highest peak, it was like a giant map, every detail sharply defined in light and shade.

They lay back and rested, talking, teasing each other, perfectly at ease. It was not until they sat down for another rest on the way down that Anamar began to talk about the Pyrenees again. When they had stopped near the summit of the Blue Stack, Maureen had wanted to hear more, accusing Anamar of keeping them on tenterhooks about her adventures with Hank, but there had been no response.

Now she began to tell them about the journey she and Hank had made to the Enchanted Mountains. The story continued during the rest of the long sunny afternoon and through the evening, while they made the meal and ate it. Anamar was still telling her tale as they sat by the lake-side and darkness drew in over Belshade.

She explained that the Enchanted Mountains are a remote part of the Pyrenees, called in Spanish, Los Encantados. It had taken Hank and Anamar a whole morning to travel on his motor-bike to the Spanish Town of Viella. To Anamar's surprise, Spanish Viella was, to her, on the wrong side of the Pyrenees. She had always thought that the Pyrenees separated France on the north side from Spain in the south. Hank had told her, however, that this was the Vall D'Aran, the only part of Spain on the 'French' side of the mountains.

In the afternoon, a narrow twisting road, only a rough track at times, climbed through the hills on a long, circuitous route over the main range. A switch-back descent on the south side and a climb up another valley brought them to an ancient inn. It was stone-built, perched on the hillside above the river, tucked in below the highest peaks.

Hank's map showed that it was the Hospital de Viella, only about 10km. as the crow flies from the town of Viella itself but on the other side of the main ridge of the Pyrenees. They had covered five or six times the direct distance to reach it.

Below was the entrance to a tunnel, obviously still in the process of construction. Men and machines moved in and out of its mouth, like busy worker ants entering and leaving the hole which led into their nest.

Hank had been here before. The tunnel would not be ready for another year but when finished, it would be 5km. long and a new link between the Vall D'Aran and the mainland of Spain. The Hospital de Viella was probably the oldest mountain inn in Europe still in use. For hundreds of years it had been the last staging post on the mule route across the mountains.

The inn had been built directly on the track, the main structure on one side, the barn and outhouses on the other. In between, the track was paved with cobbles like the street in front of the door of Anamar's own farmhouse in Donegal.

On one side of the building there was a small chapel and as Hank went into the inn to arrange for them to stay, Anamar peeped inside. It was cool, plainly furnished. There was washing hanging on clothes lines to one side but it was obviously still in use as a church. The day had been long and hot, an exceedingly bumpy ride on the pillion seat of the motor-bike. Anamar stretched to ease the saddle soreness and went into the empty chapel to sit down. The wooden seat was hard but flat, and so much larger than the pillion, it felt luxurious.

Since she had left home Anamar had attended Mass much less frequently than before. But she had sometimes found herself slipping into a church to pray for a few moments or just to sit and think. When she did attend Mass, it seemed to mean much more to her that ever before. She had discovered too, that the time on her own in church was the time she felt closest to God, as if the ceremony was keeping the priest between God and herself.

As she paused in the chapel, Anamar felt a great surge of hope. Since she had met Hank, he had worried her more than she could ever have confided to him. She had been concerned for his state of mind, anxious that he might be overcome by despair. Then suddenly, as she sat there, she knew all would be well.

Maureen and Eamon were taking in every word. Maureen had to keep stopping herself from asking questions. When Anamar was in a story-telling mood, the best thing was to let her run on. The questions could wait.

Anamar became very thoughtful as she talked on about Hank. Quietly she explained that although no one could have said that Hank was in good spirits during the journey, she had sensed a change in him. He was no longer so dejected, so defeated by life as he often had been when they had first met. He still seemed sad and needed prompting to keep him talking. When they had reached the Hospital de Viella, at the end of a long hard day's ride, she had felt tired and sore, while he was lively, as if the place had restored his energy.

They stayed the night at the inn, in a tiny room with old-fashioned beds, piled with blankets and quilts even though it was still summer. The next morning they left the motor-bike parked against the barn and walked up the valley behind the inn.

Hank carried a huge rucksack packed with food and equipment. He had lent Anamar a smaller bag, he called it his day sack. It was packed by him, with great care. He explained that this must be done properly. The weight had to be in exactly the right place, near the top. All the other items were so arranged that there were no hard edges to stick into the back. Her sack was lighter than it looked and far more comfortable than she had ever imagined a pack could be.

They turned north and began to follow a faint path which zig-zagged up a steep slope. As usual, Hank was soon some way ahead but this time he stopped to wait for her as soon as he realised she was being left behind.

'Arriba!' He was shouting down to her, cheerfully encouraging her ascent. 'Arriba! Arriba!'

He sounded so happy she could hardly believe her ears.

They kept going steadily, now at her pace instead of his. But when they reached the pass at the top of the slope, she was panting hard and her legs felt like lead weights. Hank stepped aside to let her see the view on the other side.

'This is it,' he said. 'Los Encantados.' He was trying to sound as if it was the sort of view he looked at every day. But Anamar knew better. There was a note of pride in his voice, of excitement. This was his element, his place. It had been obvious that the mountains meant a great deal to Hank, but on this day he was able to let it show, and maybe because she was there to share it.

Anamar looked past him at the most dramatic mountain scene she had ever beheld. They were on the rim of a circular depression, ringed with high peaks, joined together by cliffs and sharp ridges. At their feet was a round lake of darkest blue with little wavelets lapping at the shore.

Hank pointed at a sheltered level place near the lake.

'That's our camp site,' he said and began to walk towards it.

From his rucksack Hank produced two rectangular sheets of canvas, each with a triangular piece attached to one end. They buttoned together with a double row of buttons. In a matter of minutes they had been erected, with two folding wooden poles and about a dozen wire pegs to form a small tent.

He explained that this was the bivouac shelter used by the American soldiers during the war. Each man carried one sheet of canvas, one pole and a few pegs, so that two men could button their sheets together to form a simple tent. It was open to the elements at the front and had a pointed end at the back, formed by the triangular extension pieces, and had to be pitched with its back to the wind.

This was the tent they had used when they had climbed Vignemale but Anamar had not seen Hank erect it. Now she sat cross-legged on the ground and watched in wonder as their home for the night took shape before her eyes. Hank spread two light oilskin sheets as a floor inside the tent and laid out his sleeping bag on one.

From her rucksack he extracted the other sleeping bag. This was the inner lining which he could use inside his main bag in very cold conditions. Hank left a space between the two sleeping places and as they unpacked it became filled with the rest of their gear.

Beside the tent, dark blue gentians in full flower were scattered across the down slope and Anamar had to move carefully not to crush them underfoot.

Hank gave her a canvas bucket with a rope handle and she went down to the lake edge for water. When she came back he had lit a small petrol stove and constructed a circular wall around it with rocks, just high enough to give shelter from the wind. He filled a dixie with water, placed it on the stove and grinned at Anamar.

'Stay well back from the stove,' he said. 'This little baby's a hot-rod. Runs on petrol. Burns like a rocket engine. I call it The Bomb.'

In what seemed like a few seconds the water was boiling. Hank had two more small aluminium pots in the set of three which fitted inside each other. He made tea for Anamar in one and coffee for himself in the other and they sat at their ease and looked out over the lake to the peaks beyond.

Small white clouds streamed across the sky. Light and dark patches raced across the surface of the lake. They were now at 8,000 feet, 'more than twice as high as any mountain in Ireland', Anamar thought to herself but decided not to say. They were sheltered from the light breeze by rocks but at a much higher altitude the clouds were speeding past, borne on the most powerful of winds.

Hank's mood was changing. Now that they were camped here, he became quiet and Anamar wondered if he was concerned about the weather.

'No, not the weather,' he said with a strange, rueful look on his face. 'There's a storm on its way but it's not the weather I'm worried about. It's me.' It was as if something had disturbed him and he had withdrawn from Anamar's company to protect himself.

Eamon was fascinated by the idea of camping amongst the wild, high peaks of a range like the Pyrenees. He had been listening intently to Anamar's story and every time she spoke about Hank's feelings and state of mind he became uneasy. He rose and left them, as if answering a call of nature and Anamar continued while he was away.

She and Hank had climbed in silence from their camp to the top of a small peak above the lake. It was unnamed on the map but gave them yet another dramatic mountain view. This time it was to the west, to magnificent snow covered ridges and a great rocky summit plastered with ice. Anamar was hoping that Hank might tell her their names but he stood and stared without a word.

As they started back to their camp he suddenly spoke.

'That beautiful peak at the head of the nearest valley is Mulleres. And behind it is Maladetta, the Evil One, the biggest of them all. It's highest point is called Aneto.' His voice was low, his tone dull. He spoke as if out of duty.

Anamar turned back and climbed the few steps to the top again. He would have to wait. Unlike herself, he knew about these mountains, and having made the effort to get here, it was only fair that she should hear about them too.

'You see that valley below Mulleres.' Hank yelled up to her, 'I call it the Valley of the Three Seasons. You start in high summer at the bottom and walk back to hard winter as you climb to the top.'

Eamon returned as Anamar was describing the evening meal she and Hank had shared at their camp.

They had eaten the soup and the omelette with chunks of bread pulled from the long loaf Anamar had carried up in two pieces, stuffed down the sides of her rucksack.

Hank had told her that the Enchanted Mountains were in the old Kingdom of the Catalans. He said that was why it was sometimes hard to understand the locals, they were speaking in the old tongue. He seemed more at ease now and began a story he had been told by a Catalan during the war.

When first he came to the throne, the last king of the Catalans had made it known that his dearest wish was to cross Los Encantados, the greatest range in his kingdom. The years passed, however, and he grew old without having fulfilled his dream.

Then his family and courtiers arranged for a group of local shepherds and hunters to find a way through the heart of the mountains, which could be traversed by mules. They did so and all was prepared for the journey. The chosen day dawned fine and the King and his retinue set out in festive mood. The route across Els Encantats, as they would have called them in Catalan, was magnificent. Every time they paused on the way up, the stupendous panorama of the kingdom widened below them. The King himself was enchanted.

They stopped to feast on the way. At the highest pass, the view was to every point of the compass, to the very limits of the King's domain. For him, a lifetime's ambition had been fulfilled and all Catalonia rejoiced.

Hank began to smile as he finished the story. It was as if his spirits had risen with the telling.

'I guess I could work out where they stopped for that barbecue on the way,' he said, laughing at the look on Anamar's face when he called their banquet a barbecue. 'Before we go back to the Hospital, we'll see if we can find the King's Route.'

A great surge of happiness filled Anamar's body. To be in such a place, to hear such a tale, to feel that Hank's dark mood was brightening, brought her as great a joy as she had ever known.

Before dark, she had walked a little way around the lake to be on her own. She had crossed scree where tiny Alpine flowers grew amongst the small stones and gravel. They appeared to need no soil. Some had seeded in narrow cracks in the rocks, their little stems packed together in clumps for mutual support.

A tiny, perfectly formed fir seedling was growing in a rock fissure so narrow it seemed the stem must be flattened to let it through. There were flowers which looked like small asters, geraniums, anemones. These must be the Pyrenean versions.

There were wild strawberries, so small she only saw them when she knelt down to look for rock fragments that had caught her eye, glinting in the sunlight. The strawberry runners twisted between the stones and through other plants, their little stems hung with berries.

She had eaten a few and picked some for Hank. Remembering sunny days with Maureen and Eamon picking wild berries, she had threaded them on a stalk of grass poked through from the stalk end to the tip of the berry. How did they manage to grow here, so high amongst the mountains where the winters would be long and bitterly cold? Nobody at home would believe her. 'Strawberries indeed! Growing high in the mountains, amongst the rock and snow peaks! Who ever heard of such a thing?'

When Anamar came back to the tent, darkness fell quickly like a stage curtain dropping to hide the scene. Hank lit a candle inside the tent and made tea, The Bomb roared in its own rocky shelter a few yards away. It was the only sound and somehow reassuring in this wild place.

As they lay down on their separate sides of the tent Anamar reached out and took Hank's hand. He gripped hers tightly as if he needed to hold on but released his grasp as soon as she did.

Anamar was more tired than ever she had been in her life. It was not just the walk and the climb. Having to carry the rucksack, light though it was, had taken its toll of her strength.

But it was only now when the day was nearly over that she dare admit to herself that she was exhausted. Her legs were so weary she could hardly stretch them out in the sleeping bag. She made the effort to turn on her side and was asleep in minutes.

Suddenly a great flash of lightning lit up the night and Anamar awoke with a start. She and Hank sat up in their sleeping bags and a roar of thunder blasted the air like an explosion. Its sharp crack reverberated around the lake. The tent vibrated in the wind and the rain began to pelt the canvas.

At the next brilliant flash Hank began to count quietly. As he reached nineteen, a blast of thunder shook the whole mountainside.

'Nineteen seconds,' he said. 'That means the eye of the storm is about four miles away.' He must have sensed that Anamar was wondering how he could be so precise so he explained that the speed of sound was slower than that of light. It would take the noise of the thunder about five seconds for every mile it had to travel to reach them.

The next blaze of lightning seemed nearer. Anamar began to count. This time it was twelve seconds before the roll of thunder.

'It's coming towards us,' she said, trying not to sound too nervous. 'It's only two and a half miles away.'

Hank's laugh sounded eerie in the darkness.

'You're some smart lady,' he said. 'Quick learner. A little action always concentrates the mind.'

Hearing him speak so cheerfully eased Anamar's fear for a moment. Then the whole world seemed to explode around them.

The flash was so brilliant inside the dark green tent it illuminated Hank's face and every detail of the interior. Almost simultaneously there was an horrendous crash of thunder. The tent shook and the thunder peal echoed around their valley. A blast of wind threatened to rip the canvas from its pegs. The rain turned to hail, driven against the flimsy shelter with the force of a gale.

'This is it! Welcome to the eye of the storm, baby!' Hank's voice was calm, 'We gotta sit this one out,' he said. 'Keep off the sides of the tent. It's a tough cookie, but if you touch canvas it leaks.'

He was talking like this to keep her spirits up and Anamar laughed nervously in the darkness. She gave his arm a nudge with her elbow.

'*And how am I supposed to do that?' she asked. 'With the hurricane battering the side against me no matter where I sit.' She might be more frightened than ever she had been in her life before, but no American was going to hear one word of panic from her, not if she could help it.*

'*No place to run to,' Hank said calmly. 'Take your pick. Pray to your God or join me among the fatalists.'*

Suddenly the rain stopped and the wind dropped right away. The roar of the gale and the drumming of the hail on the canvas were now silenced.

Then a shattering eruption of light and sound brought flash and bang together in one cataclysmic explosion. Anamar was knocked sideways against the canvas wall of the tent. It was as if she had been physically hit across the shoulders by a huge plank of wood. The flash was so bright and the bang so loud she was completely disorientated. She lay still for a moment, afraid to move, then crawled back into her sleeping bag, shaken, numb with fear.

There was a strange acrid odour which she recognised at once. It was the sharp smell of flint struck on flint. Years before, she and Maureen had tried to light a fire without matches. The tinder was dry and should have been flammable but the sparks from the flints failed to produce flames. But there was a smell, a powerful nose-twitching stink, once smelt, never forgotten.

'*I guess that was it,' said Hank quietly. He too had been hit and was now sitting up feeling his shoulder. It was bruised, tender to the touch. 'Do you smell that burnt rock, blasted by the thousands of amps of electricity?'*

They held hands and waited for the next big bang. Anamar prayed, almost, but not quite silently. Then she found herself saying the Rosary. When the next flash came, it came alone and Hank counted to forty-five before they heard the roll of thunder. The storm was miles off. They breathed a simultaneous, audible sigh of relief. As suddenly as it had come, it had gone, racing away across the mountains.

Anamar dressed and crawled through the open front of the tent. The grass was wet. There were little piles of hailstones driven up against the side of rocks. The clouds had cleared. The rim of peaks and ridges on the far side of the lake were black against the dark, dark blue of the sky. The stars were from a fairy story, clear, bright, reassuringly familiar.

'*They really do twinkle,' Anamar thought, but she was too shy to say it. Hank sat in the door of the tent and watched her stand and stare.*

When she lay down in the tent again, Anamar did so without undressing. She was feeling the tiredness of the whole day, but in the warmth of her sleeping bag there was comfort, security. She took Hank's hand once more and held it like a sister. He seemed more alive than ever before. She was sure he was smiling in the darkness. 'The demons of despair have left him. Maybe they've gone off with the storm,' she thought to herself.

Maureen and Eamon had been listening without a word. Now there were the questions. 'Were you hurt? Were you not scared out of your wits? How could you stay there for the rest of the night? You could have been killed. What did Hank say?'

After the evening meal it was Eamon who encouraged Anamar to continue.

'What about the King's Road over the mountains? Did you find any trace of it the next day?' He was embarrassed to be sounding so enthusiastic.

'And here was me thinking you were jealous of Hank.' As usual, Maureen was not going to miss a chance to tease him. 'And now you're ready to follow his every footstep.' The girls laughed at Eamon's discomfort…

Anamar continued the story.

She told them she had slept so soundly, she had only wakened in the morning because the heat of the sun on the tent made it unbearable to stay inside. Hank was already up and washed. He had breakfast laid out in front of the tent. The Bomb was roaring away under a pot of water. They sat with their backs against a rock and ate in silence in the sunshine. The view across the lake was sublime. The prospect so peaceful it was hard to believe that a storm had erupted here so violently. For one awful moment it had held them, trapped in its eye. Anamar shook her shoulders to dispel the memory and smiled at Hank.

Half an hour later they struck camp and followed the lake shore to cross a pass between two small peaks to the east.

Now they could see into the very heart of Los Encantados. It was a stunning view. A short distance below, in a long, high valley there were three lakes flashing and glittering in the sun's low rays. The nearest was as large as the one they had camped beside the previous night. The furthest was tiny but the middle one was a long, narrow tarn in the most beautiful mountain setting Anamar had ever seen.

Beyond, a ridge ringed the end of the valley. Behind that, there were mountains and ridges with huge peaks, which Hank said were nearly 10,000ft. high, dominating all. The terrain rolled back into the distance as if there was no end.

'We'll camp there for the night.' Hank was pointing to the left of the middle lake. 'I reckon His Royalness must have passed thataway.' He was smiling, trying to joke with her.

They reached the lake before mid-day. As Hank lit the stove, Anamar went to look at something which she had seen from above. On the way down from the pass she had noticed a faint line, curving around the long tarn. It looked like an Irish green road. Her eye was accustomed to picking out tracks in the mountains and green roads were a part of the Donegal landscape she knew so well. They had been built and used long before tar macadam highways and many were still in use.

When she reached the line of the track she had seen from above, she followed it for a hundred yards or so. The first part of it seemed like a natural feature of the mountainside but a little further on she was not so sure. Kneeling down on the low side, she pulled the vegetation back and gave a cry of delight. She was right. The edge of the bank had been built up with flat stones to form a little causeway.

Anamar ran back towards the camp, waving to Hank and shouting.

'I've found it! The King's Road! It's over here!'

Hank laughed and joined her on the track. He gave her a pat on the back.

'I said you were some smart lady.' He was laughing out loud.

When they had eaten and pitched camp, they walked the line of the King's Road to a high pass. From there it descended steeply towards a large lake and they followed it down to the shore-line, going north over yet another pass. They climbed a small rock peak for the view and watched the King's Road twist down a valley, presumably wending its way out of the mountains.

They sat for a long time looking out over the Enchanted Mountains, each lost in thought. Their friendship had grown. They were now comrades. They were both enchanted by this place.

On a nearby peak Anamar saw a herd of tiny deer running nimbly across scree.

'They're Pyrenean chamois.' Hank seemed as pleased as she was to see them, 'The Spanish call them 'isards'.' This was his element. He was a happy man here in these mountains, and now beginning to admit it, even to himself.

In the morning, they walked back down to the Hospital de Viella by a different route, travelling slowly, saying little, needing to talk less than before, understanding more of each other.

Once again, they were the only guests at the ancient inn and the senora welcomed them as old friends.

That evening, they sat by the fire in the main room of the inn where the fire was in the middle of the floor. Directly above it, the ceiling ascended in a narrowing vault to become the chimney. There were hooks hanging down to hold hams for smoking. The logs hissed and crackled as they would have done here for centuries. The senora brought them big glasses of the dark red wine from the cask while they waited for their meal. Anamar drank the almost-black wine sip by sip.

'Hank and I both knew this would be our last evening together.' She said

softly to Maureen and Eamon. 'The parting of the ways. He was off to the Sierra Nevada Mountains in the south of Spain and it was time for me to come back to Donegal.'

There was a pause. Maureen's next question was on the tip of her tongue but she knew it could not be asked, not just yet.

'I know Eamon has to go back to the farm to-morrow,' Anamar said looking thoughtfully at Maureen. 'But why don't you stay another night? I've never talked so much in my life and I'm really enjoying the company.'

Maureen smiled and readily agreed. She wondered if Anamar had read the question in her mind and decided that there could be no answer until they were alone.

Do You Remember an Inn, Miranda?

Eamon left early, just as the others were stirring, thinking of rising to make breakfast. It was a bright morning, too good to waste. He needed to be on his way back home if he was to get any work done that day.

'Seen you soon!', he shouted into the mouth of the cave, too shy to look inside in case the girls were dressing.

By the time they came out into the weak morning sunshine, he was well on his way to the ridge. They saw him turn back to wave so often, it was easy to guess he was reluctant to go. The girls took their tea down to the lake-side and sat on grassy banks without a word, looking across the water. It was Anamar who spoke first.

'Do you see that the largest bits of gravel are all at the right hand end of the beach,' she said. 'And the way the wee waves gather speed as they roll in to the shore.'

Maureen sighed theatrically. She could contain herself no longer.

'Never mind your precious gravel and your wee wavelets,' she said, grinning. 'What about your last night at the old inn in the Pyrenees?'

Anamar began to laugh, rocking gently back and forth on her seat. Maureen kept up the pressure.

'Why do you think I arranged to get rid of the good brother? He's too young and inexperienced for this sort of chat. You owe me the full story.'

They left their cups on a stone and walked slowly around the lake. Anamar took the story back to the evening meal at the inn.

While they waited for the food to arrive at their table, she and Hank spoke about their separate plans. It had taken the senora three trips from the kitchen to bring them a wicker basket of bread, a brown earthenware jug of wine, a tomato salad piled high in a bowl and a Spanish omelette.

As they began to eat Hank smiled.

'Do you know the poem about the inn in the Pyrenees called 'Tarantella'?' he asked.

72

Anamar nodded. In her last year in Mr. Robson's class they had learned it by heart, repeating it in unison until everyone knew all the words.

'Do you remember an Inn,

Miranda?

Do you remember an Inn?'

She said the words softly and, inside her head, heard the class chanting, the sounds flowing together like a mountain stream.

'Well, this is it.' Hank pointed to the interior of the Hospital de Viella, 'Give or take a little poetic licence, this gotta be it.'

English Literature had been Hank's favourite subject at college and when first he came to the Pyrenees, he had been on the look-out for the inn in Hilaire Belloc's poem. To his own surprise he continued the verse.

'And the tedding and the spreading
Of the straw for a bedding,
And the fleas that tease in the High Pyrenees.'

'And tell me this,' Anamar said, laughing. 'Do the fleas still tease in the High Pyrenees?'

Hank raised his tumbler of wine.

'Well, this is the place to find out,' he said. 'Here's to the fleas of the High Pyrenees. And if we drink a few glasses of this, chances are they'll keep their distance to-night.'

Anamar clinked her tumbler loudly against his. At first she had found this wine too sharp, too strong for her taste and Hank had advised her to drink plenty of water with it, not mixed but in a separate glass.

'This is the 'vino negre',' Hank had said. 'It's so dark a red it's known as 'the black wine'. When Hilaire Belloc was here, walking these hills, he called it, 'the wine that tasted of the tar.'

Anamar knew what he was thinking but wanted to encourage him to keep talking. 'You always stop just as it becomes interesting.'

'That's the years without the practice, Anamar,' he said. 'It's been a long time since I felt I could talk to someone.'

They talked on quietly throughout the meal. The omelette was delicious, delicately aromatic. They guessed that the senora had cooked it with herbs from the mountain. She had smiled to see their enjoyment when she brought in the next course, a bowl of lamb chops, grilled over the open fire.

The bowl had been piled high and to her own amazement Anamar ate four chops while Hank was still at work on his third.

The senora appeared behind him, laughing.

'Quiere mas?' she said. Already Anamar was learning a few words of Spanish and knew that she meant. 'Would you like some more?'

They shook their heads and Hank left it to Anamar to do the talking.

'No mas, gracias,' she replied. 'Esto estupendo,' and they laughed together, the senora clapping gently and softly crying, 'Bravo! Bravo!'.

Anamar could not remember an evening when she had been happier. Over the weeks Hank's dark mood of melancholy had waned a little. When first it had begun to change, there had been moments when he had almost seemed cheerful. But the underlying sense of despair, of hopelessness, had remained. Now it was fading into the background, although Anamar could detect its presence virtually every time he spoke.

The change in him over the weeks had been slow and gradual, but it was a real transformation. On this trip, his conversation no longer seemed out of duty to his companion. His sharp comments of the past had become his wry good humour of the present. He smiled, not often, but frequently enough to indicate that he was happier, not only to be in the mountains but to be with her.

Hank finished the last chop and took a long drink of the wine. He looked across the table to Anamar, who was waiting for him to speak.

'You'll know by now I'm not one for speeches,' he said. 'Do you remember me telling you that,when I came back to the Pyrenees this time, it was to end my life.'

Anamar was not surprised and said nothing. There was no need.

'I think I've changed my mind.' He paused, as if the effort to speak was draining his energy. 'But, for some reason, I need to tell you why I became so low in the first place.'

It was Anamar's turn to sip the wine. She knew what he was thinking and settled back in her chair, smiling encouragingly. Since she had met him, she had been aware that something awful must have happened to have affected him so deeply. He was obviously an interesting, intelligent man who had already achieved a great deal in life. His career in the army had been successful. He had travelled widely since his student days. His mountaineering had been such an exciting and enjoyable interest. Life had been good to him. His life had been happy. Some traumatic event had changed everything.

Hank took her back to the war and his part in the action.

'You know, of course, that the United States didn't come into the conflict until the Japanese bombed Pearl Harbour in 1941.'

Anamar nodded. As an eleven-year-old she had heard the news on the wireless. As usual her mother and father had said nothing. They had both looked stunned, shocked beyond words, the war was now affecting the whole world. It was the way they always reacted to the bad news of the war, like the devastation of an Allied convoy in the Atlantic, or an horrendous battle in Russia. Although they would receive it without comment, accepting the horror, later they would talk much more than usual.

'I was at West Point at the time, playing at being a trainee officer.' Hank was speaking quickly, as if anxious to get the story told. Anamar sat perfectly still and listened.

'Pearl Harbour changed all that. We had to become soldiers quickly. Soldiers are supposed to be able to fight, to kill. Officers are meant to lead them into the fight, to teach them to kill, to make sure they do it well.'

Hank was not enjoying this step back into his past.

'On June 6 1944 we were on a troopship sailing in convoy across the Atlantic, when we heard a message broadcast over the ship's tannoy. It was from General Eisenhower's HQ in England. The 'D-Day' invasion of Europe had begun at last. Allied troops had landed in Northern France.'

Hank paused and looked reflective for a moment.

'Word spread around the ship that that's where we were headed. But it was only a rumour. Our destination was a holding camp in North Africa. Two months later we sailed across the Mediterranean as part of another invasion force called Operation Dragoon. We were to land in the South of France to divert the German Army away from the Northern Front. There were over a hundred ships carrying nearly 200,000 men.

'My division was on a British ship called the M.V. Circassia and we were to land on a beach called the Plage de la Pampleonne near Saint-Tropez. The British seamen of the Circassia had survived sea battles in nearly every ocean in the world. But it was the first time for all of us. For every American officer and soldier, this was it, the real war, kill or be killed.'

Hank stopped. He suddenly looked very tired. For Anamar, it was hard to stay silent, to keep from saying he should not go on. But she knew he needed to tell the story and said nothing.

'As we sailed towards the shore, our warships stayed further out to sea pounding the enemy positions. Their shells flew over our heads. The roar was like a thousand mock battles. On board the Circassia the decks were crowded with soldiers, every man at his station, waiting for the word to go.

'The battle hardened ship's crew had treated us well on the passage through the Med, now they stood watching us. It was our turn, our moment of truth.

'The Circassia hove to off the beach and we began to transfer to the landing craft. The first of the men from another ship were already on the shore, running

into a hail of fire. We could see smoke, tracer bullets, exploding grenades. Suddenly the crackle of small arms' fire and the bumping of the mortars would stop for a short almost silent pause, and then would erupt again more fiercely than before.

'My men were due to be amongst the last off. Nobody spoke. No need to. Then I heard a great shout along the ship's side to my left. There were raised voices and the sound of a pistol shot. One of our men had refused to leave the ship and an officer had drawn his pistol and fired over his head.

'Most of the men looked away. Some of them were swearing, wanting to get going, hating the waiting. It was hard enough to hold your own nerve without having to think of anyone else. We'd been through this in lectures at West Point. 'Panic spreads like a forest fire. Stop it or it will burn down the whole forest'.

'A young captain pushed his way down the crowded deck, having a quiet word with each officer in turn. He didn't get as far as me but I was certain he was delivering an order. 'Draw your side arm. Don't argue with any man who refuses to go. Shoot him!'

'When it was our turn, I knew who to watch. He looked far too young to be a soldier, like a boy in man's clothes, sent to do a man's job. Crossing the Atlantic he had been ill. It was not sea-sickness. The boy was a very experienced sailor from a rich sailing family, had his own yacht when he was seventeen. It was not going to sea which was the problem. It was going to war.

'The men were swarming over the side, climbing down rope ladders into the landing craft. He turned back and saw me with the gun in my hand. His face was grey as if he was already losing his grip of himself. I saw his lips form words but I couldn't hear.'

'The other men near him saw nothing. They were totally involved, concentrating on getting over the side. They struggled with huge loads of kit and arms and ammunition, down the rope ladders, into the boats.

'The boy was facing the wrong way, back against the ship's rail, his eyes pleading with me. I pointed the gun and decided to give him three seconds to go. As if he could read my mind, he turned, lurched over the side and struggled with the rope ladder, almost falling down into the boat.'

Hank paused to draw a deep breath, like a sigh passing into his body rather than out. Then he steeled himself to continue.

'I followed and heard a crew member's shout behind me, 'Good luck Yankees! Good luck to all of you!' and then in a lower voice I was not meant to hear. 'And by God you'll need it!'

'I sat in the landing craft where I could watch the boy. He was shaking. His eyes were closed but he knew I was there.

'We hit the beach running, just as we'd practised a hundred times on that beach on the other side of the Med. The boy was at the back, but he still had me behind him. We ran for the shelter of the trees, three paces between us. A machine gun clattered and I was amazed not to be hit, but he was. The boy was shot through the abdomen, the first of my men to fall.

'The enemy fire was so heavy we all had to drop flat. I had to leave him at first, then there was a lull. He was very badly wounded, dying in agony.'

Hank stopped, his face drained of colour.

'Dragging him up to the trees, I was hit in the shoulder by a lump of shrapnel, just as we reached cover. And that was the end of the war for both of us.

'I should have let him stay on the ship. He was the last man, except for myself. Nobody would have known except the sailors.

'When I came to my senses in hospital, I heard that he had been buried in a soldier's grave. I spent three months in a hospital bed in Saint-Tropez and got a medal, a Purple Heart.'

Hank put his head in his hands and began to cry softly. The senora came into the room with another jug of wine, set it on the table and left without a word. Anamar sat very still and almost held her breath in case she would make a noise.

Her heart went out to him. She wanted to stand up and hug him across the table. But maybe he needed to let the tears flow. She wanted to weep for him too, for his tortured years since the battle on the beach at Saint-Tropez.

She let him cry for what seemed a long time, then she reached out and put her hand on his arm.

He looked up, embarrassed, but Anamar was smiling.

'Real men aren't afraid to cry,' she said in a whisper. He raised his glass to his lips to drink a deep draught of the vino negre. The moments passed in silence. Then he tried to smile too.

'And that's the first time I've told anyone the story of what happened on La Plage de la Pampleonne.' Now that he had stopped, there was relief in Hank's voice. There was an air of finality too, as if there was no more to tell, he had reached the end.

For Anamar, it was still a tale only half told. What had happened next? She could understand now why he had been so depressed then, but that was years ago. Had he felt worse as time passed? Had no one been able to help him.

'It wasn't your fault,' she heard herself saying. 'Anyway, it happened ages ago.' In a few moments Hank raised his head to look her directly.

'It was Friday, August 18, 1944, four years ago on the day before yesterday, four years to the day. When you and I met in Gavarnie, I had already chosen this year's anniversary as the day I would put an end to it all. An end to the bad times I've had in the past four years.

'*I had picked the place too, Vignemale, the beautiful mountain. But you made me think again. By the time you and I pitched our tent at the lake two days ago, I realised that here we were, together in the Enchanted Mountains, instead of me being on the loneliest journey of all on Vignemale.*'

Anamar kept her lips tightly shut in case she uttered a word and stopped him speaking. Hank filled the big tumblers with wine and talked on as if he was explaining to himself what had happened between them.

'*When we started out on that wet day of our walk up the valley, the rain stopped at the Lac D'Ossoue. The sun came out as we climbed. Then we looked up and there was the great peak above us, Vignemale.*

'*I had made the decision to take my own life after miserable months in hospital and years of agonising about what had happened. I could think of nothing else. Life seemed pointless. When I had made up my mind that suicide was the only way out, I felt better.*

As *the days and weeks passed, I was sure I was right. I had caused the death of the boy because he was more afraid of me than the enemy. All the hours I spent with friends and psychiatrists only convinced me that they didn't understand. Unknowingly, they were confirming my decision.*

'*The day we saw Vignemale, you confused me. You made me angry because you weakened my resolve. Without knowing why, I began to doubt my decision. But by the end of that walk, I no longer knew for certain that suicide was the only way.*'

He paused and Anamar knew she had to say something.

'It wasn't just me,' she said very quietly. 'It was where we were. You began to change as soon as we started to climb that valley, before we saw the mountain.'

Hank looked startled to hear her voice as if surprised she was still there.

'Sorry,' he said. 'I've been so used to talking things out in my head, I had almost forgotten you were here. I guess I can't recall what it's like to be able to talk to someone.'

They left the table to go outside for a breath of air. The sky was clear, the stars brilliant. When their eyes became used to the light, they picked out a great jagged mountain to the west.

'Mulleres,' Hank said. 'My first Pyrenean peak. I call that black space below it 'the Valley of the Three Seasons'.' He sounded happier now talking about the mountains, as if his fears were slipping away.

When they came back inside they chatted about their separate plans. For a man who had been so dour, Anamar had sometimes wondered what she had to do to get him to speak. Hank was now talking excitedly, telling her about his plans to climb in the Sierra Nevada in Southern Spain.

'*Hold on!*' she said, pretending that her patience had run out. '*Just hold your whist for a minute.*'

They both began to laugh.

'*What kindova word is 'whist'?*' Hank asked. '*Is that Donegal Irish?*'

Anamar pretended to be offended.

'*At least it's a sight better than 'kindova','* she said. Deirdre Ryan hated American slang like '*kindova*' and '*you don't say*' almost as much as incorrect grammar like '*I seen*' and '*I done*' and Anamar was not happy being taught how to speak by an American.

'*OK! OK! I surrender.*' Hank raised his arms and his voice. '*I've always been told not to fist-fight an Irishman or argue with an Irish woman.*'

They were enjoying themselves so much that the senora was drawn into the doorway of the room and she stood there, leaning against the upright, sharing the fun. She was quite tall for a Spanish woman, strongly built, confident of her physical presence. When the muleteers were gathering here for the journey across the mountains, it was easy to see her dealing with any trouble which might arise.

It was obviously a rare event for her to have foreigners staying at the inn and she treated Anamar and Hank as honoured guests. Now she was enjoying their happiness. This pair would give her something to talk to her friends about in the long winter evenings.

From behind her back she produced a large bottle of clear liquid and two squat glasses.

'*Un licor,*' she explained, showing them the distinctively waisted litre bottle with a blue label. '*Marie Brizard Anisette.*' She made a little speech and handed the bottle to Hank.

'*It's a present,*' Hank said to Anamar. '*Aniseed liqueur, good for the digestion. This Marie Brizard outfit makes the best.*'

He asked the senora to bring another glass so that she could join them. At first she refused. Then she went to the kitchen and came back with a small tumbler. She had been so hesitant, Anamar felt this might have been the first time she had ever shared a drink with strangers.

Hank filled the glasses, stood up for a moment and held his glass to the others.

'*Espana!*' he said, and they drank a toast to Spain. The senora was delighted. She smiled her thanks and left them on their own. Hank held his glass up for another toast.

'*To the girl from Donegal. Who saved me an avalanche of trouble.*'

Anamar grinned at him.

'*Don't think you're going to keep me out of this round just by toasting me.*'

She said cheerily and she held up her glass and mimicked his southern accent.

'And here's to the man from Lafayette, Louisiana, who helped himself! And the little old Pyrenees who helped us all!'

They drank the toasts, laughing together, as if this was the way it had always been between them.

Maureen and Anamar had been walking slowly around Lough Belshade, stopping to look back across the water towards the shelter stone. Maureen had hardly uttered a word, except to encourage Anamar to keep talking. They had rambled along the steep western side to the southern shore and now had reached the cairn which Eamon would have passed on his way down over an hour before.

They sat down on the heather and Maureen steeled herself to wait with all the patience she could muster. Anamar was smiling, looking into the distance, knees drawn up to her chin, arms cradling her shins, still and calm as the lake. After a decent interval Maureen could restrain herself no longer.

'Go on,' she said. ' Am I to drag it out of you, like pulling teeth?'

Anamar seemed to be in a dream as she continued.

Hank wanted to know about her own plans. It was back home, to Donegal, she said, back to the farm on the shores of Lough Eske.

'And when you set out on your motor-bike down the road, I'm off across the mountains to Viella. The first stage of my journey back to Ireland.' She said it quietly, expecting some objection from Hank for proposing to tackle such a long mountain walk on her own.

To her surprise Hank smiled.

And all he said was, 'Good for you, little mountain runner. I'll give you the map, you might just need it.'

They were sharing a room not much bigger than Hank's tent but there were two narrow iron-framed beds, one against each of the side walls. The mattresses were stuffed with horses' hair. Instead of blankets there were thick quilts. A small window, set in a wall two feet thick, overlooked the valley. The door was of solid wood, with two pegs on the back of it, one for each guest's clothes. A lighted paraffin lamp sat comfortably on the window ledge and the room's furniture was completed by one straight-backed wooden chair.

Hank let her go to the room first and by the time he came in she was undressed and in her sleeping bag. He blew out the paraffin lamp and before getting into his own bed, kissed her on the hair.

'Good-night, Anamar,' he said softly. 'Be sure I'll remember you.'

Anamar wondered what Hank was thinking, what he felt about her. There was a physical gap between them. Maybe it was a gap which he was not yet well enough recovered to try to cross.

A few minutes later she heard his breathing, deep and even, and knew he was asleep. She slept too, but not for long. When she opened her eyes it was pitch dark. She turned on her back to stretch her legs inside the sleeping bag. Suddenly she realised that he too was awake. After a long pause she put out her hand and found his in the darkness between them as if he had been waiting for her.

Anamar stopped and turned to look at Maureen, feeling shy with her friend for the first time in her life. Maureen smiled. She knew that this was the end of the story for the present. Although it was against everything they had been brought up to believe, she wanted to hear that on their last night together, Anamar and Hank had become lovers.

She knew instinctively, however, that although she and Anamar had always been closer than sisters, Anamar would tell her no more for the present. She might hear later, but for now Hank's part in the tale was over.

A Pilgrim's Staff for the Pyrenees

The two girls sat at the cairn for a long time, feeling closer than ever before. Maureen's usual chatty conversation and physical restlessness were stilled. She felt at ease, content to be here with her friend, sharing her secrets.

They rose and collected a few stones from the river to make the cairn a little more substantial. It was more than a marker now.

'It's like a little mountain,' Maureen said, her voice softer, more gentle than usual.

Anamar stirred as if from a day-dream and they began to walk back.

At the cave they made tea and ate bread and home-made rhubarb jam. In the afternoon they walked north, climbing slowly up a steep side valley to the crest of the main ridge of the Blue Stacks. They brought the map so they could name all the mountains and valleys they could see.

They were all great names, 'Lavagh More', 'Croveenananta', 'Gaugin Mountain'. The day was hot, humid, sultry but high on the ridge the gentlest of breezes freshened the air.

Maureen thought about asking Anamar to continue her story but felt quite proud of herself when she resisted the temptation. They hardly spoke and Maureen was amazed to find how much she was enjoying herself in her friend's company without talking. 'It's not like me to sing dumb,' she thought to herself. 'If Rose and Maggie were here they'd think I was sickening for something.'

As they made the evening meal the sky clouded over and they sat in the mouth of the cave to eat, watching the big rain drops splash down. Suddenly Anamar began to talk again. She took Maureen by surprise by going straight to the next morning in her story. There was a bit missing. 'Maybe I'll never hear it,' Maureen thought. 'Anyway, better not say anything just now.'

Hank left early next morning. His motor-bike started at the first kick. His gear was in two side panniers and the rucksack strapped to the pillion seat. Anamar had given him back the inner sleeping bag he had lent her. Where he was headed he would need it.

They kissed goodbye and she waved him down to the service road at the tunnel. She watched and listened until he was out of sight and out of sound.

Her rucksack was packed too, and this time she had been allowed to do it herself. 'Things are looking up,' she had thought, as Hank had watched how she placed every item in the bag. 'He must think I'm no longer the helpless little girl.'

Anamar took a last look around the buildings which comprised the Hospital de Viella. They had been in use as an inn for over two hundred years. The construction was substantial, built to withstand hard winters, tucked into the hillside well above the valley floor. Beside the river was the dirt road which serviced the tunnelling. It would become the motor road through the tunnel to the town of Viella when the work was finished.

The back of the Hospital was towards the river and its front door opened out on to a cobbled street between the inn and its outbuildings. Attached to the southern end of the inn was the small chapel, like all the other buildings, constructed from stone hewn from the mountainside.

The Hospital was the last overnight stop for the mule trains on the way to Spanish Viella on the north side of the mountains. Once these mule caravans had been the only link across the range but now there was a road of sorts, the circuitous route, largely unsurfaced, which they had ridden on Hank's motor cycle to reach here. The senora had told Hank that the mule trains were fewer now, and once the tunnel was opened they would be needed no longer.

It would be another few months before the tunnel provided a short cut for vehicles under the hills, but Anamar intended to follow the ancient route which wound its way through these high peaks. All would go well if she could find the old path and keep to it. There were bound to be other tracks and no signs to tell her which was the right one. The muleteers and their mules would have had no need of markers. Anamar began to feel nervous about being alone on this journey.

She stood on the cobbled street where the muleteers would have assembled and felt a part of their history. It gave her strength. 'Anyway,' she thought. 'Hank's gone. No time for doubts. I'd better get on with the journey.'

Anamar was certain that, as she followed the trail of the muleteers, it would lead her into an entirely new part of her life.

'Did you not go into the church?' A lifetime of close contact with her religion showed in Maureen's tone of concern. There was a long pause.

'I did,' said Anamar eventually, as if she had considered the act of entering the church very seriously. 'The senora's washing was hanging on a clothes line in the back corner. I sat down for a while and thought about Hank and had a feeling all would be well with him. At that moment, I was sure all would be well with me too.

Maureen gave a quiet, involuntary sigh of relief. At times Anamar seemed so independent, so free in her mind, so strong in herself, she wondered if the church had lost her completely.

As Anamar continued she did so purposefully, as if she had seriously considered the practicalities of her walk.

The senora had given her bread, cheese, a few slices of the tasty garlic sausage and a big, firm tomato. She shouldered her pack and they shook hands. She was setting off alone. This was different from leaving home for Dublin, travelling to Lourdes, living there on her own.

This time she was facing a journey through the wilds of the Pyrenees. Hank had reckoned it would take seven or eight hours and that finding the way would not be easy.

There would be false trails, steep, seemingly unending slopes to climb, rough, rocky going, the possibility of bad weather. But Anamar had refused to be intimidated. She was excited by the adventure, by the prospect of finding her own way and having to look after herself amongst these mountains, exhilarated by the thought of making this journey alone.

As she set off along the track, there was a shout from behind. The senora was running after her. It was to give her a stick to help her on the way.

This was no puny walking cane for city streets. It was a staff, shoulder high, bark stripped and surface smoothed. 'This is a real pilgrim's staff.' Anamar thought. And the further she went, the more she felt that, with such a stick, she might be a pilgrim too.

Maureen was looking at her friend in admiration. She realised she had always thought highly of Anamar, always seen her as very capable, efficient, good in an emergency, often accepted her as the leader when the two of them were together. But when Anamar had returned home she had been a different person and she was beginning to understand why this was so.

Now, as Anamar described setting off on her journey, she appeared so strong, so at ease with herself, so self-reliant, so undaunted by the difficulties and dangers of the trip. This new Anamar was a revelation. Now Maureen knew why she was so happy in her company.

Anamar paused as if to collect her thoughts. She looked up, saw the look of delight on Maureen's face and began to laugh.

'Pride before a fall,' she said. 'Miss Ryan, as usual, was right.'

Anamar described the track winding gently up the valley, huge snow-capped peaks ahead, steep rocky slopes on her right, even steeper slopes, topped with dark grey cliffs, across the broad meadow to her left.

This was the place Hank called 'the Valley of the Three Seasons'. At this time of year, he said, it would be high summer in the meadow below. Climbing past a waterfall would lead to a higher level and a knee-high carpet of flowers in the full bloom of late spring. Anamar could see that waterfall clearly and, higher up, the second water-fall too, above which the plants would be tiny alpines set between the rocks or in clumps on the scree.

Towards the head of the valley, Hank said there was a rocky out-crop leading to a higher level where it would be full winter still. Up there, below the ice-domed peaks, were three lakes. These would be partly frozen over, even in the month of August. One was directly under the cliffs and it would have icebergs as big as houses.

Hank made it sound the most spectacular location in all the mountains. Although he had never taken her there, his words were so clear in her head she could imagine every detail of the terrain. Would she be able to look down on it later, and see the whole valley, its three seasons in the one view?

Anamar was walking quickly, stepping out along the path. After a mile or more she crossed a stream and fifteen minutes later stopped to look at the map. She had gone wrong. The stream was beyond the point where she should have turned right to climb the slope. If she kept on the way she was going, she would soon be climbing into the middle reaches of the Valley of the Three Seasons. She should have branched right before the stream and zig-zagged up the steep slope to the north.

She remembered Hank saying, 'Finding the way, like rock climbing, is always easy until you begin to have doubts, then it suddenly becomes so difficult, you feel you'll never be able to do it.' He was right. Anamar could feel the panic rising in her chest.

Maureen was laughing,

'Half an hour's walk from the inn, and the intrepid mountain traveller was lost! Some Pyrenean pioneer you were!' she said. 'I always knew you shouldn't be let out on your own. You'd have looked the quare eejit, if your precious Hank had been waiting for you half way up the mountain and watching you go wrong at the first turn.'

They laughed together and Maureen kept teasing Anamar right through the gloom of the evening, as it turned quickly to the dark of a bad night. Inside the cave, wrapped in their bedding, they were dry and snug. Over a cup of cocoa Anamar heard what Maureen had been up to. There was a list of boy friends long enough to surprise Anamar but obviously not long enough to produce one who pleased Maureen. There had been dances, days at the fair in Donegal Town, summer trips to Bundoran, parish socials, outings to the cinema in Ballyshannon.

According to Maureen, the Abbey Cinema in Ballyshannon was the centre of the world. It was 'just great, a real palace of a place'. She had gone with a crowd of six of her friends packed into the one car to see Rex Harrison in 'Anna and the King of Siam' and a bus from Donegal Town had taken them to a special matinee to see 'Snow White and the Seven Dwarfs'.

There had been a talent competition one evening at the Abbey Cinema and Rose's father had taken them in the car.

'You should have seen Maggie.' Maureen had been too quiet for too long and was enjoying herself. 'She had on this skirt and up on the stage of the Abbey it looked **so** short. She was a sketch. Eamon didn't know where to look. He was sweet on her at the time. But she's no chance now, of course. Those big sheep's eyes are only for you and well you know it.

Anamar was laughing so much, her face ached.

'And what did she do for her turn?' she managed to say.

'Oh, she sang 'Galway Bay', what else? She had the whole crowd roaring the chorus with her. There would have been a riot if the judges had given the prize to anyone else.'

It was late when they lay down to sleep. Anamar was so tired. Telling her story had drained every drop of her energy. But Maureen's conversation was like a healing balm. She might be feeling exhausted, but her mind was at ease, her body relaxed. It was so good to have been able to talk to someone.

Maureen planned to leave for home in the early afternoon and during the morning Anamar continued the tale of her epic journey across the mountains.

'I had to turn back,' she said. 'I hated that, although it wasn't very far. It was time and energy wasted but it had to be done.'

Anamar had turned and recrossed the stream and walked towards the Hospital slowly, looking for any trace of the path she should have taken. And to her amazement, there it was, a faint track heading north up the steep hillside. How could she have missed it? And what would she have done if she had not looked at the map until much later?

Across the Pyrenean Pass

The feeling of relief, now that Anamar was going the right way made her spirits rise with the track. But she knew that she must make no more mistakes. Such an error, made later when she was in the midst of the mountains, could well be serious. And particularly so if, at the same time, she were to be caught in a thunderstorm or the mist came down to cover the peaks.

The path was steep and it turned and twisted to take the best line up the slope. Anamar found herself panting hard. She had only been walking uphill for fifteen minutes but already her chest felt tight. It must be the anxiety about finding the right route as well as the effort. Her lungs gasped for air, the pulse of her heart-beat throbbed at the left side of her temple.

She stopped for a moment to give herself a chance to recover. It had been too fast a pace. What was it Hank used to say when they were walking on the French side of the Pyrenees?

'Qui va doucement, va surement. Qui va surement, va loin.'... 'Who goes gently, goes safely. Who goes safely, goes far.'

She smiled to herself. It was not much more than an hour since she had started out and already she had made two blunders.

She could hear Hank's voice in her head as she climbed. 'Doucement! ... doucement! ... doucement!', he would say over and over again as they rose into the hills. Encouraging her on every hard upward step.

Deirdre Ryan had lent Anamar a book about Eastern Religions and she had read that, when Buddhists were meditating, they often used a single word or a phrase called a mantra, repeating it again and again. Miss Ryan had told her that it was like Christians saying a familiar prayer or a decade of the Rosary.

She set a slower pace to let her breath come more evenly and the climbing felt easier. The path topped a rise and led into a shallow depression. For the first time she could see the ridge above her head, with its cliffs and rocky peaks apparently barring the way.

Lower down, the angle had been so rocky and steep she could see nothing but the slope she was climbing. Now, there was a stunning view. To her left, she looked into the heart of the Valley of the Three Seasons. Below, the slope fell away, right down to the Hospital de Viella and the mouth of the tunnel. Up ahead, across a stream, was a small lake, a tiny mountain tarn set amongst the boulders.

The path twisted and turned through the stones and scree. Often it was hard to see the next stretch, for the whole slope was so littered with rocks and rubble which had tumbled down from the cliffs. Then, to her great relief, she would spot one of the small cairns of stones built to mark the route. Such reassurance was a wonderful feeling but right away she had to concentrate on the next stretch.

As she reached the lake she looked up and saw a cleft in the cliffs. It seemed the obvious, and indeed the only way through the rock wall, but Anamar was much more cautious now.

She checked the map and it showed the pass quite clearly. It was named the Port de Toro, but she could also see that her route did not go through this gap in the cliffs. The dotted line which marked its path wound upwards from the lake to the Port de Toro. There, it turned sharply right across the face of the cliffs to another pass which, helpfully enough, was called the Port de Viella.

Although this pass was not a direct way, it had to be the right route. After all she was headed for the town of Viella.

Anamar looked at Maureen and smiled. The logic of this explanation seemed so childishly simple that her friend was laughing.

'Fair enough,' said Maureen. 'I believe you, but thousands wouldn't. And what with you being trained by that American wizard walker, I certainty would have followed you. 'Lead on McDuff!', you'd have heard me cry.'

Anamar was smiling to hide her embarrassment but it would not do to let Maureen off with this. She might never hear the end of it.

'Well, listen to the instant expert from the County Donegal,' she said. 'It's not so easy when you're out there on your own and having to make a go of it all by yourself.'

There, there, child dear.' Maureen's voice was soothing as if she was speaking to a toddler. 'Don't worry your wee head about it.' She winked theatrically, 'I won't tell a soul that, once your lovely man left, you were terrified out of your mind and completely lost up there in the wilds of the Pyrenees.'

Anamar realised that there was nothing for it but to go on with the story. She was not going to win this particular battle of words. Patiently she explained that making sense of the picture shown by the map in relation to the ground, gave her confidence a huge boost just when it was needed.

Maureen reached over and took her hand.

'Sorry,' she said, pretending to be contrite. 'I'm loving this journey and am with you every step of the way. I'm seeing an Anamar I've never seen before.'

'You're not the only one,' Anamar said. 'It was a new experience for me too, I suppose I was getting to know myself for the first time.'

Maureen settled down very close to her as if she needed the support and Anamar continued.

After a short rest at the little lake, the strain of route finding eased for the first time since she had missed the way in the valley below.

An hour later she climbed the rocky valley and scrambled through the rocks at its head to the Port de Toro, the Pass of the Bull. This time the pace was steady. She felt strong on each upward step, agile on the loose scree.

Almost without sound she had repeated the mantra, 'doucement!', over and over again, 'doucement! ... doucement! ... doucement! ...'. And her spirits had risen with the slope.

At the Pass of the Bull she looked over and saw a deep chasm of a drop on the other side. It gave her a great feeling of satisfaction to know that this was not the way. She turned sharp right as the map indicated and followed the track along the face of the cliffs.

It was a most spectacular route. The path lay across rock ledges, some natural, others hacked out of the cliff or built up on the lower side for the safe passage of men and animals. There were snow-drifts and tiny clumps of flowers in bloom, only recently uncovered as the snow melted.

The view was stupendous. To the south east was the magnificent summit of Mulleres, the peak which had been Hank's first Pyrenean ascent. It had looked impressive when they had seen it together from below, but here she was high enough to look it in the eye and it was magnificent. Behind it was an even bigger mountain, a great massif with a cluster of tops. This must be the one Hank had told her was the highest of them all, Maladetta, the Evil One.

The day was hot but at this height there was a breeze. At the Port de Viella, the breeze became a wind and it tugged at her clothes and pack as she crossed through the gap to the north side of the ridge.

In a few steps she had left mainland Spain behind and was looking down on the one valley of that great country on the wrong side of the Pyrenees. There it was, the Vall D'Aran.

Below her feet, the terrain swooped steeply down to a river gorge and thickly wooded slopes. It seemed as if it was waiting to welcome her back down to the inhabited land but it still looked a long, long way away.

Maureen lit the Primus stove to make another cup of tea as it seemed hours since breakfast. She loved to tease Anamar but sensed that this was not the right time to do so. In the telling of her story, Anamar seemed to be thinking aloud, telling it to herself as well as Maureen, so that she might understand the significance of the journey too.

Maureen found herself sitting as calm and quiet as her friend. She knew she had always been restless, finding it hard to sit still in church or at the cinema or even when someone was telling a good story. Her mother used to ask, not in the hope of an answer, but with an air of resignation, 'Were you born a figit or do you just do it to keep me on eggs?'

She was aware that she would have to leave for home soon and Anamar might not have finished her tale.

They both sat silently, Anamar as if in a day dream, Maureen waiting for her friend to continue. A little shower of rain passed over the lake and they took shelter in the cave. At last Anamar spoke.

On the north side of the Pyrenean ridge there was shelter from the wind below a rocky outcrop and she sat down to rest and eat. She took out her water bottle and the bread, cheese and chorizo the senora had given her. Eating the big tomato like an apple, she laughed as the juice squirted out to one side. Her scarf was keeping the sun from the back of her neck, now it was needed to wipe her hands and mouth.

A sense of loneliness, like a draught of wind from the far side of the pass, made her shiver. She was missing Hank. In spite of the depth of his depression, meeting him had brought her the most exciting times of her life. She would never forget the ascent of Vignemale or the wonderful days they had spent in the Enchanted Mountains. And that last night at the inn ... She felt so close to Hank now. Was this what people called love? And what did he feel for her? Neither of them had entrusted the other with their secret thoughts. Was it just shyness? Was it being unused to intimacy? And they had parted so easily. Did that mean there was no deeper feeling to be shared?

A discomfort, much more distressing than the cold wind could ever have been, made her rise, pack her bag and move off down the slope.

The descent from the pass was long and hard. It took hours of patient, careful walking down scree and rock. The heat of the day rose rapidly as she descended. She planted the stick firmly in front of her feet and found it helped to keep balance. The pilgrim's staff was proving to be like an extra leg and it was at its most useful when her own legs began to tremble with tiredness on a steep descent.

There were sheep in a high meadow but no shepherd. She sat down beside the river to rest and saw seven animals on a rock-strewn bank on the other side. They were marmots, looking like big, powerful rabbits, playing together like children.

Suddenly one of them whistled in alarm. It was a fierce shrieking scream, alerting the others to the approach of another marmot from above. Immediately the largest of the group gave chase. The two marmots rushed across the slope, leaping up small cliffs, dodging through gullies, disappearing from sight behind great boulders. The intruder managed to escape to higher ground and his pursuer returned triumphantly to the family group.

After a time Anamar stood up to go and the marmots scurried back into their holes. There was no shade, neither was there the cooling breeze of the higher slopes. The baking heat of the sun was on her back sapping her energy. She walked slowly on easier ground, trying to pick the best line of descent.

Eventually she reached the forest and the welcome shade she had been heading towards for hours. Anamar needed a rest, a much longer rest than before and she lay down under a tree on the very edge of the river. She must have slept for half an hour and wakened feeling thirsty but ready for the last part of the walk.

She splashed her face with river water and at once was surrounded by a swarm of black butterflies. They landed on the droplets of water she had sprayed on the warm stones of the river. They sat on her rucksack and perched on her arms and shoulders, so tightly packed, it was as if she was covered by thick black velvet.

It had to be the very best of omens. Since she was a child Anamar had been fascinated by butterflies. Near her Grannie Mac's cottage there was a patch of nettles which Rose had forbidden Anamar's father to clear. 'I tell him I need them for soup and nettle champ,' she had whispered to Anamar one day. 'But the nettles bring the butterflies and the butterflies bring beauty and hope to us all.'

Anamar's desire to get the walk finished was tempered now by a strange sense that, once it was over, her time in the Pyrenees would have ended. It made her feel sad for the passing of the happiest time in her whole life. She gathered her things together and an hour later she was on a gravel road and nearing the town of Viella itself.

There was no feeling of elation, no great sense of achievement now the journey was over but she was no longer sad. It was as if she had completed a stage of her life and was heading towards a future which, at that moment, was a wonderful, exciting prospect.

On the edge of the town, at the corner of a narrow street, there was a fonda, a small inn, advertising rooms and meals. In ten minutes Anamar was upstairs, in a room of her own, lying flat out on the bed, enjoying the pleasure of well-earned rest.

'Weren't you just great?' Maureen could contain herself no longer. 'Your fancy Yankee man would have been delighted with you. It's well seen you were born and raised in the hills of Donegal. If you had been city bred from the likes of Dublin you'd still be wandering around the Pyrenees, like a lost soul crying in the wilderness.'

'So that's it,' said Anamar, as if she had not heard Maureen speak. 'I went back to Lourdes to get my things and leave my job. The train and boat brought me home and the rest of the story you know.'

Anamar sighed, as if every last puff of air in her lungs was being expelled. Her tale was told. It was only now she realised that she had spoken the words for herself to hear, for her own ears first and foremost.

Lunch was easily made and it was time for Maureen to go. She had very little to bring back with her. Eamon had taken the two blankets and the creel and most of what they had brought up to Belshade had been for eating.

'And here's me like a grand lady,' said Maureen. 'Heading off back down to civilisation with my two arms the one length.'

'Well, that was not how you came up,' said Anamar. 'Your arms were full. You and Eamon brought everything we needed and more.' She paused and continued very quietly. 'And I won't forget the way you've listened to my ramblings. I had to tell someone and it could only have been you.'

Maureen shook her finger at her. 'Haven't I always told you I was a grand listener and you've never believed me. I wouldn't have missed it. But you've still a wee step to go with that story and some day I'll wriggle it out of you. At that inn, where the fleas don't tease, what happened when the lights were out ?'

They both began to laugh, Anamar shaking her head and trying to hide the fact that she was enjoying being teased.

Anamar walked back with Maureen to the cairn at the mouth of the lake and then down to the cairn at the Corabber River. She hardly spoke. There was no need to. Maureen chatted and gossiped as if with relief at being able to talk freely without having to worry about interrupting Anamar's story.

She was going to the Abbey Cinema in Ballyshannon on Sunday evening to see the Jolson Story. There was yet another talent competition there the following week. She was having a dress made for her by Mrs Feelin in the town, for the next parish social. She thought she had a date with a fellow they had gone to school with but was not certain. She would have to find out for sure without sounding too keen.

They parted at the cairn with a kiss and a long hug.

'Don't stay too much longer,' Maureen said gently. 'You've had your quiet time. You could do with a bit of fun.'

Anamar smiled. Maureen was right. She knew that for sure. Something was holding her at the lake but it would not be long until she, too, was on her way down from Belshade, back to her home on the shores of Lough Eske.

That evening, Anamar was truly lonely for the first time since she had walked up to the lake three weeks before. It was an empty, aching loneliness, the like of which she could not remember feeling since she was a child.

She tried to keep busy, doing little jobs neglected over the past few days. Deliberately, she took much longer than usual as she made her evening meal. She boiled potatoes and mashed them with some of Eamon's scallions to make the poundies again. There was plenty of butter and cheese and she stuck a wedge of each in the mound of poundies on her plate.

It looked good and had the most appetising smell but her appetite had gone. A cup of buttermilk was cool and satisfying, but the poundies sat untouched.

She tried to read from the few pages of the Donegal Democrat which she had so carefully preserved but that made her feel even more lonely and isolated.

In her canvas bag, she discovered the copy of the poems of T. S. Eliot given to her by Father Jack. Deirdre Ryan used to say that Mr Eliot's poems could sound very bleak, but when she read them her spirits always rose.

The book opened half way through 'A Portrait of a Lady'.

'Now that lilacs are in bloom
She has a bowl of lilacs in her room'.

Anamar read the lines aloud. When she was a young child the lilac had been the flower she had liked least. For years her mother had admired a lilac bush beside the never-used front door of a friend's farm. The bush had flourished and flowered unnoticed and unloved except by Una. But when she had shown it to Anamar, her daughter had been repelled by the smell. Una loved the lilac's perfume but for Anamar, the lilac had an odour far too strong to be wholesome.

Then a cutting of the bush, taken secretly by her mother, had taken root and over the years Anamar had watched the bush grow so very slowly. When it flowered she had been the first to find the blossom. To her surprise the aroma of this first bloom had been so fresh and delicate that the lilac had become one of her favourite flowers.

By the light of two candles she read on. Deirdre was right, the verses were often bleak but Anamar had no feeling of depression even though the words were painting a solemn, dismal scene.

'April is the cruelest month, breeding
Lilacs out of the dead land, mixing
memory and desire ...'

There the lilacs were again, but at least they were growing. Even in the dead land there was always a blink of hope. Although, like Father Jack, Anamar felt she could not claim to understand these poems, she knew they were speaking to her. She was moved, comforted, cheered by them to the point where the loneliness slipped quietly away without its absence being noticed.

She warmed the cold poundies over a pot of boiling water and they tasted good with another cup of buttermilk. When she lay down in her little nest, the cave seemed so warm and comfortable. It had been an important day. Through talking to Maureen she had been able to speak to herself. She knew herself much better now and had discovered nothing which left her disappointed. She regretted nothing.

Sleep came stealing in as gently and easily as friendship had between her and Maureen when they were very young.

The Pilgrimage Plan

As the early morning light filtered into the cave, Anamar lay quite still, completely at ease, in that half-awake, half-dreaming state in which we almost know how we feel and are almost sure what we need to do. She was glad the story was told. It was a relief not to have it still surging unbidden through her mind, sometimes out of control, often confusing every other thought.

Telling Maureen had been easy. The whole saga had presented itself in such an ordered fashion, but true to her feelings at the time. It had been the chance she needed to relive those days away from home when she had grown from a girl into a woman.

For the first time since she had arrived at Belshade, she felt no compulsion to be up and about. She stretched her full length under the coverlet and wriggled around to reform the hollows in the heather bed in exactly the right places.

When she rose at last, it was because she felt hungry. There was still plenty of food. Both Eamon and Maureen had hearty appetites but they had brought much more than they had eaten. When she came here first, Anamar had little interest in food. She ate to live, but that had changed as the time had passed. Making the meals had become a most significant part of her day. When her friends had come to stay every meal had been a joy.

She boiled an egg and experimented by trying to toast a slice of wheaten bread on the Primus stove. Having speared the slice on the point of the knife, she held it near the side of the stove with the help of a forked heather twig, to catch the heat escaping from under the boiling pot. She smiled, knowing that when she was telling Eamon about it, she could never claim that the result was perfectly toasted bread. But at least it was warm and singed a little on both sides and she could smother it with butter.

The result delighted her. She cut the buttered toast into slender soldiers and dipped them in the yolk of the egg. It took her straight back to the good times at home, when she was much younger.

She saw her mother kneeling on a mat in front of the turf fire, with a slice of bread on a long home-made toasting fork. It would never happen at breakfast, her mother was much too busy then. But sometimes at supper time Una's face would be red with the heat, a straggle of hair falling forward across her temple, toasting fork held out towards the red-glowing embers. When she rose, she did so stiffly, with a well-done piece of toast clasped in one hand, pushing herself up with the other. She would be muttering, quietly complaining about having to kneel and rise with each slice. But Anamar knew her mother secretly enjoyed making this simple treat.

Anamar saw the morning and afternoon slip past like the fast skeins of thin, white cloud across the sky. Maureen's suggestion that she should soon think of returning home came to mind. She felt much better about that now. The day she had left for Belshade, the distance between her parents and herself had seemed immense, unbridgeable. Now it was different. They could not have been expected to know how she had changed from the wee girl who had left them a year ago.

She had thought they would know what was in her mind and be able to divine her thoughts. Perhaps Maureen was right, it was time to go back.

She spent the evening with the book of Eliot's poems. At first she took it up the hill-side to a little sheltered spot she often used. But then the sky darkened and it looked like rain so she scurried back to the cave. As the light faded, she lit two candles and jammed one high in a crack. In her mind it took her back to Lourdes, a part of the great stream of flickering lights of a candle-light procession to the Grotto after dark.

As she moved to find a place for the other candle, the shadows darted through the cave, making the very stones of its walls dance around her. She remembered Deirdre Ryan telling her about the great Amber Fort of Jaipur, in India. Deirdre had been there with her father and described this magnificent palace of amber stone, on a hill, surrounded by a huge wall like the great Wall of China. They had climbed the steep road to its gates on an elephant and been bewitched by its wonders. But the greatest wonder of all was the sleeping apartments. They were set high to catch the wind, arcaded, the arches and walls decorated, inside and out, with thousands of tiny mirrors, fragments of coloured glass, semi-precious stones.

The guide had shut the door of a small circular room and lit a candle. As he moved the flame, the walls and ceiling had flashed, the shadows had flickered, as if the solid structure was moving. Even her father had been astonished by this extraordinary experience. For Deirdre it had been a magical moment.

Mr Eliot's poems rolled into one another when Anamar read them later. There were lines which made her catch her breath. Sometimes he made her smile. When she read again of J. Alfred Prufrock, she had a picture in her mind of a city gent in pin-stripe suit, bowler hat and black, patent-leather boots, carrying a rolled umbrella, tip-toeing through the muddy streets of an English market town, with his trousers rolled up a few inches to keep them out of the gutters.

The frightening images never made her scared. 'The Hollow Men' drew her back and she read it again, still with no real understanding of the meaning. Yet the sound of the words spoke to her, giving her strength, even when they seemed to lead to the end of the world.

She blew out one candle and eased gently into bed so as not to disturb the comfortable hollows of the morning. The loneliness was gone. This was the time to think, to let her mind roam back to the talk of the past two days.

The pleasure of being on her own again was heightened by the fact that the following day was a Sunday. She was certain there would be more visitors.

The next day the weather was perfect. For a week it had been unsettled, but the early morning mists had cleared quickly. Blinks of sunshine had been dimmed by dark clouds scudding in from the west, born on stiff, sudden winds, threatening rain, or bringing it in short showers, each one a small downpour. Every day she had felt the rain on her skin. It was typical Donegal, end-of-summer weather.

On this Sunday morning there were high, fleecy-white clouds drifting slowly across from the north-west. The sun warmed the air early. The weather had settled, clear, bright, but not too hot. There was a welcome breeze and that would keep the midges from being too active. Anamar laughed, thinking of how Maggie loved a day like this. 'Thanks be to God them wee midgets hate the wind,' she would have said, with feeling.

The first group of people appeared at the mouth of the lake soon after noon. There were five of them, all waving. Although she could not recognise any of them at that distance, Anamar was sure that she would know them. The waves were the greetings of friends.

Maureen's mother, Mrs McGinley, was leading the party, striding out across the heather clumps and banks with her companions following in her wake. Anamar went to meet them. Rose and Maggie had been amongst her first visitors and Lena O' Driscoll had been with Ellie McGinley on her previous visit. Bringing up the rear was a tall, angular, softly-spoken man dressed in his Sunday best. Anamar knew that he was a relation of Lena's called Dan Byrne. She had seen him often at Mass but had never spoken to him except to pass the time of day.

Ellie McGinley shouted a greeting as Anamar crossed the boulder slope towards them and hugged her when they met. Rose and Maggie nodded in friendly fashion, without being too demonstrative, as was the way of the young. They both looked hot and out of breath, not enjoying the effort of the walk up to the lake on such a warm day.

Lena and Dan shook hands with Anamar and Lena was the first to speak.

'I don't suppose you expected to see us up at the lake again after the struggle we had to get here the last time. I could do with a cup of tea. Is that good stove of yours still behaving itself?'

When they reached the cave, Dan offered to light the stove. The pump had given Anamar a little trouble that morning but Dan had it unscrewed, fixed and reassembled in a matter of seconds.

Ellie gave Anamar a nudge with her elbow.

'He's a very handy fellow that Dan,' she said. 'So if you've any other wee jobs that need doing, Dan's your man. He heard about the trip from Lena this morning at early Mass and asked if he could join us.'

The visitors had brought sandwiches for a picnic and bread, eggs, milk and buttermilk for Anamar's stores. Maggie took the provisions inside the cave and stacked them neatly on the flat rock on which Anamar kept her supplies.

Ellie explained that Eamon or Maureen had both intended to come but their father had needed them to help repair a fence damaged by the cattle the previous night.

However, when Lena, Rose and Maggie had called at the McGinleys the previous day to discuss coming up to Belshade, and without giving any secrets away, Maureen had been regaling them with stories of Anamar's adventures in the Pyrenees.

'Here we are again,' said Ellie, obviously delighted to be up at Belshade. She was smiling, wagging a finger directly at Anamar, pretending to be bossy. 'And have we got a great idea for you?'

'Just a minute,' said Lena, laughing. 'You sound like an advert in the Donegal Democrat for the latest film. Anyway, it's not like you to hide your light under a bushel. Tell her it's your idea and we've been all press-ganged into supporting you.'

Suddenly Ellie seemed embarrassed. The others were surprised. It was not like her to be shy. Rose took over for a moment.

'It's back to Lourdes for you, my girl,' she said to Anamar. 'Only this time you'll have the whole crowd of us with you. Mind you, Maggie is only going because she thinks Eamon will be there.'

Maggie thought she had heard enough from Rose.

'Just a minute,' she said. 'I'm only going in the hope that I meet a gorgeous American. If Anamar can do it, you never know, we could all be in with a chance.' They laughed and Ellie was relieved that the girls had introduced the idea without sounding too solemn about it. She began to tell Anamar about the plan.

'We could go as a parish pilgrimage,' she said. 'It wouldn't be too difficult to take a small group of invalids with us. We could start saving now and raise money at functions in the parish hall over the winter. Then, come the spring, we would all head off to Lourdes on our Pilgrimage.'

Anamar smiled. It was a wonderful scheme. She would be delighted to go with them. Ellie's confidence was growing.

'That's the good tidings,' she said. 'Now for the bad. Father Brogan will want to go too. In fact, I think he'll insist on going.'

'What's wrong with that?' said Anamar laughing. 'He and I had a little disagreement, that's all. Anyway, I would have thought that, seeing it's his parish, he would need to be one of the first to be asked.'

They could all hear Ellie's breath expelled in relief. When the idea had come to her mind as she came down from Belshade on her previous visit, she had been wondering how she could make sure that Anamar would agree to go, even though Father Brogan would have to be asked too.

'I haven't told him yet. However, I just happened to mention to him one Sunday that you had been telling us all about Lourdes,' she said archly. 'I told him that you talked about the reasons why people went on the pilgrimage. He was most interested. Says he want to discuss it with you, if you please. Imagine that ! Our Father Brogan wanting to discuss religious thinking with a woman.'

They all laughed. Ellie was no religious rebel but they would all have heard her speak her mind about the church being ruled entirely by men.

As they sat around in the sunshine after the picnic, a solitary figure appeared on the ridge at the mouth of the lake. It was a man, moving quickly, travelling across the hillside like a young deer. It was Eamon, his work on the fence finished and knowing that his mother would be mentioning the pilgrimage, he was anxious to hear Anamar's reaction.

Maggie jumped up from her comfortable seat in the heather and reached him a cup of tea. He was just in time for the important part of the discussion. The questions, mainly from Ellie, brought Anamar into the conversation. How much would it cost? How would they travel? How many could go? How would they raise the money? How would they look after the invalids travelling with them?

They talked about the pilgrimage for an hour. Lena and Ellie both knew older people who had been to Lourdes before the war but Anamar had not only travelled with a party, she had lived there for a few months. She would know the ropes.

They were so involved in the discussion that none of them saw the next little band of walkers on its way to Belshade, until they heard the sound of voices close by.

There were five of them, three women and two men, all unknown to Anamar except one of the men. He was Father Jack, the young priest who had shyly given

Anamar the copy of T. S. Eliot's poems when he had been here with two of his friends.

Anamar left her friends to meet the newcomers. One of the women did the talking.

'We're from Pettigo in County Fermanagh. Father Jack mentioned you at Mass last Sunday,' she said, to Anamar's astonishment. 'When we spoke to him afterwards, he said we should visit you here. So we joined him when we heard he was coming to-day.'

'He was saying you have been to Lourdes.' It was the man speaking. He sounded troubled, as if he was anxious to say what was on his mind. He held out his hand towards one of the women to include her in what he was saying.

'We have a boy who has T.B. He's fourteen now. He's supposed to be cured but he has lost a lung and seems to get worse, not better, as the months go by. Do you think it would do him any good if we took him to Lourdes?'

Anamar smiled.

'It would be almost certain to do him good,' she said gently. 'Whether it cures him or not. You've come at the right time. We've just been discussing a pilgrimage to Lourdes next spring.' She motioned towards Ellie. 'This is Mrs McGinley and it's her idea. She'll tell you all about it.'

Ellie went over to sit down beside the man and his wife.

Anamar looked up and saw more people coming around the lake, all heading in their direction. As Ellie began to explain her idea for a pilgrimage, Anamar rose to meet the new arrivals. There seemed to be three different parties, about fifteen people in all. She knew only a few of them, some had been before but they all acted as if they knew exactly who she was.

It was a shock for her to realise that they had made the journey up the mountain to Lough Belshade for one reason only. It was to meet her. The surprise made her catch her breath and she had to stand for a few moments to collect herself; so many people on the one day, making the effort to climb the mountain to see her.

Rose and Maggie had the Primus stove roaring, making tea, handing it around, using the same mugs, quickly rinsed out each time one was free.

'It's like a fair day in the Town,' Rose whispered to Maggie. 'The world and his wife have made the trek up here.'

'You have it the wrong way round,' said Maggie. 'It's the world and her husband. Well, one husband, doing his duty to his good woman and keeping his nose clean.'

The two girls giggled and Eamon gave them a look. He had not heard a word they had said but he suspected they were up to something.

Soon Ellie had to begin her explanations again. Each time she made the case for the pilgrimage, she was more sure they could make a go of it. She knew she was sounding more confident each time she spoke.

Anamar was pleased that someone else was doing the talking. It was hard enough coping with the thought that they had come here to see her. It would have been embarrassing to have been the sole centre of attention. She was relieved to find that she only had to speak when someone asked a question. What was the Grotto like? Why had the shrine been set up in the first place?

Father Jack came across to speak quietly to Anamar.

'I remember you saying that the crowds don't just flock to Lourdes in the hope of cures. Were you not surprised? I thought that most people who went there were only interested in the miracles.'

'That might have been true before the war,' said Anamar. 'But since then huge crowds have come on special occasions, like the Great Pilgrimage of 1945, when thousands of people, who had been imprisoned or deported, came to Lourdes and formed a great procession to the Grotto as an act of thanksgiving for their freedom.'

Father Jack was not aware of it, but most of the others had ceased talking. They were now sitting quietly, listening to his discussion with Anamar. He had just begun to talk about the importance of self-discovery, in a world increasingly divided by the pursuit of money, when he suddenly became aware of the silence. He looked up and there they were, sitting attentively, hanging on his every word, as if he was preaching one of his best sermons.

He stopped and looked embarrassed, wondering if what he had said sounded pompous, even patronising. Anamar smiled.

'Good for you,' she said. 'You'd better give your name to Ellie and sign up to come with us. We'll need a few thoughts like those.'

Ellie was delighted. She could let the others do the talking. For the moment, her work was done.

Towards the middle of the afternoon the visitors began to take their leave. Anamar spoke to all of them in turn, feeling close to each one, even those she had met for the first time. She knew that there was something about being here which made it easy to make contact with people.

All the usual barriers were down. For once in their lives these visitors, mainly from Donegal, had not been too solemn when they were talking about something spiritual. They had been able to speak as they felt, without embarrassment. And Anamar had enjoyed sharing their freedom.

Ellie's party, which now included Eamon, was the last to leave and Anamar walked with them to the mouth of the lake. There had not been a moment since he had arrived when there had been a chance for her to speak to Eamon. He seemed in very good form. Although he had said nothing when the pilgrimage was being discussed, Anamar knew he was thinking about going.

They parted at the Belshade Cairn and Ellie had just started to leave when she turned back.

'I nearly forgot,' she said. 'I brought you a book. I saw it on the second-hand book stall at a church sale in the town last week. It cost me all of a silver sixpence.'

It was a small hard-backed edition of some of Chaucer's Canterbury Tales. Anamar could hardly believe her eyes. One of Deirdre Ryan's most prized books was a copy of the same edition. On the fly-leaf on this one was a name and date inscribed in pen, 'Pollie Ashworth, June 1886'. It had probably been a school text-book for there were tiny, neat notes in pencil in the margins.

'The local priest saw I'd spotted it,' Ellie said dryly. 'Now there's a few good stories about a pilgrimage,' says he with a twinkle in his eye. 'Just in case you ever think of going on one.'

Suddenly Anamar remembered reading from Deirdre's identical copy. 'It's always best to read Old English aloud.' Deirdre would have said.

> 'Whan that Aprille with his schowres swotte (in the margin it
> said, 'sweet')
> The drought of Marche hath perced to the roote,
> ....
> And smale fowles maken melodie,
> Than longen folk to gon on pilgrimages.'

Anamar spoke the words from the first page of the Prologue to Ellie and they hugged as they said their good-byes.

As she walked back to the cave, Anamar's spirits soared. One happening really did lead on from another. When she had first left home, like the butterfly struggling out of its chrysalis, she had entered a new and entirely different existence. Now all these friends seemed to accept that existence as her way, as if there had been no other, as if it was the true path for her.

Walking down beside the river, Ellie's mind raced ahead to the pilgrimage. She was a little way behind her party as they trooped down the mountain. By the time they reached the Corabber Cairn at the river junction, she had decided that Father Brogan must be invited to be Spiritual Director of the pilgrimage. She would form a committee and would make sure that she herself was appointed official organiser. Everyone on the committee would have to help. Each one would be allocated a job. She would control the whole thing.

She knew now that Anamar would be certain to want to go with them. Her advice would be crucial. But Anamar would have no need of an official title. Everyone would accept her. The cream would rise to the top.

Lena O'Driscoll was sure to go. Ellie knew her friend well and an outing like this was not to be missed. Rose and Maggie would probably want to go, and as for Maureen, if Anamar was on the list, she would be on it too.

Ellie counted them up on her fingers. Including herself, she made it eight possibles. 'And what about Dan Byrne?' she asked herself. He might have said nothing all day but then men like him never said a word that would give the slightest clue to what they were thinking. She had been watching him, however, and he was another candidate.

Then there was the couple who had heard Father Jack mention Anamar at Mass. They had come up to Belshade specially to ask Anamar about taking their young invalid son to Lourdes. They were another three. And maybe Father Jack too, It would be great to have a young priest with them. He would understand that the young ones would not want to be serious all the time.

Ellie smiled to herself. She had just started counting and already she had nearly a dozen possibles. It would be easy to set up a committee out of this lot, she told herself. She would sound them out over the next few days.

Lena was a little ahead, as they came to the good track further down. She stopped and waited for Ellie.

'It's easy to see you're well pleased about something. You've borrowed the Cheshire Cat's grin.'

'Don't worry yourself,' said Ellie. 'You'll hear all about it as soon as I'm ready. I'll have chapter and verse for the whole crowd of you. It's a great scheme and I intend to be head and tail of it.'

Lena laughed.

'If past experience is anything to go by, you mean that you'll be the head of it and I'll be the tail of it.'

The two women linked arms and tripped lightly down the track like young ones, laughing and teasing each other. At the end of what should have been a strenuous walk for both of them, they were feeling younger than Rose and Maggie, and happier than they had been for as long as either could remember.

The Figure on the Ridge

When she reached the cave Anamar's spirits were still soaring. There had never been a time in her life when she had enjoyed the company of people more. And it was not only because her close friends had been present, there had been others, unknown to her, but they all had been able to talk together as if they had known each other for years.

Then there was Ellie's idea for the pilgrimage. How could Ellie have known that her own dearest wish was to return to Lourdes? Now her friends were planning to go there and were set on taking her with them. It seemed as if everything she could have hoped for was happening without any conscious effort on her part.

To celebrate, she made poundies yet again for her evening meal, but this time with a special flavour. Eamon had given her the idea when he gave her some tender young nettles, wrapped in newspaper, with his scallions. She boiled the nettles with the potatoes for a few minutes and cut them into the poundies with the scallions. This was the real thing, champ as it should be made, as you would never taste it in the likes of Dublin.

As a treat, she opened a tin of Spam, a form of tinned, cooked pork called luncheon meat, easy to slice and quite good to eat when hunger was the sauce. Anamar sat down on a bank looking out across Belshade and sipped buttermilk from the big mug before she began her meal.

All at once her spirits fell. They had been soaring happily like a peregrine across the hills, now it was as if a chance shot had winged the bird and it had fallen in the heather.

Why did it always happen when she was about to eat? It was worse than before. She felt an awful depth of loneliness, not just a sense of being alone, but of being cut off from every one she knew and cared for. It was like the home-sickness of a young child, a hopeless, sickening fear of being totally out of touch with any other human. The nausea rose in her stomach. She set the plate of steaming poundies down on a flat rock, her appetite gone.

And the worst of it was, she thought, that it was her own fault. Her friends had not deserted her. As they had all happily planned for the future, she was the one who had stayed behind and let the rest of them go.

She rose and walked away from the cave and her fine meal. At the lake's edge, the only sound was the splash of ripples of water on the tiny beach. At this moment of dejection she thought of the kitchen at home and her mother resting in her chair beside the fire. At those rare times when Una allowed herself to sit down for a quiet pause in her busy life, her hands would be folded together in her lap, her ankles crossed under the chair and her head held erect, eyes staring at the fire. Anamar was suddenly aware that it had been a long time since she had left the farm and walked up the mountain to Belshade.

Since then, Maureen had acted as the go-between between mother and daughter, keeping both informed. Just over a week before, according to Maureen, Anamar's mother had left suddenly for a village near Sligo. Her sister Kathleen's only daughter was about to give birth to her first child and, as Kathleen had been a semi-invalid for years, Mrs Cassidy had gone to keep house and supervise the confinement.

The baby had been born within twenty-four hours or her arrival, a beautiful five and a half pound girl. Mother and baby were well and Una Cassidy was to be the child's godmother. But the latest news was not so good. In a quiet moment that afternoon Ellie had taken Anamar to one side to tell her that her mother had felt ill and was returning home from Sligo the following day.

Anamar dipped her hands in the lake water and put her wet fingers over her eyes. The drops ran down her cheeks like tears. She had a strange feeling of knowing that this would be no passing indisposition. She had a feeling her mother might be seriously ill. She had no choice now. She would be needed at home.

It would be hard to leave Belshade. But as she stood at the edge of the lake she knew that, whether her mother was well or ill, whether she wanted to leave here or not, it was time to go. In the morning she would gather together as much as she could carry, the rest of the baggage would have to wait until Eamon and Maureen could help her bring it home. In the afternoon she would leave the lake and return to the farm.

The decision to do something lifted her depression a little and she began to feel the need of food. In a few minutes she was back at the cave, the Primus stove lit and water boiling in the pot. She placed the enamel plate holding the poundies on top of the open pot and then put the pot lid on top of the food.

When the poundies were ready she could bite into the scallions and the nettles added a subtle, delicate flavour unlike any other herb or vegetable she had tasted. Even the Spam was good.

For the first time, sleep did not come easily that evening. There were strange noises outside. The total darkness of the moonless night failed to come. Through the cave opening she could see a faint, misty, eerie light over the lake. Anamar dozed, rather than slept. She twisted on the bed and the hollows under her hip and shoulder deepened as the padding of grass and fine twigs of heather was pushed to the side. Soon her body was resting on the hard floor of the cave.

She rose much earlier than usual and made tea. The loneliness returned as soon as she wakened and she had no appetite for breakfast. Anamar knew she had to go but lacked the will to do so. The very thought of sorting out some of her belongings to take with her drained what little energy she had. She sat on a stone in the mouth of her shelter and cupped her hands around the big, warm mug of tea.

Time seemed to hover without moving as she sat there, although when she looked at her wrist watch, another hour had passed. It was nearly noon. She would have to make a start. It might be difficult to leave but another lonely night here did not bear thinking about.

Anamar rose and came out of the cave to walk down to the beach. Washing her face in the lake water might bring her back to life. She glanced across towards the ridge beyond the mouth of the lake. There was a solitary figure silhouetted on the sky-line. It was a tall person, almost certainty a man, standing erect near the location of the cairn.

Anamar washed her face and was returning from the waters' edge when she stopped and looked again. The man was moving forwards and backwards along the little ridge. Each time he stopped it was to face in her direction, as if he was staring across to her corner of the lake. The figure was too far away to identify but again the man walked a few steps to one side. Suddenly Anamar recognised the movement. It was her father.

She ran across to the highest, near-by boulder, scrambled on to its top and began to wave. The figure waved back and started towards her, moving quickly. Anamar jumped down and walked slowly towards the almost-running figure. She was right. It was her father. As he drew close she could see him panting for breath. His face had lost its normal weather-beaten tan, an almost grey pallor showed through the stubble on his chin. He looked his age, all sixty-three years of if. The hard labour of the hill farm showed too, in his limbs and stance, for the first time in Anamar's memory.

They stopped a few yards from each other, glad to have met, but without a spoken greeting or any kind of physical contact. Anamar was amazed to be confronted by her father, of all people, up here in the hills. It must be something serious.

'What's wrong?' she asked. 'What's happened?'

'You're needed at home. Your mother's ill.' John Joseph Cassidy had been worrying what he would say to his daughter when they met. He need not have bothered. It all came out so easily.

'She was taken poorly at your Aunt Kathleen's in Sligo. She was meant to come back to-day but she arrived late last night in a taxi. We had to get the doctor this morning, first thing.'

Anamar turned back towards the cave and her father followed. She climbed in through the entrance and was surprised to find that there was so little she needed to bring with her. There was the coat, like a cape, which had sheltered her from wind and rain by day and had been thrown across her bedding to keep her warm on cold nights. She folded it carefully and tied it with string, so that she could carry it across her shoulder.

She put the two little books of Eliot's poems and Chaucer's Canterbury Tales in her haversack with her soap, towel and toothbrush and the few items of underclothes that Maureen had brought up for her. And that was it. The rest could wait until Maureen and Eamon came up with her to help clear the cave.

John Joe Cassidy stood some distance away while his daughter was inside her cave. He showed no desire to see where she had made her home for the past few weeks. This was her private place, her young woman's place which no father should enter.

On the way down they hardly spoke. Anamar felt she could understand his worry. But there was a lack of closeness between them. There always had been.

To him, it was the natural distance there had to be between a man and his daughter. As Anamar began to grow up, he sensed that she was aware of the true nature of his relationship with his wife. He and Una were together because they were married. If there had been love, it had gone, long since. There was a kind of companionship they both needed, a comfort in knowing someone else was there, a dependence on each other for survival.

Father and daughter passed the cairn at the mouth of the lake.

'Ellie told me about the wee piles of stones.' John Joe was trying to think of something to say.

Anamar nodded. It was not that she was withholding her conversation. There was nothing to say. In her mind, there was an image of her mother sitting up in bed, not complaining, being a good patient.

'Who's looking after her while you're up here?' she said and her father began to talk as if this was the invitation he needed.

'I went for Maeve last night and she was here when the taxi arrived. She came back first thing this morning on her bicycle.' Maeve was another of Una's sisters. She lived less than three miles away on the other side of Lough Eske. 'She's staying the night. The doctor doesn't seem to know what's wrong with your mother, or if he does, he's not telling us.'

They trudged down beside the stream to the Corabber Cairn and the good path which dropped steeply away to the road. The track seemed longer to Anamar than it should have been. Near the road, they took the short cut across the fields and scrub land to the McGinley's farm. The dog barking brought the McGinley family out of the house. They stood awkwardly in a line, Ellie and her husband, Maureen and Eamon, waiting for John Joe and Anamar to reach them, not sure what to say.

'When you're ready to go back to Belshade, we'll give you a hand with the rest of your stuff.' Eamon broke the silence. 'Just tell us when.'

Ellie could see that John Joe was exhausted.

'Faith and it didn't take you long to scoot up to the lake," she said to him, trying to raise his spirits. 'The Outlaw O'Driscoll must have been on your heels.'

They all laughed except John Joe, who just about managed a smile. 'O'Driscoll of Darra - The Outlaw of The Mountains' was the current serial story in the Donegal Democrat. Even Anamar had read two of the episodes in the pages of the paper which had found their way up to Belshade as wrapping for food or supplies.

'Don't worry about cooking this evening,' Ellie shouted after them. 'Maureen and I will bring you round some stew. I've a big pot of it swinging on the crane.'

In her mind's eye Anamar could see the hearth in the McGinley's kitchen. A big black pot like a witch's cauldron would be swinging from a wire crook hooked to the metal bar. This was the crane, which allowed the pots and the kettle to be swung over the turf fire. It would be a lamb stew with onions, carrots and potatoes, of course. It was such a reassuringly familiar image that she began to feel a bit brighter for the first time that day.

She and John Joe walked on across the path to their own farm. Aunt Maeve met them at the door. She spoke quietly as if she did not want the patient to hear.

'She's feeling a bit better this afternoon,' she said. 'A wee sleep this morning helped her but don't be encouraging her to talk. The doctor says she's better just to be quiet.'

Anamar led the way into the kitchen. The door through to the inner room was open and a bed had been made up for her mother near the far wall. Anamar came close and her mother's eyes were closed. Her arms and shoulders were so thin. Anamar wondered why she had not noticed when she had come home from France. Or had it happened since then? If she could have seen herself, Una Cassidy would have said she was 'failed'. The skin of her face was palest yellow, drawn tightly over the cheek bones. The eyes opened and she turned her head.

'So it's you,' she said. 'You've come back home.'

Anamar put a hand on the arm resting on the patchwork quilt. Her mother's other arm came slowly across her body and the hand rested on top of Anamar's.

'Do you remember the time of it we had making this quilt?' Mrs Cassidy spoke slowly but although her voice showed her weariness, there was no weakness in it. 'I could have seen it far enough but you were the one determined to see the job finished.'

Anamar felt the gentlest pressure of her mother's hand on hers. The gap between them was closing. It needed no words from either of them to prove it. The days when they seemed to need to distance themselves from each other were over.

Mrs Cassidy grimaced as she turned her head to look at her daughter.

'I've a tiredness on me, Anamar.' Anamar could not remember when her mother had called her by her chosen name. She had a remarkable gift of addressing her without calling her by name. 'I've a tiredness on me like a load of wet turf on my back,' she said. 'And the like of it I never felt in all my days.'

'Can I get you anything?' Anamar asked, not wanting to encourage her mother to talk. But the eyes had closed again and when Anamar looked across towards her Aunt Maeve, the nod indicated that they should withdraw and let the patient sleep.

They sat down around the fire in the kitchen, the door to the inner room ajar. John Joe was in his own chair to the right of the fireplace and Anamar in her mother's place on the straight-backed chair to the left. Aunt Maeve preferred a kitchen chair and she sat in the middle, suspecting that they would need her if there was to be any conversation at all.

Maeve held her tongue at first to encourage Anamar and her father to talk, but both were deep in their own thoughts. The silence was no surprise. Although she and Una had always been close, she favoured Anamar as much or more than her own daughters. But she and John Joe had never had anything to say to each other. The day he and Una were married, she remembered telling her mother that the only thing the groom had in his favour was a fair farm of land. Her mother's reply had been so sharp, Maeve knew she must have been too close to the mark for comfort.

She began to talk to Anamar about Una's illness.

'It seemed to come on her so suddenly. When she went off to Galway less than two weeks ago she was in good form. I was here when she came back and we had to carry her in from the taxi. Your Aunt Kathleen was with her. She said that your mother seemed fine the morning the baby was born. But that afternoon she had collapsed in a heap, as if she had been holding herself together for days. She wouldn't hear of going into hospital, however, insisted on coming back here the next day.

Maeve rose and crossed to the doorway of the inner room. She peeped in to check that Una was asleep, closed the door softly and came back to her chair. After a moment or two she looked at John Joe and then at Anamar.

'Your father doesn't know yet but the doctor told me this morning he's almost sure it's cancer.'

In the silence, the pendulum clock's tick seemed too loud, then a lump of turf fell softly on to the front of the hearth stone. Anamar looked across at her father and his face was so dark and still it might have been carved from bog oak.

'Is it incurable?' she said quietly as if she expected no answer. Maeve shook her head. She felt a sadness far greater even than her sorrow for her sister's plight. What would happen to this small family if Una died? There was little enough between them as it was, but whether the other two knew it or not, Una was like the hearth before them. If the fire died, the stones would cool, the very life of the farmhouse would be extinguished.

'I don't know,' she said. 'The doctor told me it was a case of 'wait and see'.'

There was nothing else to say and they sat for a long time so quietly that they might have been asleep. The dog barked and they heard voices outside in the farmyard. The door opened and Ellie's face appeared.

'Anyone at home,' she said cheerfully. 'We brought the stew, hot and tasty. I hope you're all hungry.'

Maeve was up and laying the table almost before Ellie and Maureen had come into the kitchen. She was delighted to see them. There had been too much despondency in this house over the past twenty-four hours. The door opened again and Eamon came in. He had stopped to pat the dog. It was always a good idea to be on friendly terms with a neighbour's dog.

The McGinleys brought their cheerful, good-spirited chat with them as well as the stew. They had already eaten, but accepted cups of tea while Maeve, Anamar and John Joe enjoyed the food. John Joe surprised himself by taking a second plate of stew and then he remembered that he had hardly eaten since the middle of the previous day. Una wakened a little later and when Maeve inquired if she would like something to eat, she asked for panada.

Ellie and Maeve sat with Una while Maureen watched Anamar make the panada and Eamon talked with John Joe. Anamar knew just how her mother liked it. When she was feeling ill for any reason, Una always maintained that it was the only food she could stomach.

Anamar put half a pint of milk into a pan and heated it on a trivet at the side of the fire. As the milk warmed she added small chunks of buttered bread, some sugar and a good dash of cinnamon powder. The milk began to simmer and she lifted the pot back to let it cool. The panada was ready. Her mother's favourite bowl was the big white one with blue stripes and a lattice work of minute cracks around the rim. She poured the panada carefully, making sure that there was not even one drip down the side. Ill or well, her mother would have been sure to notice and to remark on it.

In the inner room Una was sitting up in bed, smiling. It was such a rare occurrence for her to let herself go in a smile that Anamar laughed gently in surprise. Ellie's good company was working its magic

An hour later it was time for Maeve to settle the patient down in the bed again. They left the door of the room open to let the sound of their voices keep her company and sat around the fire talking into the night. When it was time for the McGinleys to go, Ellie spoke to Anamar at the door.

'When you're feeling low in bed to-night and maybe not able to sleep, just have a wee think to yourself about our pilgrimage.' She squeezed Anamar's arm.

Maeve had made up a bed for herself on the long couch in the inner room. Years ago, before she was married, she had been a nurse. Nursing might have changed during the time that had elapsed since then, but she knew that Una trusted her and had need of her.

Tucked up comfortably in her bed in the little room under the eaves, Anamar found sleep hard to come by. She took Ellie's advice and thinking about the pilgrimage cheered her spirits. When she wakened, it was after nine o'clock, well into the morning, much later than would have been usual for her at Belshade.

Anamar's Return

It took Anamar over a week to find her bearings again at the farm. Her father was quieter than ever. He kept himself busy working around the yard, in the fields, checking the sheep up the hill or walking over to a neighbour's house.

Aunt Maeve was there every day and stayed most nights. In the past Ellie had never been a frequent visitor, now she called every day, sometimes two or three times. Maeve was glad of her company and Anamar realised that it was the presence of her aunt and Ellie which was helping her lose the feeling of being a stranger in her own home.

She fed the hens and helped her father with the milking. The two big earthenware crocks in the cool scullery at the back of the kitchen were full of the thick, creamy top of the milk. Her father seemed pleased when she offered to make butter. It had always been her mother's job but Anamar had helped before she left home. Now she would be in charge.

When she was making butter, Una called the scullery her dairy and everything had to be especially clean. Anamar boiled a great pot of water and washed her hands using a little brush her mother had bought for the purpose. She scrubbed the wooden table top and everything she intended to use. When she was satisfied that all was prepared, she scooped the cream from the top of the crocks and put it in the wooden churn.

Some people said they hated churning, it was such a tiring, monotonous job. Anamar loved the rhythm of it. 'Plunge and lift and don't forget the twist.' She could hear her mother's voice instructing her all those years ago when she was old enough to manage the plunger.

When the little globules of butter began to form, she kept the plunger going to get the best from the cream. The soft yellow lumps were easy to scoop into a dish lined with muslin. She lifted the cloth by the corners and squeezed it to remove the excess milk. It needed a little salt, but not too much, her mother said that country butter should always have a hint of salt but it was easy to spoil it.

Then came the part Anamar enjoyed most. She kneaded the formless mound with her hands then, with the two wooden paddles, she slapped and shaped the

112

mass into manageable blocks. When the last of the excess moisture was expelled, there it was, a pale buttercup-yellow lump of the finest country butter.

She worked on until the crocks of cream were empty and the churn could yield no more. The oblong blocks she wrapped in grease-proof paper from her mother's precious store and, using a mould with an indented shape, she turned out handsome circular pats decorated with a thistle motif.

Mrs Cassidy had an arrangement with Willie Joe Mullins of Donegal Town, sole proprietor of Mullins and Son, High Class Grocers. Willie Joe would never have said as much, but he thought Una Cassidy's butter far better than the best he imported to the town in wooden butter boxes. Una had found him a ready buyer for both her blocks and thistle pats but it always annoyed her when she saw in his shop the mark-up added to the price he paid her.

'Overheads! Mrs Cassidy dear, overheads!.' Willie would say when Una challenged him. 'As you well know, Mrs C, I provide the very best of comestibles for the more discerning palates of this town. But you could have no idea of the vast sums I am liable to pay for that privilege.'

The smell of the buttermilk, left when the churning was done, was fresh and delicate, slightly sharp. It had been the delicious memory of it which had drawn Anamar back into the dairy. She poured the buttermilk into big delph jugs for storage on the coolest shelf in the dairy, until it would be needed for baking bread or for drinking. Anamar liked buttermilk rather than milk with her meals and, on the day it was made, it was the most refreshing drink she had ever tasted.

Now the job was finished, she had the great satisfaction of having done it on her own for the first time. Completing it had somehow settled her back into her home again. She realised now how much she had missed the farm when she had been away in France. And how much she had missed her life here in this corner of Donegal.

In the kitchen, Maeve had just finished making bread on the big iron griddle. The griddle was slung on three chains from the crane where it could be swung over the fire or away from the heat as need be. Maeve was happy making griddle bread. It was so satisfying to be able to see the dough rise and the bread bake before your very eyes. Her face was red with the heat and she fanned herself with the feathered turkey wing used for dusting the top of the griddle before each batch of bread was placed on it.

She and Ellie had known what Anamar was doing in the scullery but had left her to it without advice or comment. Now they were full of praise for the butter. Ellie split one of Maeve's soda farls and the heat escaped from it in a vapour. The new butter melted into the bread as she spread it. There was home-made rhubarb jam to top it off and she suggested that Anamar should take some into her mother with a cup of tea.

Una smiled when she saw her daughter with the fresh, buttered bread on the tray.

'It's our own thistle top butter,' she said examining the soda farl. 'I heard the slaps of the paddles in the dairy and knew it had to be you. Make sure that Willie Joe Mullins gives you a fair price when you take it into the town.'

Anamar went back for her own tea and another split farl of the soda bread and sat by the bed. Her mother ate half of hers and then stopped, but not because she was no longer hungry. She was tired. Even eating seemed to tire her these days.

'I've little or no pain now I've had the doctor's medicine,' Una said quietly. 'Even the rheumatickey fingers aren't a bother. But I'm like a washed out dishrag, not an ounce of energy in me from head to toe.'

To save her mother the effort of speaking, Anamar began to talk. It was the first time that she had said more than a few words to her since she had come back from Belshade, and not because there had been nothing to say. The gap that had always existed between them made her hold her tongue. Now, as she had sensed the previous evening when she had held her mother's hand, the distance was diminishing.

She began to talk about the cave at Belshade and how, on her last day there, she had seen this figure pacing about on the ridge on the far side of the lake.

"I couldn't believe it,' she said. 'It was father himself, nobody else has his walk.'

'He knew rightly where you were,' her mother said sharply. 'Ellie and Maureen had talked enough about your wee nest under the big stone at the lake. But that's your father for you. Sometimes he needs an invitation to come in out of the rain.'

She asked Anamar about the people who had visited her at Belshade. Who had made the trip? What had they said? Why had they come? Realising that her mother would not have heard of the large number there had been on the previous Sunday, Anamar told her about that crowd first.

As they talked, Anamar was working her way backwards into the story. The earlier events would have wait their turn. It was the right way to talk about it. To start at the beginning was not her mother's way. They would both be much more comfortable taking the roundabout route. As Ellie McGinley had said to her daughter, Maureen, in the secrecy of their own kitchen, 'Una Cassidy will want to know the seed, breed and generation of everyone who was there and every nod and wink of the conversation, without showing that she had the slightest interest in any of them'.

After a quarter of an hour or so Maeve looked in and Anamar took it as a signal that it was time for her mother to rest.

'We'll have the next instalment later.' Una was smiling at the ease of Anamar's conversation. As a child, her only daughter had been sociable, lively, even noisy at times when she was outside playing with her friends. Inside the house, however, she had been very quiet, hard to talk to, becoming more serious as she grew older, keeping herself to herself.

In the long years she and John Joe had been married, Una had never been certain that she wanted to have children at all. But, had she to give birth, it was her prayer that it would be a quiet, biddable youngster. She herself had been brought up to believe that children should be 'seen and not heard'. However, as Anamar had grown up, there had been times when Una had wished that, in their quiet household, at least the young one would have had something to say for herself.

But this young woman was a different person. She was easy in herself, easy to listen to, able to talk about what she had been doing in a most interesting way. Una felt a wave of regret for all those years when she and Anamar might have been able to talk to each other.

The sadness lasted for a brief moment only. She was tired but felt better for the chat and much the better for feeling a new sense of closeness with her daughter. Before Anamar left the room, pulling the door behind her, her mother was asleep.

Every few days the doctor made his visit before noon. They could hear his car in the lane and then the dog barking. Dr Corr hated dogs and the Cassidy's dog, Timmy, smelling an enemy, always showed his best or, if you happened to be Dr Corr, his worst territory-protection instincts. With this particular visitor, Timmy thoroughly enjoyed himself, barking and snarling, trying to snap at the doctor's ankles. It was the same for Dr Corr at other farms. Even the friendliest of dogs would put on the fierce-guard-dog act every time he arrived on their premises.

Someone would have to go out into the yard to escort the doctor from the car to the door. It annoyed John Joe that Timmy created such a fuss but it amused Maeve and Anamar to see the good doctor, a self-confessed expert on almost every aspect of farm life, so discomfited by one of the softest dogs in the country.

Mrs Cassidy could hear the commotion in the yard and it pleased her so much she was always smiling when the doctor entered the room.

Dr Corr wore a Donegal tweed suit and a canary yellow waistcoat. His tweed hat had a large fishing fly stuck in its band and his boots were highly polished, custom made, best brown leather.

'And aren't you the great patient, Mrs Cassidy, always a ready smile for the old saw bones.' The doctor had cultivated a bluff, jokey manner for his farming patients. His fear of encouraging a too familiar response, however, meant that sometimes he found it hard to ask the questions which would elicit a helpful response. As a result, his skill was never fully appreciated by his patients.

As a young man he had worked in hospitals in Dublin and London. He had been particularly interested in scientific methods of diagnosis, keeping himself up-to-date with the latest testing techniques and treatments. Having worked in Dublin for some years, he had taken over a practice in Donegal Town in middle life and intended to bring modern medicine to this corner of Ireland.

It had been a simple matter to convert a scullery beside his surgery into a small laboratory. There, with his test tubes, chemicals and microscope, he was able to test his patients samples of blood or urine as well, or better than most hospitals in the country outside the very largest and most modern. Dr Corr was a better doctor than he was ever given credit for, in either the town or the country.

He took Una's pulse and listened to her chest and tried his best to be reassuring without telling lies. He knew, now that he had completed his tests, that Una had but a short time to live and it was time to tell the family. Apart from advising wholesome food and rest, there was little he could do. The medicine he had left with Maeve would be a help if Una was in pain. He felt a vague sense of helplessness but this patient was appreciative and it was a help to know that he could make those last days as pain free and comfortable as possible.

When he was leaving, Anamar left him to his car. Timmy had been waiting but when he realised that the doctor was accompanied, he hid his disappointment by slinking back into the shed as if he had seen nothing.

'Is there a cure? Will she get better? Is it just a matter of time?' Anamar had not meant to be so direct but, as they had reached the car, she had to ask.

'Go round and sit in the car with me for a minute.' The doctor's joviality had gone. 'You're very close,' he said. 'Those are the questions and you're right to ask. The answer to the last one is 'Yes'. I'm as sure as I can be that it's leukaemia. It's a form of cancer which affects the blood. Your mother has days to live, not weeks, well maybe a week or two at the most.' He paused to let Anamar take in the news.

'I think your mother knows the worst, but she's pretending she doesn't. It's best to go along with her. Your father is down in the low field and I'll stop and tell him before I leave. Try to keep her as happy as you can. Your aunt knows what she's about. I've left her some more medicine which should help if she feels pain. I'll call every three or four days to see that she's not in discomfort.'

Back in the kitchen, and with the inner door closed, Anamar repeated the doctor's news to Aunt Maeve and Ellie.

'It's only what I expected,' Maeve said, allowing herself to show signs of her weariness. 'We'll just keep on as we're going, as if we know nothing. One of us can take the bike down to the priest and tell him.'

Father Brogan knew that Una was ill. He had called since Anamar had come down from Belshade but there had been no discussion of the time they had met in the farm kitchen before she had left for the mountains.

He called again that evening. Anamar had cycled down to the parochial house and had left a note with the housekeeper to say that her mother was gravely ill. John Joe made himself scarce when he heard the car at the foot of the lane. It was out of no disrespect to the priest. He always found something urgent to do outside if he had warning of any visitor's arrival.

Maeve had cycled home to catch up with her own work and was not due back until later, so Anamar was alone when Father Brogan arrived. She brought him into the kitchen and made tea. Her mother was sleeping and the door to the room was closed, so she was able to tell him the doctor's news.

The priest sat in John Joe's chair and she took her mother's place on the other side of the hearth. As a child she had often thought, as they rested before the fire, that her parents always sat as far apart as possible. Now she and the priest were obeying the same rule. Father Brogan nodded in understanding as Anamar told him of her mother's condition. He asked the right questions and assured her of his concern.

'You must try not to worry,' he said sympathetically. 'Your aunt knows what to do. She will be able to help you and your father, whatever happens.'

His attitude to Anamar had changed. When they had met here on the day she had gone to Belshade, he had seen her as the young girl he had known before she first left home. It had been a startling surprise to find she had become so self-willed. Now he had heard a great deal about her from some of those who had visited her at the lake. They had been deeply impressed. Without spelling out any precise reason, they obviously expected him to be pleased. It would have been impossible for him to ignore parishioners like Mrs McGinley and Mrs O'Driscoll. Indeed the talk of the three young priests, who had stayed with him, had been of her presence and her inspirational effect on those who came to visit.

However, he had not forgotten the scene when her mother had called him to their home. Anamar had defied him without saying a word. It had rankled. It was not what he would have expected from a young woman of his parish. Its effect had been to increase the instinctive wariness which he felt when he was alone with one of his female parishioners. Although he needed to make it clear that he was her parish priest, he would be magnanimous. He decided to make no reference to the earlier confrontation. He would start afresh.

'I hear you're planning to take a group to Lourdes,' he said and Anamar smiled at the tactic of placing her in the front pew.

'Is that what you've heard?' she was doing her best to sound friendly. 'It wasn't my idea. Credit where it's due. It was Mrs McGinley who suggested the pilgrimage. I would love to go. But it will take some organising. We'll all need to help if we're to make a go of it.'

There was the tapping of a stick on the floor of the inner room.

'That's my mother,' she said. 'If you go in now, I'll make fresh tea for her and I'll bring you another cup, if you'd like.'

Father Brogan smiled his thanks. He was pleased that Anamar seemed to bear him no ill will. He had not been looking forward to meeting this young woman again.

He went in to see the patient, heard her confession, gave her communion, spoke quietly to her. Conversation had never come easily between them but he sat beside the bed, talking to her, until relief arrived as Anamar came in with the tea. He invited Anamar to kneel with him and prayed a simple prayer. There was a pause before they rose and Anamar added a prayer of her own, silently.

Timmy paid no attention to Father Brogan as he left the house. The priest had been born on a farm but had never been interested in animals. Neither man nor dog took the slightest notice of each other.

Una smiled as Anamar cleared away the tea cups.

'The good father keeps us all well beyond arm's length but he treats you like a Mother Superior.' She laughed gently at her own little joke. When Anamar joined her, she could not remember a time when they had laughed out loud together. Una began to cough wheezily and Anamar raised her head a little to help her settle. In a few moments her mother was calm again, but now very tired, and Anamar left her to rest.

Every morning, afternoon and evening Anamar spent half an hour or so, sometimes much longer, with her mother. Their conversation was in snatches, five or ten minutes at a time, depending on how the patient felt. When she had heard enough, Una would close her eyes and rest. But when they started again, Una always remembered where they had left off. She wanted to hear every detail of Anamar's story and quietly led the talk, first to what had happened at Belshade, then later, to the time in France.

As the tale unfolded, Anamar found herself able to recount what had happened much more openly to her mother than she would have expected. Even when it came to Hank and their adventures in the Pyrenees, she was able to speak almost as freely as she had to Maureen. They both looked forward to this time together and the gap between them narrowed once again. In a few days it seemed to have closed completely. It was as if it had existed before only in the darker corners of their imaginations.

John Joe spent little time in the house. Although he came in to see Una frequently and was ready to do anything to help, he never stayed long in the sick room. Maeve was fascinated by Anamar's story and took to joining her and Una as it unfolded. She was pleased beyond words that mother and daughter had become so close. It might be late, but it was never too late.

When it seemed as if the life was slipping away from her, Una would rally as Anamar talked. If she was very tired she would lie back with her eyes closed but Anamar would know, by the press of her mother's hand on hers, that she should go on speaking.

One evening Maeve called her into the room and her mother was lying back, eyes shut, face expressionless, drained of all colour. Anamar sat on the edge of the bed and her mother's eyes opened.

'Help me up,' she said, and they raised her gently on extra pillows. She seemed intent on speaking to Anamar.

'We're more alike, daughter dear, than anybody knows.' Maeve and Anamar hardly dared to breathe in case they missed a word. 'The difference is, I've kept myself hidden all my life, God alone knows why. But you're going to wear your heart on your sleeve and you'll live a life beyond the wildest dreams of anyone from this corner of Donegal.'

Anamar looked at Aunt Maeve to see if they should be encouraging her mother to rest. Maeve's whispered in her ear.

'Let her talk. She needs to tell you. It'll bring her peace.'

'You have dreamed your dreams,' her mother continued, going back to the time Anamar had spoken out, squeezing her daughter's hand until it hurt. 'You can see the past in a person's eyes. I know now how you'll change the world. You've changed yourself and that's changed the whole world for you.'

She paused as if she had finished, and then began again.

'When I was young, I had the gifts too, but I never dared to use them. I know for sure you'll never make a display of them to impress the crowd that would love to be impressed. You will dare to use them where I didn't. But only use them rarely. You've already found a power for good within you which can help those in real need of it.'

She took deep breaths as if to energise her body.

'This jaunt to Lourdes will bring grace and blessing to the whole of this parish. When it's finished, you'll find you have another pilgrimage in front of you. It will span countries. There'll be rivers and mountains to cross, shadeless plains to travel. You'll feel the baking heat, hunger, thirst, fear, doubt, a tiredness you've never known. But before the journey's end, you'll find your reward.'

Her eyes closed and she clasped both Anamar's hands in hers.

'Let me sleep,' she said. 'Now we've both had our say, I can rest easy.'
Maeve settled her back in the bed.

'She'll sleep well to-night,' she whispered as they left the room. 'But it's my guess she's not long for this world. And maybe it's thank God for that. It could be a sweet release.'

The Dark Hour Before the Dawn

It must have been hours later, but Anamar felt as if she had just laid her head on her own pillow, when she felt a hand on her shoulder. It was Maeve, holding a candle stick in one hand and shaking her awake with the other. Maeve was worried. There was no look of concern on her face. It was the sound of her voice that startled Anamar. Her aunt could hide her anxieties better than anyone she knew, but she could clearly hear them now.

'You'd better come down,' she said. 'It's four o'clock. Your mother always dreaded 'the dark hour before the dawn' as she calls it. She was in labour with you at four in the morning and was terrified that only one of you would live to see the light of day.'

Anamar slipped on a pair of shoes and pulled her big coat around her shoulders like a cape. While Maeve went into the other upstairs room to waken her father, she lit a candle and came down to her mother's bedside. The room was lit by two small oil lamps, bright enough for her to see that her mother was agitated, her body twisted in the bed, rigid with pain.

Anamar placed the rosary beads across the clenched hand and her mother's face turned quickly to see who it was.

'What time is it?' Una's voice was demanding. 'What time of the night is it, at all?'

Maeve had come in silently behind Anamar and took over, patting Una's arm.

'There, there,' she said quietly, as if the patient was a child in pain. 'There, there, there.' She reached for the bottle of medicine and the spoon. 'Here you are child dear,' she said, holding a spoonful to Una's lips with a towel tucked just below her chin to catch the drips. Una sipped the dark liquid and closed her eyes. In a quarter of an hour the potion was having its effect and the tension eased, but her strength seemed to flow away with it.

John Joe sat at one side of the bed and Maeve and Anamar at the other. At six o'clock Maeve took Una's pulse.

'It's too late for the doctor,' she said calmly, all trace of fear gone from her voice. 'One of you will have to get the priest.'

'I'll go,' said John Joe, on his feet and on his way to the door before Anamar could move. 'I'll take Anamar's bicycle. It's all downhill. It'll only take me twenty minutes.'

Maeve looked at Anamar, as if in apology for having to tell her father what to do.

'You'd better tell Father Brogan that it won't be long now. And while you're there you should ring Dr Corr. ' She set about straightening the quilt on the bed and tidying the room.

Anamar stayed with her mother and Maeve went into the kitchen to rekindle the fire. She stirred the ashes and added a few whin roots from the pile in the corner. As the wood crackled into flame she stacked turf like an Indian tepee over the whin and hung a pot of water from the crane.

In less than an hour Father Brogan's car drove into the farmyard. John Joe was with him, they had wedged his bicycle across the open boot of the car.

The priest bent low over Una, anointing her, whispering the litany of the last rites, by now as much a part of his persona as the stole around his neck. He was aware of the power of familiar prayer at times like this, and not least for himself. His faith could help him. But how could he help others?

'She waited for me to come,' he said gently, reassuringly, now that he had prepared Una for death.

'I knew last night,' Maeve said, looking over her shoulder at John Joe and Anamar as if sharing a secret. 'I knew she had decided she had held on long enough.'

Una sighed softly and died as she had lived, quietly, without fuss, as if her time had come.

When he stepped back from the bed, Father Brogan's words of consolation would have sounded trite to some, but not here. It seemed sad to Anamar that it had taken the death of her mother to let her see the caring man within the overbearing priest.

Father Brogan and John Joe drank a cup of strong tea laced with a tot of whiskey from a bottle Maeve had brought with her in her basket. The priest shook hands with the three of them and after a decent interval, took his leave.

Maeve left Anamar alone with her mother in the inner room. She and Una had never been as close as most sisters seemed to be. Although it was not a cold day she pulled her chair close to the fire and prodded the lumps of turf with the poker. She cried softly, knowing that John Joe and Anamar, for very different reasons, would both find it hard to let the tears fall.

Anamar took a chair to the tiny window which overlooked Lough Eske. A feeling of numbness detached her from the view and she watched the light across the lake.

These farm houses were not built for the view. They were set into the hillside to be at the heart of the holding, to take what shelter there was from the lie of the land. But this was a beautiful prospect. She looked across the lake to the far shore. The water glowed brighter than the sky. The trees and bushes sheltered the houses and cottages. The white walls of Maeve's home gleamed in the middle of the picture and she thought of the happy times she had spent there, feeling a part of a family more than she had ever done here at home.

She startled suddenly, realising how guilty she felt at that thought. She tried to banish it by thinking of the conversations of the past few days. But that only made her angry. Her mother's death had occurred at the moment of reconciliation. What about all those wasted years when neither had been able to speak or be heard. Who was to blame? Was it her mother? The more she thought of it, the more it seemed obvious that she would have to blame herself.

Anamar put her head in her hands and wept dry tears for the wasted years. She felt a rawness inside, a sickening sense of despair. There was no denying it had happened and it was her fault. The chance had gone. There would never be another. Her mother was dead. And she herself was the guilty one, guilty by default. She should have been able to make it work between them. If it had not been possible before she left home on her travels, it certainly should have been when she returned.

Maeve had left the door ajar and peeped in to see if Anamar was all right. Her niece was sitting near the window, head in her hands, as still as a rock on the mountainside. She decided not to intrude.

Two hours later Dr Corr arrived. He had been out on a call when the priest had telephoned and came as soon as his housekeeper had given him the message. Timmy looked out from the shed but decided to make no move towards the enemy.

Maeve stirred at the sound of the car and she met the doctor at the door with the news that her sister was dead.

'I'm sorry for your trouble,' he said kindly. 'Believe me, it's for the best.'

He came out of the inner room a few minutes later and, to Maeve's surprise, joined them in the kitchen for tea. Dr Corr was not one for sitting down in a patient's kitchen for a social chat. Maeve was pleased. She decided to produce the whiskey and offer him a drop in his tea.

'Well, well, isn't that very kind of you,' he said. 'I don't usually indulge before evening but a wee nip in the tea could hardly be said to break a rule.' He chuckled, finding himself far more at ease in this house than ever he would have expected.

'It must have been very hard to see her fading away so quickly, a bit weaker day by day and nothing you could do.' He was talking quietly, needing no response, trying to ease the pain. 'Take my word for it, it could have been a great deal worse. She could have lingered on and suffered more.'

'I know,' said Maeve. 'Had she been in bad pain, and us able to do nothing …' She hesitated, not knowing how to put that awful possibility into words.

Dr Corr was one of Miss Ryan's small circle of friends in Donegal Town. For years the best efforts of local gossips to spread rumours about a serious, romantic attachment had failed. They were friends and also the hub of a small group of like-minded companions, who met regularly and thoroughly enjoyed each other's company.

'I hear that, come the spring, you're off to Lourdes again.' The doctor might appear to keep his distance from his patients but he missed little of what was happening in the locality. It was just enough to draw Anamar into the conversation and she began to talk about Ellie's idea.

'Easy girl,' said Maeve. 'You'll have the doctor signed up as medical officer to the pilgrimage before he leaves.'

Dr Corr was on his feet, ready to go.

'Do you know, that might not be such a bad idea,' he said. 'There's many a good invitation made in jest. You might just keep me posted.'

Anamar left him out to the car. Timmy waited until she had gone back into the house and then raced down the lane after the car, barking frantically.

Maeve was so taken aback by the doctor's reaction to her suggestion that she sounded flustered when Anamar came back into the kitchen

'Declare to God! Nobody will believe us,' she said. 'Our man the doctor sitting down in the kitchen, taking tea with a nip in it, chatting away to us as if we were his cronies in the town.'

Anamar smiled. If Dr Corr's intention had been to cheer them up he had succeeded.

'It's you, m'girl,' Maeve continued. Neither priest nor doctor know what to make of you, so you have them at your coat tails. You'd do well to keep them both guessing.'

Each in its own way, the visits of priest and doctor had helped them over the worst moments in the aftermath of death. Even John Joe, who had exchanged not a word with either man, seemed less troubled.

During the next few days the doubts and despair returned to torment Anamar. On the afternoon after the funeral she went to the graveyard and sat on the grass by the new grave. The fresh soil was strewn with fresh flowers. The soil would settle and eventually a green sward would grow, but soon the flowers would wither and die. The real tears came and she cried as never before since she had been a child. Without a handkerchief, she wiped her wet cheeks on her sleeve.

Then she almost smiled, remembering what would have happened if she had hurt herself when she was young and had started to cry. Her mother would have spoken to her quite sharply. 'There's no point snivelling,' she would have said. 'There's plenty with far more pain to bear than you.'

The sun warmed her back and she looked across the lake up to the peaks of the Blue Stacks. There was a stillness in the air, a calmness, a sense of peace. Her stifling depression began to lift. There was no joy in the moment, but the sadness was no longer so overpowering. It would take a long time for her to come to terms with the guilt, but for now it was contained.

The house had been full every evening since the death and all the help Anamar needed had been readily given by Maeve, Ellie and Maureen. The previous evening, neighbours and friends had arrived, sombrely offering their condolences. Then the conversation and the food and drink had taken over and cheered up the proceedings. When the last of the stragglers had departed in the early hours, they left the house a more peaceful place. Now, she and her father had to face the future by themselves.

When she came back from the cemetery, John Joe was alone in the house. He had been waiting for her.

'I was thinking of going out for the evening,' he said quietly. 'Will you be all right? You could always go round to the McGinley's. Maureen was here looking for you.'

Anamar was pleased. She had not been looking forward to the prospect of a silent evening with her father, sitting at the fire. He left on his bicycle and it was easy to guess he would be going to the pub with a bachelor friend. There was no need to worry, come what may they would look after each other.

Now the fuss of the funeral was over, Anamar felt quite content to be in the house on her own. She made herself scumbled eggs, adding the chopped scallions the way Eamon had done at Belshade. She smiled, remembering how pleased he was to have added his own little touch to his mother's method.

It was after seven-thirty when she followed the track to the McGinley's.

'You're the lucky woman,' said Ellie as soon as she saw her. 'We were going to give you another fifteen minutes. If you hadn't shown up by then, Maureen and Eamon were going round with the wheel barrow to kidnap you.'

They all smiled and Maureen and Ellie began to tease Eamon and Anamar, pretending that they were sweethearts. Eamon was annoyed to start with, but when he realised that Anamar was enjoying the banter, he relaxed and discovered that he was well pleased to be thought of as her boyfriend even though it was all meant to be in fun.

Ellie turned the conversation to the plans for the pilgrimage to Lourdes. That very morning she had spoken to Father Brogan.

'I suppose I shouldn't have been surprised, but he seems to know as much about the idea as I do,' she said. 'Anyhow, he's all for it. Expressed himself very happy to join us, if you please. He was also very keen to hear if you intended to go.' She had turned to address Anamar. 'Seems to think it's important that you do. Maybe he feels you need to spend a bit more time on your knees.'

Ellie's good form was infectious. Even Eamon, who was keen to go with the group but worried that he might be one of very few men amongst a horde of women, allowed himself to show some interest.

A meeting had been arranged for the following Monday evening in the school. Ellie had invited people she knew were interested and intended to make them the organising committee. Father Brogan had said he would look in to see them. She had written to Father Jack in Fermanagh to tell him about the meeting. She was elated. They were about to take the first step on the way to Lourdes.

It was nearly mid-night when Maureen and Eamon left Anamar home. Her father had not returned. She was not surprised. If he had any sense he would stay the night with his friend.

She lay down in her little room under the eaves and let her mind go back to the Pyrenees and her last night there with Hank at the Hospital De Viella. When she had left the inn the next day, it had seemed as if a chapter of her life had ended. Now another chapter was finished but, as before, when one closed another was already opening.

F. B. O'Boyle - The Experienced Pilgrim

Ellie was hoping the meeting would be a success when the unbelievable happened. Everyone turned up early. It was unheard of in South Donegal. It augured well for the success of their venture. They sat around a table at the top end of the room and Ellie spoke first.

'When I told you all it would be a seven o'clock start, I thought you'd still be rolling up about half past eight,' she said cheerily. 'You must be keen. I've no doubts now that we have the right crowd here to organise this pilgrimage.'

There were a few chuckles around the table. Like Ellie, everyone was in good form. They were as excited as children hearing about an excursion to the seaside at Bundoran.

Ellie had come with Maureen and Anamar. Lena, Maggie and Rose had met them at the gate. As they had greeted each other, Father Jack had arrived by car, accompanied by the man who had been with him on his last visit to Belshade. Anamar remembered him as the father who was keen to take his son to Lourdes. His name was Peter Heaney.

'The parish priest said I could take the motor,' Jack had said, almost as an apology. 'He thinks it's a grand idea and hopes some of our parishioners will want to join you.'

Ellie had never run a meeting before and, to keep them to the business, she had made a list of the points they should discuss. Asking if they thought that the pilgrimage to Lourdes was a good idea seemed the obvious way to start. An hour later they had not only agreed that it was, but had talked about the best time of the year, how they would travel, how much it might cost and how many they might expect to go.

Anamar told them that groups usually spent four or five days in Lourdes and described what the pilgrims did on each of the days they were there.

They were deciding who would help Ellie find the travel information they needed when they heard a car draw up outside the school. The door of the room opened and Father Brogan entered, accompanied by a small, neatly-dressed man, known to most of those present as the proprietor of a haberdashery shop in the Town.

Father Brogan smiled.

'I'm sure most of you know Mr O'Boyle,' he said briskly and then, with the slightest possible movement of his head towards Ellie, he continued. 'I took the liberty of inviting him so that we could avail of his expert knowledge. He's not a man to step into the limelight of his own accord but, in his youth, he had the great good fortune to be a member of the Second Irish Pilgrimage to Lourdes in 1924.'

Francis Brendan O'Boyle stepped forward to Father Brogan's side. He was a tiny man, neatly dressed in a navy blue suit with a white shirt and a plain dark blue tie. In his breast pocket the tip of a white handkerchief showed, but only he knew, although others suspected, that this was merely the hemmed corner of a piece of white linen and not part of an actual handkerchief.

Mr O'Boyle thought he was smiling at the company but only his mouth moved. He deemed it a great honour to have been invited here by the priest. Most of the women present were known to him as customers and he was wary of them. He was wary of everyone in this part of Ireland, young or old, man or woman, rich or poor. It was fifteen years since he had come from Dublin to Donegal Town to manage a shop owned by his great aunt. O'BOYLE'S HABERDASHERY sold clothing and dress-making materials, buttons, thread, wool, cloth by the yard.

F. B. O'Boyle, as he liked to be known, was a man who kept himself to himself. Outside church activities he had virtually no contact with local people except in his shop. Father Brogan was not his parish priest but he had been pleased to see him when the Father had telephoned to invite him to the meeting. F. B. O'Boyle accepted that it was his religious duty to attend and, although he regarded himself as a shy man, reluctant to hold forth in company, he intended to fulfil that duty.

'Pleased to meet you,' he said civilly. 'Father Brogan tells me that you hope to organise a pilgrimage group to go to Lourdes. He feels I may be of some assistance to you. Should your efforts be rewarded by God with the opportunity to visit Massabielle, the Shrine of the Holy Mother of God, I would also consider accompanying the party.'

'Massabielle's the name of the rock where the Grotto is,' whispered Anamar to Ellie, who was looking puzzled.

There was a silent pause. Father Brogan looked around for a chair and Mr O'Boyle scurried to the back of the room to bring one for him and made a second journey to fetch another for himself.

'You'd think he could have managed a chair in each hand to save himself a double run.' Maggie was addressing Rose in a stage whisper, so loud they all heard, and Father Jack put his hand over his face to hide the smile.

They were sitting in a semi-circle with Ellie at one end of the curve, Father

Brogan and Mr O'Boyle drew their chairs to the side where the three men were sitting and arranged them as part of the arc of the circle. As he sat down Father Brogan spoke.

'Perhaps we could begin by inviting Mr O'Boyle to tell us about the wonderful National Pilgrimage of 1924.'

F. B. O'Boyle tried to smile and shyly rose to his feet.

'But we've already started,' Ellie said sharply. She could see control of the meeting taken from her hands as soon as the priest had spoken. 'We've been hard at it for an hour and have our plans laid for the next stage, but I'm sure we'd all enjoy a break from the work to hear Mr O'Boyle.'

F. B. O'Boyle seemed flustered. He looked at Father Brogan, who gave him a brusque nod as an indication that he should continue.

'Well, of course, it was different …' F. B. O'Boyle stopped as if he had forgotten what he intended to say. Then the words came with a rush.

'It was a very large pilgrimage in '24. There were four thousand of us. We were in three contingents, one leaving from Dublin, a second from Belfast and the third from Rosslare. There were five hundred invalids with us. I was one of the fifty members of the St. John's Ambulance Corps. We went as part of the medical staff to help the doctors and nurses.'

He stopped again and looked at Ellie this time. Maggie and Rose were stretched back in their chairs trying to show that they were bored. Father Jack was embarrassed. Father Brogan was staring at the back wall. Ellie smiled, feeling sorry for poor Mr O'Boyle. If he was Father Brogan's secret weapon, he had gone off like a damp squib.

'That's very interesting, Mr O'Boyle,' she said, realising that this was her chance to take charge of the meeting again. 'While you're collecting your thoughts, I'll just bring Father Brogan and yourself up-to-date on what we've agreed so far.'

'We've decided that we should go next Spring and that the party shouldn't be too big, say about thirty or forty. We plan to spend four or five days in Lourdes itself with a proper programme of activities. The travelling would be on top of that, of course. Within the group, we would hope to have a small number of ill and disabled people. You might be surprised to hear that Dr Corr has expressed an interest in accompanying us.'

Ellie paused. Those who had been at the meeting from the beginning were as startled as the late comers. Not everything that Ellie was now mentioning had been discussed. Nor had all the arrangements been agreed, but she was using her notes to good effect and making it seem as if the committee had been very businesslike.

The news of Dr Corr's interest was a surprise and not only because it was the first time it had been mentioned. The doctor was a Protestant, not a regular church attender, but a member of the Church of Ireland, none-the-less.

It was not a point about which anyone present would have wished to comment, least of all Father Brogan. The doctor had always been most helpful when their duties brought them together. When they happened to meet of an evening in the hotel in the Town, they found each other very affable company over a glass of whiskey. But control of this pilgrimage was slipping away from him like an unhooked fish might slither out of his hands, back into the water of Lough Eske when he was indulging in his favourite form of relaxation.

Peter Heaney broke the silence which followed Ellie's speech.

'I take my hat off to Mrs McGinley,' he said. 'She's brought us together and kept us strictly to business. If the pilgrimage goes as well as this evening, it's set fair to be a success.'

Father Jack nodded in agreement but said nothing. Ellie looked down at her notes.

'Only two more items of business,' she said. 'I'm very pleased Father Brogan has honoured us with his presence. It allows me to ask him in person, and on behalf of all of us, to be the Spiritual Director of the pilgrimage.'

Father Brogan had played Gaelic football in his youth and knew that, although he might score a few points if he tried hard, Mrs McGinley had already scored enough goals to settle the match.

'I accept with pleasure,' he said gently. 'How could I refuse such a gracious invitation?'

Father Jack and Peter led the applause, although F. B. O'Boyle clapped loudest once he saw that everyone was joining in.

'Thank you Father,' said Ellie. 'And before I ask Mr O'Boyle to address us again, I just want to suggest the date of the next meeting.' She suggested an evening four weeks away and promised to report on the enquiries she, Maggie and Rose would make on travel arrangements and costs.

'And now it's over to you again, Mr O'Boyle.'

F. B. O'Boyle rose to his feet and began to rock backwards and forwards in his highly-polished, patent-leather, black ankle boots, from the rim of his heels to the tip of his toes. He looked towards Father Brogan, whose eyes were examining the paint on the back wall.

'Sit yourself down like the rest of us,' said Ellie gently. 'Tell us what you did when you were there in '24.' And she gained in F. B. an ally who would stand her in good stead in the months ahead.

F. B. resumed his seat and began to talk about the huge undertaking which had been the second national pilgrimage officially organised by the Church in Ireland and led by eight bishops. He opened his attache case and produced his green be-ribboned Irish Pilgrim's Medal, holding it aloft for all to see. Ellie rose and crossed the room to where he was sitting.

'You should be sporting your medal on your chest,' she said and pinned it to the lapel of his coat. 'It'll inspire us all.'

F. B. sat an inch taller in his seat. He beamed with pleasure.

'Our St. John's Corps made such a good impression the two Superintendents were invited back to Lourdes the next year to be specially decorated.'

He hesitated, unsure if this might sound like boasting.

'The doctors and nurses were in charge, of course, and they were wonderful. We helped in the Aisle Hospital and the Baths.'

F. B. rummaged in his case again and produced a large leather bound book.

'I brought my scrap-book,' he said. 'There were reports in the Irish Independent, written by their special correspondent, Jacques, who was travelling with the Dublin Section. My mother kept all the papers for me.'

Anamar had not said a word since the two men had arrived.

'Why don't you read to us from your scrap-book,' she said encouragingly. 'We'd love to hear what Jacques had to say about you all.'

F. B. opened the book near the front and quoted Jacques in full flow.

'We are off to Lourdes', was in the tramp of the feet along the pier. 'We are off to Lourdes', was in the lilt of the hymns they sang as the vessels speeded out of the harbour. In many years' experience of crossings I have never found the demons that stir up trouble in the Irish Sea in nastier humour ... In the sloppy, chilly darkness of the morn we assembled at Holyhead Pier - a green-ribboned medal on every breast ...

'The trains were marshalled to meet us - Blue Train, Green Train, Yellow Train - and every coach, on every train, had printed numbers all in order posted on the windows. A school child could go alone on a journey worked out on simple lines like this. Cook's man did not need to guide us; he came around simply to ask if we were comfortable.'

F. B. O'Boyle stopped again, but this time he was neither agitated nor in the least flustered at having to be the centre of attention. The others began to clap. F. B. had never dared to dream that others people would receive what he had to say so kindly.

'Thank you,' he said diffidently and stood up to bring the scrap book over to Ellie. 'I thought you might like to borrow it for a wee while.'

When the meeting was over, Father Brogan told Ellie it was unlikely that he would be able to attend many of the meetings, but he hoped she would keep him informed of progress. They were both well aware now of their relative positions in the project. Ellie would be in charge of the organisational details of the venture and, although the Father was withdrawing into the background, he would retain his divine right as their parish priest to be the final arbiter in all matters. As he and Mr O'Boyle were leaving F. B. shook Ellie's hand.

'It's God's work you're doing,' he said. 'And I'll do what I can to help.'

Father Jack and Peter Heaney left to drive back to Fermanagh and Dan Byrne headed home on his bicycle. Ellie locked the outer door of the school and joined the other women where their bicycles were propped against the school wall. Lena looked at Ellie and shook her head in mock amazement.

'I don't know how you do it,' she said. 'You're a different woman since you got that bee in your bonnet about Lourdes. Father Brogan thinks you're taking over the parish and he's away back to the Town to drown his sorrows in the hotel bar. He'll probably meet Dr Corr and get another earful about how marvellous Anamar is too.'

They all laughed. Ellie was well pleased. She would get Maggie and Rose to help her. They both worked in the Town. By the next meeting they would have chapter and verse about the travel. She would plan a notice for the Donegal Democrat, announcing the pilgrimage. And in the meantime, she had F. B's wonderful book to study.

It was only nine o'clock and Anamar suddenly had an idea. She had spoken to Deirdre Ryan at her mother's funeral, but there had been no opportunity to have a proper conversation since she had come back home from Belshade.

She left the others, knowing that the meeting just finished would keep them in chat for ages, and cycled down to Miss Ryan's house on the main road.

It was the only home Anamar visited where she went to the front door and Deirdre was delighted to see her.

'And here was me thinking you'd forgotten where I lived,' she said. 'I've been waiting patiently to hear about your foreign travels and as for this sojourn in the mountains, where you lived like an anchoress ...'

She paused, thinking Anamar's look was quizzical and continued in the voice which she always used when she was pretending to be the stern school-mistress. 'For your information, Miss Cassidy, 'anchoress' is the feminine of 'anchorite', which you will be well aware, of course, is synonymous with 'hermit'.'

They laughed together and hugged and Anamar wondered why she had waited so long to make this visit.

Cassoulet De Donegal

Deirdre made tea. She brought the tray into the sitting room and placed it on a low table near the fire. To Anamar, this was the most beautiful room she had ever been in. There were paintings on the walls, not prints, but original paintings, most of them by artist friends of Deirdre's. There was a group of five water-colours of village life in Donegal on the wall opposite the window and a large oil of a clown above the mantelpiece. Near the door, there were nine miniatures arranged in rows of three. These were tiny portraits of famous Irish figures and of friends from Deirdre's circle, including Dr Corr in a deerstalker hat and Deirdre herself with a dramatic Edwardian hairstyle and blouse.

Polished mahogany book-shelves lined the wall facing the fireplace and in a niche amongst the volumes, a bronze bust of Oliver Goldsmith, nearly a foot high, looked out across the room. There were carvings in wood and bone on a brass-topped table and inlaid boxes on the window ledge. Five small oil lamps with coloured glass shades lit every corner of the room with a subdued, tranquil light. The carpet was of an oriental design and its darker shades set off a luxurious, brightly-patterned Persian rug in front of the fire.

They sat in comfort in deep, easy chairs, one on either side of the fire. Anamar often sat on the Persian rug, but never when she and Deirdre were taking tea. Deirdre poured the tea into China cups. She addressed Anamar in her most dignified voice but with a little smile to remind her that, as their own little joke, they always celebrated ceremonies, like serving tea, in the grand manner.

'It's Assam so I didn't bring the milk,' she said. 'In the hope that your sojourn in France had accustomed you to taking tea in the proper way, without milk to destroy the delicate taste.'

Deirdre was right. Anamar's tastes had changed. The French often made tea without letting the water come to the boil, but while she was there, she had learned to enjoy the fresh flavour of tea without milk, sometimes with a tiny slice of lemon.

'And what's more,' she said. 'When you offer me coffee, I'll be glad to have the real thing, rather than a spoonful of coffee essence in a cup of boiling milk!'

They both laughed. Deirdre liked to make coffee from freshly ground beans, specially ordered from a grocer in Dublin and ground in her own grinder. Anamar had always thought it was a very roundabout way of making a simple drink. However, her stay in France had ensured that she had developed the taste for what Deirdre called, 'proper coffee'.

They settled back with their cups of Assam tea and Anamar regaled Deirdre with the proceedings of the Lourdes Committee that evening.

'You should have seen Father Brogan's face when he arrived to take over the meeting, with his henchman, F. B. O'Boyle, the Haberdasher. Ellie stopped the pair of them in their tracks. That poor man O'Boyle didn't know where to put himself.'

Deirdre wanted to hear of every move and counter-move. She nodded in appreciation when she heard how Ellie had listed the committee's decisions to Father Brogan, whether the decisions had been discussed or not. She was intrigued to learn of Dr Corr's interest. 'He's been keeping quiet about this trip,' she thought to herself, but said nothing. She laughed until the tears ran down her cheeks when Anamar stood up and rocked back and forth on her heels and toes recounting F. B's contribution.

'Stop girl!' she cried through the tears.

Later, Deirdre listened with hardly a comment when Anamar told her why she had left so hurriedly for Lough Belshade and what had happened while she had been there. Then, they both realised that it was late and Deirdre had not yet heard about Anamar's stay in France.

'I'm only allowing you to stop there,' she said. 'On condition that you come back on Saturday evening and join me for the evening meal. I'm enjoying your escapades, but I've a feeling the best is yet to come.'

They hugged again on the doorstep and Deirdre had the last word as Anamar was leaving.

'Maybe you could borrow that scrap-book of Mr O'Boyle's from Mrs McGinley and bring it with you when you come to dinner. I'd love to see it.'

Anamar had always enjoyed Deirdre Ryan's company but, now she had lived away from home, she and Deirdre could talk together on equal terms.

Her father had wired up the lights of the bicycle so that the red tail light and the head light worked off the same battery. No one else in this part of the country ever used bicycle lights, even when it was pitch dark, but her father had always insisted she do so and Anamar was grateful to him as she pedalled slowly home.

When she went back to Deirdre's on the Saturday she had the scrap-book wrapped in brown paper in the basket at the front of her bicycle. Dinner was almost ready when she arrived. Deirdre had made a lamb casserole with onions and carrots in a rich sauce. The table had been laid for two with silver cutlery, a cut-glass water jug and tumblers, wine glasses in plain glass and an opened bottle of red wine in a silver coaster.

After a first course of smoked salmon sprinkled with herbs, Deirdre served the casserole with small potatoes boiled in their jackets. On their plates it looked like a dish Anamar would have been served in France when she had been out for a special meal. She said so and Deirdre smiled.

'And I'm the one who is more than pleased to have her cooking appreciated. We shall call it, 'Cassoulet de Donegal', Deirdre laughed, filled the glasses a little over half-full and raised hers in a toast.

'Here's to good food, fine wine and congenial conversation.'

Deirdre meant it to sound joyful but she said it so seriously, with almost a quiver in her voice, that Anamar wondered whether, within the fascinating, cultured, cultivated life that Deirdre led, there might be something missing. She knew that, in the unlikely event of her entrusting the thought to Maggie or Rose, the immediate reply would have been, 'Sure all that one needs is a man.' Anamar knew instinctively, however, that they were wrong. Deirdre had many friends, of both sexes, and seemed to enjoy their company immensely.

At school, the gossip had been that Miss Ryan must be nearly forty so, as far as the pupils were concerned, she was really quite old. Now they were friends, to Anamar it seemed that Deirdre was younger than some married women she knew who were in their twenties. She was convinced that the serious tone and the quiver in Deirdre's voice had nothing to do with the fact that she was un-married.

At Belshade, Anamar had been aware of a strange yearning to find herself, of a need to fulfil herself, of having to set herself challenges which would allow her to find out who she really was. When she had been telling Maureen about her walk alone across the Pyrenees, she had known then that it was only the first step on a longer journey.

In a way, her flash of understanding of Deirdre's feelings had not been too difficult, and the more she thought about it, the more probable it seemed. Deirdre, too, longed for a challenge which would take her beyond her teaching career, her interests and social life in Ireland, her exciting travels in the long school holidays.

Anamar smiled. Just one simple toast, proposed by her friend, but the circumstances in which it was said, and the tone of saying it had managed to communicate so much.

'I envy you,' said Deirdre. 'With your whole life in front of you and nothing but freedom in your head.'

Anamar laughed aloud and wagged a finger at her friend.

'Listen to who's talking. There's no freer woman in the whole country and you're thirty years younger than the ancient school-marm who used to put the fear of God in us every time we got one spelling wrong.'

For the first time in their friendship, Anamar was hesitant as she tried to tell Deirdre of the yearning she had sensed in her.

'You have a wonderful life,' she said respectfully. 'But don't you feel the urge sometimes ...'

'To kick over the traces,' Deirdre laughed as she finished the sentence.

'No, I didn't meant that,' Anamar was a little embarrassed. 'To do something different ... '

She stopped, wondering if she had gone too far, aware that she was blushing at her presumption.

'I'm sorry Miss Ryan,' she said. 'I didn't mean to be so forward.'

'Nonsense gel! You were not in the least forward. Should you be so, I would be the first to remark upon it.' Deirdre was affecting her grand voice, as if she were gentry addressing someone in trade, but smiling broadly.

'It would be a poor friendship if you and I were not able to be open and frank with each other. And, by the way, did we not agree to address each other by our Christian names when you were but a slip of a girl?'

They both laughed loudly, Anamar with relief, Deirdre with the pleasure of feeling so comfortable in this friendship.

'Come along now,' she said. 'We'd better attack this Cassoulet de Donegal before it's stone cold.'

The casserole was delicious and they talked as they ate and enjoyed the wine. For pudding, Deirdre had baked an open fruit tart, with concentric circles of apple slices, glazed with apricot jam, in the French way, and served with fresh cream. When they had finished, Anamar shook her head, almost lost for words. She tried to thank Deirdre but her friend interrupted gently to make it easy for her.

'You and I will have many a good meal together. But now it's time for Mr O'Boyle's scrap-book.'

They cleared the table and sat side by side, poring through the big volume. They reached the page from the Irish Independent on which Jacques' description of the Dublin Section's departure for Lourdes had been given a prominent position.

'That's the piece about the Blue, Green and Yellow Trains which Mr O'Boyle read aloud at the meeting,' said Anamar.

'I remember Jacques in the Independent when I was at home and still at school,' Deirdre remembered. 'I always thought it was very sophisticated for a columnist in an Irish paper to write under a French pseudonym.' She was as excited as a school-girl.

'Do you see what happened on the way through France?' She began to read further down the column by Jacques.

'A few miles on the north side of Orleans, some thoughtless person broke the alarm signal on the Blue Train. The train at once stopped far out in open country … This caused a delay of over an hour at midnight … it threw the time-table out of joint … We should have arrived at Lourdes at 12.50 p.m. We did not reach the station until 3.45 p.m.'

Deirdre looked up from the page.

'Trust Jacques to tell us about the pranks as well as the pious hymns,' she said and switching to her grand voice. 'I trust that none of the clergy were involved in this sky-larking.'

They laughed and leafed through the book together. There was a list of the organising committees - Executive, Music and Literary, Invalids, Associates. There were illustrations of the front and back views of the Pilgrims' Medal and a much larger one of the National Banner. The sole item on one page, and placed in the centre to denote its significance, was a list of the eight bishops who were attending the pilgrimage with their full titles, no doubt correct to the last colon and comma.

In his report on the activities of the second day at Lourdes, Jacques had written.

'A sky blue as the waters of the swift-flowing Gave smiled on us … It was our first really fine, dry day since our coming to Lourdes. So Ireland streamed through the town and awakened it to its presence. Cork accents mingled with Belfast, Scottish-Irish with Connaught, Dublin with Liverpool-Irish and London-Irish. All roads led to the Rosary Church, where High Mass was celebrated … A blaze of purple robes lighted up the altar …

Anamar and Deirdre were enthralled.

'Can't you just feel that you're following the procession, the whole way to the altar? said Deirdre. 'Now, come along, my girl, what's the collective noun for a company of pilgrims?' She was using her school-teacher's voice.

'What about a pack of pilgrims?' Anamar had always enjoyed Miss Ryan's collective noun quizzes at school, not taken too seriously.

'Quite good,' said Deirdre. 'But some might say that pack would be better associated with priests, and for reasons that would be best left unexplained.'

'I know,' said Anamar. 'What about, a see of bishops?'

Deirdre smiled, bowed her head in acknowledgement and clapped softly.

'Well done,' she said. 'I'm glad to see you didn't waste my time entirely when I had you chained to a desk.'

They both laughed and then continued their study of the scrap-book in intrigued silence.

'It's a fascinating record,' Deirdre said at last. 'And put together with such loving care. I'm sure it's unique. Once your pilgrimage is over Mr O'Boyle should consider placing it in the archives of a university library.'

Anamar offered to leave the scrap-book with Deirdre for a few days to give her time to peruse it properly. She knew Ellie would not mind, it would not be needed until the next meeting.

The wine bottle was still almost half full and Deirdre replenished their glasses.

'It's from Languedoc,' she said swirling the red liquid in her glass. 'Hardly the most fashionable of the wine-making districts of France but one of my favourites. One sip and I'm back in the sunny south just north of your beloved Pyrenees.'

She paused and arched her eyebrows theatrically.

'And when pray, am I to hear of your adventures amongst the high peaks? Am I right in assuming that, like the biblical host, you've saved the good wine to the last?'

They took their wine across to the easy chairs at the fire and Anamar began her story with her meeting with Hank in the book shop. She tried to leave out nothing of significance but this was a much briefer version. In the first telling, she had told the tale as much for herself as for Maureen, or Eamon and the other girls, when they had been present.

Deirdre had been the perfect listener. Having travelled extensively in France before and since the war, she could clearly imagine Anamar's circumstances living in Lourdes. Although times had been hard and there had been shortages since the German surrender in 1945, the French were a people close to the land. The country's pre-war reputation for good food had depended upon the availability of high quality farm produce. Now the war was over, visitors could enjoy the legendary haute cuisine of France once again.

Deirdre showed no inclination to discuss Hank. Like Maureen, she knew that Anamar would tell this part of the story when she was ready. She was intrigued, however, to hear that he had mentioned Hilaire Belloc's Tarantella and that he thought the Hospital de Viella was the inn mentioned in the poem.

'You were glad then,' she said with a smile. 'When your brave boy mentioned Tarantella, that Master Robson had drummed the words into your head at school.'

They laughed at the memory of it. Jamie Robson believed in the power of repetition and the chanting by a class of spellings, or arithmetic tables, or lines of poetry was a music of youth Anamar would never forget.

Anamar's walks in the mountains with Hank were of the greatest interest to Deirdre. The year she was sixteen, her father had taken her walking in the French Alps. They had stayed in a village, walking up into the high valleys and even climbing a snow peak on the last day. It had involved the crossing of a glacier, a long, ascent using steps kicked in the snow by a previous party and an easy scramble up rocks and scree. At the top was a tiny ledge beside a jagged rock which was the actual summit. The view had been magnificent. They were high enough to see into the heart of the Dauphiné Alps. It had been an experience she would never forget.

Deirdre questioned Anamar closely about the solo walk across the Pyrenees. Her father would have seen it as foolhardy. Hank should have advised her against it. But before she could say anything to doubt the wisdom of it, she suddenly realised that Anamar had gained a good deal of experience in a short time. Although Hank had not been teaching her mountain skills directly, she had been learning by being with him. But most important of all, Anamar had needed to do this journey at that precise moment in her life.

Deirdre brought a huge atlas to the table and they pored over the map of the Pyrenees. They found Lourdes and Gavarnie and there, amongst the high peaks, was Vignemale. Further to the east was Viella, the Spanish town on the 'wrong' side of the Pyrenees. The scale of the map was just large enough to let them trace Anamar's route through the mountains with the aid of a big magnifying glass.

'It looks such a tiny distance on the map,' said Anamar, sounding disappointed.

But Deirdre would have none of it.

'Listen to me, my girl,' she said. 'I know from hard experience on my own two feet, that it can take a long time to travel a short way, once you're amongst the mountains.'

'In other respects you travelled, a long, long way in the space of a few short months,' she said when Anamar had finished her story. 'And maybe we have too, this evening.

Deirdre suggested they go for a picnic some Sunday, driving to the coast. Anamar had never been in Deirdre's car and was delighted to be asked. It was now time for her to go home.

It had been a wonderful evening and as she cycled up the road, Anamar was aware of a great feeling of inner strength which seemed to come from having good friends. You could be yourself with them and happy to be who you were.

One Man's Pass

At the second meeting of the Lourdes Pilgrimage committee the only absentee was Father Brogan. He had spoken to Ellie after Mass on the previous Sunday.

'I know you won't have need of me at every one of your little gatherings, Mrs McGinley,' he had said, in conciliatory fashion, using his I'm-sure-you-know-how-busy-I-am voice. 'But please feel free to keep me informed and don't hesitate to let me know if my presence is required for a special reason.'

Ellie had smiled with relief, and also, it has to be said, with a small measure of secret satisfaction in having won the first skirmish.

The meeting was a success. Maggie and Rose had helped Ellie with letters to travel agents. The replies had been helpful, but indicated that firm prices for the following year would not be available until after Christmas. The Committee decided, provisionally, that the Pilgrimage would be scheduled for the middle of May.

F. B. O'Boyle recommended Thomas Cook, the well-known London travel agent.

'Cook's men did us proud in '24,' he said. 'They were efficient and civil, and you might say, the divil you know …' F. B. paused, wondering if he had gone too far by recommending an English firm. No one seemed to take exception and that gave him the courage to continue.

'You have to say that Cook's are the crowd with the experience.'

'That's very helpful, Mr O'Boyle,' Ellie said. 'Cook's is one of the agents we've contacted. If they can give us the best price when the time comes, I don't see why not.'

When the meeting was over, F. B. asked Anamar if he could speak with her privately. They went outside and he came straight to the point.

'I hope you don't think I'm too forward, Miss Cassidy,' he said confidentially. 'But I'm expanding my stock just at present and have need of an assistant. Now that you're back home, I was wondering if you might be interested in the position.'

Anamar was so surprised she found herself staring at F. B. in open-mouthed astonishment.

'It's very good of you to consider me,' she said at last. 'I've been looking for a job but I've no experience of drapery, Mr O'Boyle, none at all, except of course, as a customer.'

F. B. smiled broadly and rocked back and forth on his heels and toes.

'Very droll, Miss Cassidy, very droll,' he said mischievously. 'And where would we poor drapers be, pray, without our customers.' He laughed quietly. This young woman was just what was needed to brighten up the business. He had been running it on his own for too long. He had been too serious for too long, far, far too long.

'It's not experience of the trade I need, Miss Cassidy, it's youthful energy and ideas. This is no time to live in the past. We must move towards the future.'

F. B. had been reading the trade journal, The Modern Draper ... Official Organ Of The Drapery Trade In Britain. The journal had a new editor who was trying heroically to raise morale in the trade at a time when post-war austerity was suffocating business.

'Energy' and 'Ideas' were the journal's watch-words. 'Modernisation' was its unashamed theme. F. B. was a convert. He dreamt of a bright, new Donegal, flourishing as a market town, inundated with tourists. There, all his long hours and hard work would be suitably rewarded. His business would prosper beyond his highest hopes.

F. B. had made up his mind about this prospective employee. Not wanting to take the risk of losing Anamar at this stage, he made her an offer of pay in excess of what he thought he could get away with, had the candidate been some other girl of the same age. Anamar accepted and they agreed that she would start on the following Monday.

Each morning she would cycle down to the main road and into the town. It was about six miles altogether and would take longer on the way back, but she was used to cycling. Some of the girls she knew had to cycle ten miles or more to their jobs in the town.

Her father looked relieved when she told him. He seemed to have lost interest in the farm and was selling off the stock. On one of the few occasions when they were at the house together, he had talked about selling the farm. He was thinking of going to join his brother in Glenties, who seemed to make a good living dealing in sheep and cattle.

'This wee job in the town will give you a regular wage to live on,' he had said. 'And if I part with the farm there'll be a few pounds for you in your hand. You have Granny Mac's cottage anyway, so you'll have somewhere to live and nobody to look after except yourself. There'll not be many young ones of your age better placed.'

It had been the longest speech John Joe had ever made to his daughter. At first Anamar had been so overcome with surprise she had shaken her head in disbelief. Then she had felt the pain of the final disintegration of their little family, of leaving the house which had been her home for all of her life.

But her father was right. Already their ways had parted. Had it been her idea, Anamar would have felt the pangs of guilt. But, coming from him, it was easier to admit to herself that she would not have wanted to stay at home just to look after him and the hens, running the house and that part of the farm which was traditionally woman's work.

Of course he was right. Living in her Grannie's cottage and tending the garden, she would still have her foot on the land. The walled field behind the cottage was hers too. She could plant a few apple trees and fruit bushes. The place could take care of itself when she was away for a day or two, or even longer.

On the Sunday of the picnic it was overcast but dry. Anamar was ready early. She was so excited she walked down the lane and on to the road to meet Deirdre. It was the most beautiful motor-car Anamar had ever seen, a Riley tourer with wire-spoked wheels, painted dark-green. Deirdre always called it 'British Racing Green' with a twinkle in her eye, knowing that not everyone she spoke to, would be comfortable with the idea that Britain was using Ireland's national colour as their motor-racing livery.

They folded the hood into its little compartment behind the seats at the back and drove in open topped style down through the town and along the coast to Killybegs on the north side of Donegal Bay. The day became brighter as they travelled westwards. The road surface was poor, so Deirdre drove carefully and the car gently bounced and swerved around the humps and pot-holes. Deirdre loved driving her Riley. She had her hair tied up in a head scarf and wore leather driving gloves with mesh panels in the backs. Anamar's hair swirled around her face.

They turned off into a side road like a lane and climbed steeply on a narrow track to a headland overlooking the sea. Deirdre parked the car and they carried a rug and a picnic hamper to a sheltered ledge near the cliff edge.

The view was magnificent, looking south and east across Donegal Bay to the hills behind Bundoran and west across the Atlantic Ocean. The sun came out, the breeze dropped and the air became warm.

'Who would believe it? The summer's gone and winter's nearly on us, and it's a perfect day for a picnic?' Deirdre was thinking aloud.

They placed stones on the rug in case the wind rose again and walked a few steps around a corner. Anamar could hardly believe her eyes. Below a mountain to the north, a rim of cliffs dropped directly down to the sea. It was a huge broken wall with vertical rock faces and scree slopes, so steep it seemed impossible that stones could lie at that angle without plunging into the sea below.

'It's called Slieve League,' Deirdre said quietly, as if as much in awe as Anamar. 'Those crags stretch for three miles. I think they're meant to be the highest sea-cliffs in Europe.'

'By the way, this spot is called Amharc Mor,' Deirdre shook a finger at Anamar as she spoke. 'And I hope you know that means, 'the great view', otherwise all those Irish lessons were a waste of time for both of us.'

Anamar smiled. She was always happy when Deirdre teased her.

"I certainly did,' she said cheerily. 'And I suppose you're going to let slip that Slieve League means, 'the mountain of the flagstones' just to keep me on my toes.'

They walked back to the picnic spot, arm in arm, and Deirdre laid out the food. The wicker hamper was fitted with compartments and pockets to hold food, drinks, glasses, crockery and cutlery for a party of four. There was home-made bread and scones, hard-boiled eggs, mayonnaise in a screw-topped jar, slices of cooked ham, two chicken drumsticks, apples and pears, mustard, salt and black pepper in a pepper mill. Deirdre opened a bottle of her own apple wine and filled two glasses.

Anamar was staring at the delicious spread, arranged so casually but so expertly.

'How many did you cater for?' she said distractedly. 'We'll never be able to eat all this. It's like a banquet.

'Don't worry your little head, my dear.' Deirdre was using her grand voice. 'Try this wine from Chateau Ryan. Fresh air improves the appetite and the palate, and you and I deserve a small treat every once in a while.'

It was a perfect site for a picnic. They took their time over the food and sipped the wine while they talked. When they were almost finished, and although the autumn sun was still shining, the air cooled quickly with a breeze from the sea. In a few minutes they had packed up and taken the hamper and rug back to the car.

They retraced their steps along a path towards Slieve League and climbed, following the line of the cliffs to the north. They kept well away from the edge although little variations from the main track showed that others had ventured much nearer to the edge of the abyss. When Deirdre saw that Anamar was interested she identified the rock faces as slate, conglomerate, quartz, all stained by mineral deposits, wisps of vegetation clinging to the precipitous slopes.

They crossed a narrow rock rib for a few yards, with a sheer drop on the sea-ward side. Deirdre went first, walking confidently, nimbly, picking out each step like a climber, obviously accustomed to heights and Anamar followed quickly. They paused when they were both on easier ground.

'That bit is called the One Man's Pass,' Deirdre said. 'After your treks in the Pyrenees, I knew you'd enjoy it. You and I will have to go mountain walking together. There's no better place in Ireland for striding across the hills than Donegal.'

They sat down in the shelter of big rocks to admire the view. The waves dashed against the base of the cliffs, surging in on tiny beaches, swirling around pillars and huge sea-bound boulders Deirdre called, 'The Stacks'. Wisps of foam floated upwards on the air currents. The roar of the breakers was pierced by the shriek of sea-birds. It was a prospect so different to the mountain fastness of the Blue Stacks above Lough Belshade or the dramatic snow and rock peaks around the King's Lakes in the High Pyrenees. Anamar wondered aloud if they might be compared.

'Don't worry,' said Deirdre in her gentlest voice. 'There are no comparisons between the unique. You and I will visit all three. With our walking boots on and our rucksacks on our backs, we won't need words or photographs to share them.'

They sat quietly for ten minutes or more and Deirdre asked Anamar why she had changed her name.

'Years ago Grannie Mac took me on an excursion to Bundoran,' Anamar explained. 'We went in a four-in hand to Ballyshannon and took the train from there. It only cost two shillings for Grannie and I went for half fare. We had a great day, with ice cream in the afternoon and fish and chips for our tea.'

Anamar paused, wondering if Deirdre might be bored, hearing about Bundoran, after all the places she had been. But her friend urged her on.

'Don't stop now,' she said. 'For years I've been dying to ask why you changed your name and never dared mention it until now.'

Anamar laughed.

'It was quite simple, really. The return train was not until nearly eight in the evening and Grannie and I walked down to some rocks at the edge of the sea. We dipped our hands in a pool and Grannie Mac ran the water from her cupped hands over mine. She said to me, 'Grand-daughter dear, I see you as the Spirit of the Sea, the power of the water, one of Nature's four great elements. We should have called you Anamar.'

And that was it. Anamar I became and have been ever since, and never mentioned my old name again.'

Deirdre looked thoughtful.

'When you were at school,' she said. 'I was always aware that you were an unusual child. You had a sense of your own worth, a quiet confidence, an inner strength. Most people would never have noticed. Changing your name could have been one of the reasons. It might have released the power within you.'

They walked back to the car in silence. When the conversation returned, it was the gentle sharing of friends. The car ran smoothly, whatever the surface of the roads. They were returning by the same route, but everything looked quite different going the other way. People stopped to look in admiration at the open-topped sports' car. Anamar waved and Deirdre laughed.

'You were born to travel in style,' she said. 'Maybe we all were.'

As the miles passed, it was as if they were coming back into the heart of the county after being perched on a wild cliff at its furthest extremity.

Deirdre left Anamar home to the farm and got out of the car to make friends with the Cassidy's dog. Timmy was suspicious of this strange creature, in a strange car, speaking nicely to him, trying to touch him, unafraid when he had barked his loudest. He decided to make an exception this time and allowed himself to be stroked. Deirdre was delighted.

I always had pets when I was young,' she said happily. 'But farm dogs are a special breed. They usually don't like to be petted. I'm well pleased your Timmy seems to have taken to me.'

Anamar began to laugh.

'You should ask your friend, Doctor Corr, what he thinks of our Timmy. When my mother was ill, the good doctor was glad to get away from here with the seat of his fine tweed pants still in place.'

When Deirdre slid in behind the steering wheel of her car, Anamar thanked her for the trip and the picnic.

'It was a great day, Deirdre,' she said. 'It's a day I won't forget. You and your sporty car are some partnership.'

'You and me too,' shouted Deirdre, as she took off with a roar from her car's exhaust, the gravel flying, and Timmy, who had been about to pee on her front wheel, scooting into the shed out of her way, chastened as well as unrelieved.

Then everything began to happen quickly. Maggie met Maureen and Anamar one evening and told them she was getting married. Neither she nor her husband-to-be had a choice. She was expecting his child. They had met at a dance in the town and seen each other, secretly, a few times afterwards. He was the second son of a Protestant farming family down near the coast, reputed to have one of the largest land holdings in Donegal. The wedding was only a few weeks away.

Without another word to Anamar, John Joe Cassidy put his farm on the market and Maggie's prospective father-in-law bought it at once, sight unseen, for his son. It was far enough from the home farm to let the fuss die down quickly, but not so far away that his wife would give out to him when the baby was born and she wanted to see it as frequently as possible.

Maggie was delighted. All the family trauma caused by the pregnancy had been swept away. She was going to have a white wedding and a baby and a new home to walk into. When she moved in, Anamar would be her neighbour in the cottage above. She had even begun to like Tom, the husband-to-be. At first she had found him far too quiet and serious and had only agreed to go out with him because he had a car. Once she discovered she was pregnant and he had accepted responsibility, she came to realise very quickly that he would make a far better husband than any of her previous boy friends. Anyway, she would soon liven him up, now that everything was settled and she knew she loved him.

The next time Anamar visited Deirdre, she was driven into the town to meet one of Deirdre's artist friends in the hotel bar. Dermod Muldowney was aware that he was regarded by women, particularly those of a certain age, as an extremely handsome man. It was the way they looked at him on the first meeting. He was not so certain, however, of how he was perceived by younger women. He was often uneasy in their presence. In fact, the more presentable they were, the more they unnerved him.

Dermod found Anamar most discomfiting. He saw her as a beautiful young woman, so assured, so at ease in Deirdre's company. But this was not just a social encounter. He was well aware that a commission was in the offing, should Anamar feel sufficiently at ease with him to allow him to paint her portrait.

Dermod was in his late twenties, about ten years younger than Deirdre and an occasional member of the circle of friends in the town, of which she and Dr Corr were the leading lights. He was tall and thin, with slender fingers which described graceful gestures when he spoke. His hair was much longer than would have been usual for young men of his age and station. He wore a green linen suit with a dark green shirt, a yellow tie and highly polished, elastic-sided, brown leather boots and was apparently unaware that his clothes pronounced him 'an artistic young man'.

Having failed to impress in the family business, one of the most prominent firms of auctioneers and estate agents in Dublin, Dermod's father had arranged for him to work for an old friend, who was principal of a similar business in Donegal Town. In return for contacts and commissions from Dublin, Dermod would receive a level of personal supervision only possible in the much smaller operation. It was his father's heart-felt hope that working in Donegal would introduce Dermod to 'the real world', and enable him to develop some vague semblance of 'the common touch'. For his part, Dermod saw himself as living in a form of exile in Donegal, only relieved by his contact with Deirdre and her friends.

When she was introducing him to Anamar, Deirdre came straight to the point. 'Now here's a real beauty to test that talent of yours,' she said. 'I want to add my young friend to what has been regarded, up to now, as my rogues' gallery. She hasn't been asked to sit yet, I thought it best to come from the artist. So I leave you both to it while I order a drink.'

Dermod looked so confused and self-conscious that Anamar suppressed the urge to tease him. She agreed to sit for the portrait and made it easy for him to arrange the sittings. He had set up his studio in the large, airy attic of the house in which he lodged in the town, and Anamar offered to make herself available for an hour after work for as many sessions as he required.

Deirdre's commission was for a miniature, but Dermod decided to do a life-size portrait first. Once it was finished, he could do the miniature without further sittings. He asked Anamar not to look at his work until it was completed and when they were ready she expressed herself thrilled with both pictures.

Deirdre arranged a dinner party at her home to mark the hanging of the portrait. It was to be placed at the end of one of the rows of miniatures on the wall of her sitting room. Dermod and Anamar were the guests of honour and Dr Corr and three others from their circle made up the party.

It was another of Deirdre's wonderful meals, prawns in garlic followed by leek and potato soup, with poached salmon as the main course and pears in red wine for dessert. In preparing and serving the meal, Deirdre had the help of Mary Rice, the young local girl who helped to keep the house tidy. She introduced her as they offered sherry to the guests before the meal. Mary served the red and white French wines with the food and Dr Corr helped her with the Benedictine liqueur, as she poured the coffee.

In this company, it was Anamar's turn to be shy. She felt uneasy at being attended by a servant in someone's home. It was different in a hotel or restaurant but in a friend's house, here in Donegal, it was disturbing.

Dermod was in his element. He had brought the life-size portrait with him and it was displayed on a table top, leaning against a wall. Everyone admired his paintings and he was enjoying the attention, showing off outrageously as he talked about his work and the marvellous arty crowd who had been his friends in Dublin.

'Before you lose the run of yourself entirely, Dermod,' Deirdre said with a little smile. 'We should ask the real star of the evening to tell us about this Parish Pilgrimage to Lourdes we're hearing so much about.'

Anamar was very hesitant at first, then as she realised that most of the party were very interested in what she was saying, she began to speak more freely. She told them about her own time in Lourdes, outlined Ellie's idea and the plans to visit the shrine the following year, with some invalids amongst their number. At one point Dermod tried to get himself back into the limelight.

'Surely you don't believe all those stories of 'miracle' cures?' he said with theatrically raised eyebrows. 'It's religious hysteria, provoked by the church to keep its grip on the masses.'

Whether they agreed with him or not, the reaction of the other guests was to treat this outburst without any reaction whatsoever. Deirdre said nothing, but smiled at the company. Anamar was unperturbed. She knew Dermod was feigning incredulity for effect.

'You've been to the Grotto, then? she said. 'And talked to the pilgrims about why they've come. You must meet our Committee. We've heard nothing so far but glowing reports. It's always important to hear a contrary view.'

Dermod blushed and the others smiled. They all admired his talent and liked him for trying to be himself, but he could be such a pain at times. As one of them put it afterwards, 'Once Dermod gets to the front of the stage, he forgets to come off.'

'Well no, I haven't,' Dermod said lamely. 'I've just read about ...' He felt his almost-cured stutter coming on, and stopped.

Everyone felt sorry for him and Dr Corr spoke.

'Dermod may have a point, but then I haven't been there either. Perhaps I should go sometime and make up my own mind.'

Deirdre began to laugh.

'Aren't you the sly one,' she said. 'A little bird told me the other day that you intend going with our parish group. That is, of course, if they'll have you, you being outside the true church. You've been keeping very quiet about this trip for a man usually so keen to tell us all of his future travel plans.'

'It's only a fool would try to keep a secret in this country,' Dr Corr said, pretending to be embarrassed. 'Short of having to turn my coat to get there, I do intend to go next year.'

The doctor was laughing now, too. Everyone was in good humour. Anamar was enjoying Deirdre's friends, their cheerful banter, the switch from serious conversation to jokes or irreverent comment.

When it was all over, the others went back to the town by car. Anamar was the last to leave. She had refused a lift for herself and her bicycle. It would be good to have the fresh air of the trip back home.

Deirdre left her to the door and Anamar must have looked lost for something to say.

'No need to say anything, child dear,' Deirdre spoke gently. 'I know you enjoyed the evening and I've never had a better one myself since I came here.'

Anamar cycled up the valley road, gliding along without real effort, as if the wind was in her back and the bike had one of those tiny motors she had seen on the rear wheels of bicycles in France.

The Donegal Town and District Pilgrimage

The monthly meetings of the Pilgrimage Committee continued during the winter. There was always a good attendance. Ellie involved the members in fund raising, interviewing prospective pilgrims and making arrangements. All decisions were discussed and approved at meetings. She kept Father Brogan well informed and, in his turn, he mentioned the Pilgrimage at Mass every two or three weeks, sometimes giving the impression, albeit modestly, that the burden of the work was falling on his willing shoulders.

Thomas Cook had been chosen as agents for the entire venture but, on Ellie's suggestion, it had been decided to appoint Hassett and Purdy, Authorised Travel Agents in the Town, to act on their behalf with Cook's. This meant that members of the Committee could make arrangements by calling into the local office rather than by letter or telephone to Cook's in London.

Anamar found her job in the drapery shop most interesting and, at times, even exciting. Within weeks of her starting many more younger women were coming into the shop. F. B. O'Boyle was impressed. After a month he suggested that he call her Anamar, rather than Miss Cassidy, and she refer to him as F. B., if she wished, although not in front of customers, of course.

Anamar found that she and F. B. could work together very satisfactorily. He was a good businessman and knew the trade. He was also prepared to listen to her suggestions for change. F. B. kept his books up-to-date on a weekly basis. The figures confirmed what his eyes had already told him. Turnover was rising, and better than that, even when his new assistant's wages were allowed for, profits were rising too.

After Christmas they had a Grand New Year Sale. It was Anamar's idea. They would try to get rid of as much old stock as possible, so that they could bring in more up-to-date lines. F. B. had never had a sale before and he was more excited than he had ever been in his whole life. Some of the stock in the store room was pre-war. It would be a wonderful chance to 'clear the decks for action', as he told Anamar when they were marking down the sale items.

Anamar acted as window-dresser, with F. B. standing out on the pavement, hands clasped behind his back, rocking backwards and forwards on his heels and toes, nodding approval. On the Monday, the first day of the sale, the shop was packed. By Friday they were almost sold out of sale items. It had been a huge success. F. B. was so overwhelmed he wanted to hug Anamar.

'I don't know how to thank you, Miss Cassidy, I mean Anamar.' He was almost beside himself with joy. 'We've done more business in the past six days than I would expect to do in the first two months of the year.'

When they closed the shop on Saturday evening after a hard week's work, F. B. was on his tip-toes, skipping around a shop now almost empty of stock. Anamar was expecting him to ask her to dance a reel.

'I rang the travellers this morning,' he said, rubbing his hands. 'They're coming for the orders next week. I've told them we want to see the top of the range items. And I want you to guide me, Miss Cassidy. I'll look at quality and workmanship but you must choose the styles.'

For Anamar too, it had been a fascinating week. She had a feeling of achievement and also a sense of her work being appreciated, which she had never felt at home on the farm. As she was leaving, F. B. stopped her, smiling.

'I should tell you now, Anamar,' he said. 'This little enterprise will result in a bonus for you, to be paid at the end of the month. I can't say yet just how much it will be, but you can take it that, at the very least, it will be sufficient to cover the sum you will be required to pay to go on the Pilgrimage.'

He began to laugh heartily, as usual rocking back and forth on his heels and toes.

'You could say, sister pilgrim, that the profits of our sale will be taking us both to Lourdes.'

F. B. knew he was being generous and glowed with the virtue of it. He could not remember feeling like this before. Why was it so enjoyable? Why did it make him seem younger in himself?

Having Grannie Mac's cottage as her home restored to Anamar the sense of security she had lost when her mother died and her father had moved away. She had always felt at home in her Grannie's wee cabin. And it was not so wee either. She had a large kitchen, which led to a snug bedroom with its own fireplace. The roof was of blue slates and the whole place was in good repair. There were no fewer than four outhouses, three quite small and the fourth large enough to act as a stable if required.

On her half-day she kept the vegetable garden tidy and planted some young apple trees and soft fruit bushes in her walled field at the back. She would have loved to own a dog, Timmy had gone off with her father to Glenties, but she was away so much during the day, it would not have been fair on the dog. A neighbour gave her an orange and white male kitten as company, and the pair of them found that their lives fitted together to the satisfaction of both.

When she came to visit, Deirdre referred to him as The Marmalade Cat, and Marmalade he came to be called. He slept in the largest of the outhouses where Anamar had made a bed for him on a broad ledge about five feet above ground level. When the bottom half of the half-door of the cottage was closed, he would jump over it, deftly using the top edge, first with front paws then with back, to help him on his way. If she was going to be away for more than a day, Anamar knew that she could ask Maggie to feed him.

Shortly after Maggie and Tom moved into the house below, Tom's mother came to call. As Maggie would say later, 'more an inspection than a courtesy visit, but she's not the worst. She'll want to make sure I can look after her good son and her wee grandchild to come.'

Anamar was invited down to the house to meet Maggie's mother-in-law, Mrs Johnston. She noted that Mrs Johnston called her daughter-in-law, Margaret, and was not best pleased when Tom missed his cue and referred to her as Maggie.

Once she had finished questioning Maggie about how she intended to run the house, she turned her attention to Anamar.

'So you're the one who has them all stampeding to Lourdes,' she said dryly, but although she sounded sceptical, she was smiling.

'I was going to object to Margaret going,' she continued. 'But a wee dose of religion never did anyone any harm. Anyway, as the child will have to be brought up a Catholic, it'll do him or her no harm to be blessed before birth as well as after.'

She began to laugh and pointed at Maggie swelling abdomen.

'You'll be seven months pregnant by then and you'll need a minder in foreign parts. There's nothing for it. I'll have to go with you.'

Maggie's face went slack with astonishment.

'I had no idea you were thinking ...' she started to say.

'It's all right,' said Mrs Johnston. 'Don't thank me, thank the boss.' She meant, of course, her husband. 'He says I can go as long as I don't turn my coat when I'm away.'

Anamar sat back in her chair and shook her head in disbelief. Lourdes had a power in Ireland, felt across the boundaries, even, it seemed, of religion.

Mrs Johnston was enrolled in the group shortly afterwards and that brought the numbers up to thirty-six. By March, a few had dropped out and other applications had been accepted. Barring last-minute changes, it seemed as if the party would be thirty-seven, all told.

There were four priests, led by Father Brogan as Director of the Pilgrimage.

The Invalids' Group numbered eight, all accompanied by at least one close relative. Four were in wheel-chairs, two were mentally disabled and the remaining two, although frail, could walk unaided.

Dr Corr was Medical Officer to the Pilgrimage. He examined everyone in the Invalids' Group and certified them all as fit to travel. The medical team also included five nurses, one was recently retired but very experienced, two were hospital sisters and one a well-known local mid-wife.

The evening before they left, Father Brogan preached at a valedictory Mass for the pilgrims. Ellie had arranged for those who had some distance to travel to be put up for the night by others who lived nearby.

The church was so crowded people had to stand in the aisles, in the doorway and on the steps outside. The front pews had been kept for the pilgrims. Dr Corr sat with Anamar, and Mrs Johnston had the support of Maggie on one side and Rose on the other. As he came into the church and down the aisle, Dr Corr was aware of rows and rows of heads turning, seeing him here for the first time. He had a curious sense of suddenly becoming closer to these people. Many were his patients, but attending them in his professional capacity had never given him the feeling he had when he came into their church.

Father Brogan announced the Bishop's approval for the Pilgrimage and conveyed his blessings to the pilgrims. In the course of his sermon, he told the story of the fourteen-year-old peasant girl from Lourdes, called Bernadette, and her visions. He spoke simply of the nature of pilgrimage, of its trials and rewards. Normally his voice would rise as he sought to drive home a point, but on this evening, his was the passion of the quiet pilgrim. Some of the congregation were visibly moved. Ellie was delighted. As she left the service, friends told her that it had been Father Brogan's finest sermon, as if she was responsible for enabling him to preach it.

The next morning the Donegal Town and District Pilgrimage to Lourdes assembled on the platform of the railway station at 9:30 a.m. Both Mr Hassett and Mr Purdy of the local travel agents were there to see them off. The Party would travel by County Donegal Railways on the 10: 40 to Strabane, continue by the 12:46 p.m., Great Northern Railway's train to Belfast, and sail overnight to England on the Liverpool boat.

F. B. O'Boyle was in charge of the time-tabled arrangements and, although he had yet to use the title, saw himself as Director of Transport Arrangements. He rushed around carrying a sheaf of papers with the details, encouraging everyone to 'be on their toes' for a quick boarding of the train, an exhortation which caused an exchange of dry witticisms between two of the pilgrims in wheelchairs. He had three helpers, two responsible for the Invalids' Group, all personally briefed by F. B. himself. He kept himself at full stretch overseeing the mountain of luggage, checking with Ellie and Mr Hassett and rechecking with Mr Purdy, looking harassed but enjoying himself hugely.

It was dull, dry and windy in Belfast and the night crossing on the Liverpool boat was the pilgrims' first trial. The Irish Sea was in a bad mood. The sailors seemed happy, they knew their ship had withstood far worse weather than this. Nearly everyone in the Pilgrimage Party was sea-sick. Most of those who had bunks retired early but there were others in the bar, trying manfully and womanfully, to force down the one cure which seemed popular, hot rum punch.

Father Brogan had warned them the previous evening at Mass that there would be trials. He had said it would be foolish to expect their journey to the Blessed Shrine to be 'plain sailing'. Danny and Jerome, the two men in wheelchairs were enjoying themselves again. They had wedged their wheel chairs between fixed seats and were both unaffected by the violent pitching, rolling, twisting movements of the boat, but they had noticed that Father Brogan was most uncomfortable.

The senior priest was pale and hunched, clinging to the armrests of his seat, rising unsteadily every so often to lurch out on deck for 'a breath of fresh air' and returning paler than ever to reapply himself to the cure.

'It's great to know that our Spiritual Director could predict it wouldn't be 'plain sailing' to-night,' said Danny.

'And to see that a divine can be human too,' said Jerome and if others wondered what they were laughing at, they were too ill to ask.

On the early morning train to London, most of the party slept the whole way. When they reached the city, two men from Thomas Cook's were waiting for them. F. B. introduced himself. Together they saw that everyone was transported by bus between railway stations to catch the boat train to Paris.

The English Channel was kinder than the Irish Sea and they were met in Paris by two more of Cook's men who, with F. B's help, of course, shepherded the whole party to the overnight train to Lourdes. Ellie joined Father Brogan in the first of the Party's carriages as the train left the station in Paris. They had both recovered from the crossing of the Irish Sea and she could not have been more pleased with the way things were going.

'F. B. O'Boyle is a tower of strength,' she said. 'I don't know what we would do without him.'

'Experience, Mrs McGinley. You can't beat experience. His pilgrimage in '24 is standing us all in good stead.' Father Brogan was relieved to see all was going so well.

'And you deserve your share of the praise too, Mrs McGinley,' he said. 'I have to admit I have little faith that committees will do anything but talk. But in the case of your Pilgrimage Committee, I was wrong and you were right.'

The whole carriage suddenly went silent. It was a remark from their priest given enormous weight, simply because it was so out of character.

'Well said, Father. It takes a sound man to give credit where it's due.' It was Miss Murphy, one of Father Brogan's most fervent supporters. In her eyes, he was the Church within her world. So unwilling was she to miss any kind of devotional event, she had gone to live as close to the church as she could find a vacant cottage. If there were difficulties in the days to come, Miss Murphy could be relied upon to set a good example by accepting things as they were. When there were discussions within the party about being a pilgrim, everybody agreed that she was, 'the real thing'.

F. B. knew precisely where Anamar was seated but, once the train left on the long journey south and he was doing his rounds, he would come upon her as if by surprise and ask, solicitously, how she was coping with the trip so far.

Anamar had slept on the Liverpool boat, on the train to London and intended to sleep again on the way to Lourdes. She was sharing a carriage with Maureen, Rose, Maggie and, of course, Mrs Johnston, Maggie's mother-in-law. In the end Eamon had decided not to come with the group when he discovered that there would be no other young men of his age.

In Anamar's carriage the others were asleep when the carriage door would open and she would have to acknowledge F. B's presence. On the second visit, Maggie wakened, nudged Anamar and whispered.

'Like it or lump it, my girl, but you have a follower there. Take it from me. We married women know about these things.'

The others stirred and began to giggle. Anamar was embarrassed.

'Have a bit of sense, woman,' she said very quietly. 'F. B. is just behaving like a gentleman.' But her friends were still laughing.

The train fled south through the night. As the day brightened, the pilgrims awoke and, for the first time since they had boarded the boat at Belfast, were in lively mood. Many had been very apprehensive about going abroad. But this was the way to travel. At 8 a.m. breakfast was served in the station café when the train stopped for an hour at a small town. There were hampers of food on board for lunch. These had been loaded and transferred from train to boat and boat to train by F. B. and his team.

The scenery rushed past the carriage windows, changing as they rattled through rural France. There were huge fields, as if without boundary fences, vineyards, great forests and so many coppices of trees. France was a much more wooded country than Ireland, perhaps it was as Ireland once had been.

During the afternoon they neared Lourdes and saw the snow-capped peaks of the Pyrenees, a glorious skyline above the Pilgrim Town. Then suddenly they were upon it. There was the river, and the Grotto, and the crowds of people around it, some in invalid carriages, others with lighted candles, though it was still daylight.

The train steamed into a station large enough to serve a city, and stopped at a huge platform, only one of many. The Donegal Town and District Pilgrimage to Lourdes had arrived.

Lourdes

They tumbled out of the carriages, travel-weary, stiff after the long journey, bemused by the local voices, bewildered by unfamiliar signs, apprehensive now that they were in this strange place so far from home. It was only here that most of the pilgrims felt the shock of being in a foreign country and, for virtually all of them, for the very first time.

It was all so confusing, to some even frightening. The natural reaction was to keep together and for that small mercy Ellie was grateful. F. B. and his team were already fully engaged with the baggage. She knew she could rely on Mr O'Boyle. That job would be done well. Fortunately, Father Brogan, although not tall, was an imposing figure and, without prompting, the flock gathered around him like the sheep and goats around the shepherd in Biblical times.

Anamar could speak French and Ellie looked around to see where she was. They would need to enquire about transport to the hotel. Anamar called to her from the back of the crowd.

'You're needed over here, Ellie!' she shouted. 'You and Father Brogan. There's a reception committee.'

Waiting at the back of the platform, in order not to be in the way of passengers descending from the train, were four local clergy, a nun and two women from their hotel. They were smiling in welcome, stepping forward to shake hands with the Director of the Pilgrimage and the Organiser, and as many of the pilgrims as they could manage.

They were speaking to Anamar in French. 'Yes, all was in order. The bus was waiting to take them to the hotel. Any help they needed with their programme would be readily available. They could be assured that they were most welcome to the town of Lourdes and the Domain of Our Lady.'

At the hotel some of the staff spoke English, and that was a comfort. After they had settled in very few of the pilgrims ventured out to see the town before dinner. 'If we go out for a walk, how will we find our way back to the hotel? What will we do if we're lost?' It was much safer to stay where they were and go out together later, with the whole group.

Anamar took Maureen, Rose and Maggie out to show them where she had lived. She explained that there were three parts to Lourdes. The Domain, which contained the Grotto, five churches, the Baths, the accommodation for invalids and the Esplanade. The Low Town, the commercial centre for pilgrims and tourists, which provided hotels and souvenir shops, and the oldest part, the High Town, very much like any other French provincial town. Her room had been in the High Town near the castle. It was in a narrow, steep street, two floors above a café.

With the security of Anamar as a guide who could speak the language, the girls were enjoying themselves. But as they looked up at the room Anamar became very quiet. Her tiny lodging had been one of those places where she had felt comfortable, totally at ease, even here in this foreign town. The view from the window had been across the Low Town, the Domain and the River Gave to the forests and hills beyond.

Suddenly she was thinking about Hank. 'How had he fared in the Sierra Nevada? Where was he now? Would she ever see him again? She felt that all was well with him, but even so, she must say a prayer for him at the Grotto.

She looked around at the girls and they were laughing.

'Don't let us disturb you, wee day-dreamer,' Maggie was being mischievous. 'Now you're back where you met your lovely American soldier, we were just thinking that, when you looked up at your room, it brought back memories you daren't tell us about.'

Trust Maggie to be embarrassing. Anamar felt herself blushing. She had just started to protest her innocence when the proprietor of the café saw her in the street and came running out to meet her. They kissed each other enthusiastically on both cheeks and Maggie's eyes were wide open in wonder.

'I thought they only did that in films,' she whispered to Rose and found herself being introduced to Monsieur Boutin who shook hands, greeting her volubly in French. Although they understood not a word, the three girls were charmed by his exuberant welcome. He invited them into the café and treated them to coffee. He chatted to Anamar, gesticulating with a great sweep of his arm to include the girls in what he was saying, while they stared at him blankly and Anamar laughed.

'He wants to know if you're married, Rose,' she said. 'I've told him you're as free as a bird, but he'll have to be quick, you're only here for a few days.'

When they left Monsieur Boutin's café, it was with the promise that they would come back the next day. Maureen gave Anamar a nudge with her elbow as they walked to the hotel.

'Now we know why you stayed on here last year,' she said in a theatrical whisper. 'You let the group go back to Dublin and learned French so you could understand all the nice things the men were saying to you.'

Rose and Maggie acted in unison, as if they had rehearsed it. They pursed their lips, nodded in agreement and each wagged a finger at Anamar.

'We've always known Miss Goody-Two-Shoes was worth a-watching,' said Maggie to the others. 'But I didn't know she had lost the run of herself entirely when she was here before.'

'And that was even before she met her Yankee.' It was Rose's turn and the three girls continued to talk about Anamar the whole way back, pretending to ignore her, gossiping about her as if she was not even there.

After dinner the whole group assembled outside the hotel and walked down to the Domain to take part in the Torchlight Procession. All the other pilgrimage parties were there. They were from Italy, Spain and France and walked behind their banners. The Donegal Town and District Pilgrimage had no such banner. F. B. O'Boyle had suggested having one at a committee meeting but no one else had been very keen. The feeling was that it might be 'a bit showy' for a first time pilgrimage group and they had decided not to bother. Now Ellie was sorry they had not taken F. B's advice but she said nothing, except to mention quietly to F. B. that the other groups' banners were a nice touch.

Father Brogan and the other priests led the group and Ellie ensured that the invalids were in the forefront of their party. Everyone had a lighted candle with a little shield to protect the flame from the wind. They joined with the other groups in the singing of Ave Maria, quietly at first, then much louder, gaining confidence. They became a part of the throng of hundreds of pilgrims and their waves of sound, marching slowly around the long processional route through the Domain.

The great column stopped before the Church of the Rosary and was hushed to silence before beginning to sing again, this time in unison. When the Ave Maria was finished the French pilgrims led the chant of the Credo.

'This was the battle-cry in '24.' F. B's. voice was shaking with emotion as he whispered to Ellie. He was almost overcome, reliving the days when he had been here before, all those years ago.

The chant finished and the crowd began to disperse. The Procession Aux Flambeaux was over but the Donegal Town and District Pilgrimage held its ground. Others might be familiar with the town and able to find their own way back to their hotels but this was the first night for the Irish crowd and they were sticking together. They would wait until all the other groups of pilgrims had gone so that they could leave as a party, no need for marshals, they would be on the heels of the ones in front the whole way back.

'Would you ever take a look at us,' said Jerome. 'We're like a column of ants on the move.' He and Danny were whizzing along in their wheelchairs propelled by willing helpers.

'More like a flock of clegs,' Danny whispered to him. 'In search of a big cow clap.'

As they reached the hotel, F. B. stepped to one side and let the others file in. He was waiting for a chance to speak to Anamar.

'I was wondering if I might have a word with you. I need to speak to you privately,' he said nervously. 'Perhaps after Mass to-morrow morning?'

Anamar was mystified. She had no idea what might be on F. B's mind. Perhaps it was to do with the programme for the next few days. She and F. B. had helped Father Brogan and Ellie plan it, and he took these responsibilities very seriously.

F. B. sighed audibly with relief when she agreed to meet him the following morning.

Everyone knew there was a full programme and they were looking forward to their first full day in Lourdes. They would go to High Mass in the Church of the Rosary at 10 a.m. In the early afternoon the Invalids' group, attended by as many as necessary, would go to the Baths. All would be present for the Blessed Sacrament Procession at the end of the afternoon, which would end with the blessing of the sick. After dinner they would again join the Torchlight Procession. It would be a very busy day, but that was why they were here.

During his sermon on the evening before they left home, Father Brogan had told them about Bernadette and her visions and of Our Lady telling her that she wanted people to come here in processions. If that was Her wish, here they were doing their best to fulfil it during their few days in Lourdes.

After Mass, Anamar walked with F. B. O'Boyle up to Monsieur Boutin's café near the castle. F. B. was aghast when Monsieur Boutin greeted her with kisses on both cheeks. 'I could have done without this,' he thought to himself. 'I was nervous enough to start with. There's no need for all this embracing in public.' By the time coffee had been served, he had recovered himself. There was nothing for it. It was the only chance he might have to speak to her privately.

'Miss Cassidy …' he said and stopped, flustered. He always seemed to call her 'Miss Cassidy' when he was agitated.

'I'll come straight to the point,' he said bravely. 'Latterly, I've been giving some thought to my circumstances. As you know, I'm not a poor man. You might say that, one way and another, I'm fairly well fixed. As you are very well aware I have a business geared to the future but, thank God, thriving well in the present. And I'm no longer a young man.'

F. B. stopped again, suddenly. He had meant this last comment to be a recommendation, indicating that he was now beyond the excesses of youth but somehow he felt it might have given quite the wrong impression. F. B. was in his late forties, at an age which, to many a man in Donegal, would have seemed time enough to be thinking of marrying, unless, of course, he had to. F. B. did not want the comment to be taken as some kind of apology for his years. He decided to do as he had promised and 'come straight to the point'.

'Miss Cassidy, I wish you to consider a proposal of marriage.'

Anamar flopped back in her chair and its legs skraked on the wooden floor. She gripped the arm rests to steady herself and tried to speak, but only managed to breathe out audibly.

F. B. quickly realised that his proposition had taken Anamar unawares. She looked bewildered. He raised his hands in what he thought was a calming gesture.

'Please, Miss Cassidy, Anamar, don't distress yourself. Forgive me for being so impetuous. I should not have been so hasty.'

He was certain that it was only the unexpectedness of his overtures which had affected Anamar. He never considered the possibility that it might be the nature of his offer which had so obviously shocked her.

He smiled reassuringly. His role in arranging and directing the pilgrimage had given him a confidence he had never felt before in his life. He knew the group needed his experience and expertise in organising. Things were working well. Everyone from Father Brogan and Ellie to the rank-and-file members of the party were fulsome in their praise for his efforts. He had not intended to approach Anamar until the last day and then, when she accepted, Father Brogan might announce the engagement at Mass on their final day in Lourdes.

However, the euphoria of the successful arrival, and the deeply moving Torchlight Procession on the previous evening had precipitated events. As F. B. had walked through the Domain, one of a huge crowd of pilgrims, bearing his candle like a raised sword, he had caught sight of Anamar and decided that he must act immediately.

Anamar was staring at him, pale-faced, still speechless. F. B. raised his arms again and placed his finger tips together.

'No need to say anything now, my dear,' he said, astounding himself at this newly-found confidence, which allowed him to address her so intimately. 'We'll say nothing yet, just keep it to ourselves for a few days. But we must meet privately like this every day. Don't worry, I'll take care of everything, my dear.'

There, he had said it again. F. B. sat up straight in his chair. He felt taller, more self-assured. His reflection in the café window looked boldly back at him. Come to think of it, he was quite an imposing man in his own way, he thought, with a degree of pride he was certain was quite justified by the occasion.

He rose and went up to the counter to pay the bill, holding out a large note and thanking the proprietor in English, speaking loudly so that the Frenchman would understand. Anamar was on her feet and ready to go. As she shook hands with Monsieur Boutin he whispered to her in French, asking if all was well. She nodded and smiled wanly as she and F. B. left.

'Mr O'Boyle,' she said nervously. 'I'm very grateful to you for ...' She meant to say 'Thank you but no thank you, I can't accept your proposal' but F. B. had already turned towards her and interrupted.

'Don't thank me, Anamar my dear, and please call me F. B. Your modesty does you great credit. You may rest assured that I will do my utmost to make you happy when we are man and wife.'

They were almost back at the hotel before Anamar found the strength to stop F. B. in his tracks. She turned to face him and he was amazed to hear her voice so firm and direct.

'Hold on a minute, Mr O'Boyle,' she said gently. 'I don't mean to sound rude but you've run on ahead of yourself. I was going to thank you and tell you I can't accept your proposal. We hardly know each other. I've no thoughts of marriage. No harm to you, Mr O'Boyle, you've been very kind to me and I'm flattered, but I just can't ever see myself as your wife.'

It was F. B's turn to be bewildered. He had thought of the idea of proposing to Anamar in Lourdes, weeks before they had left Ireland. In the euphoria of the pilgrimage and his newly-found confidence, he was certain she would accept. He had never considered rejection. Now he felt humiliated, deflated. Everything had been going so well. He had been in such good form since they had left home. Everyone seemed to appreciate his efforts. And now this.

Anamar thanked him again and, still in shock, F. B. held out his hand to shake hers, hardly aware of what he was doing. She walked on to the hotel but he stood on the same spot, mystified as to how he had gone wrong. Then he began to feel irritated with himself. 'Pull yourself together' he said, almost aloud and then, rising on his tip-toes, he straightened up to his full height and marched back to the hotel for lunch.

The rest of the day proved to be very busy but Anamar took the opportunity when they were alone, to tell Maureen what had happened that morning. At first Maureen had laughed as if she found it all completely unbelievable but when she heard the whole story, she whistled soundlessly with relief.

'Thanks be to God you spoke out when you did,' she said. 'That idea needed to be nipped in the bud. No wonder the oul cod was in such good humour with himself on the journey out. He thought he had nothing to do but say a few prayers for the good of his soul and scoop up a young wife to keep him warm next winter.'

That evening before dinner, Anamar went out for a walk on her own and happened to meet Sister Teresa, the nun who had been in the welcoming party at the station on the afternoon they had arrived. They talked for over an hour and a half, walking the Esplanade in the Domain and sitting on a bench there in the weak sunshine.

Sister Teresa had come from the West of Ireland fifty years before, at the age of seventeen, to enter the French Order of the Sisters of Charity. She had gone first to the mother house of the order at Nevers, where the body of Saint Bernadette still lies. Then, after her profession, she had been sent to Lourdes and had remained there since, ministering to the sick.

Anamar found that she and Sister Teresa were at ease in each other's company. They could talk together as if they had been friends for years.

Sister Teresa told her of her work with the invalids, as if it was a labour of love recurring every day. She made her smile when she told her about the Irish pilgrims. They always brought great quantities of food from home, particularly for the invalids in their group who were staying in the special accommodation in the Domain.

Doing their own catering had become a tradition. They said they could not stomach the foreign food so they brought their own sausages, rashers, tinned milk, tea, coffee, sugar, even eggs. They seemed to fry every meal in lard. But it was a tradition which came in useful immediately after the war, when food was scarce in France. It certainly was not in short supply amongst the Irish. They brought their own grub, great hampers full of it.

Anamar told the sister of her visit to France the previous year, and of the confrontation with her mother on her return home, which had led to her sojourn at Lough Belshade. Sister Teresa smiled in understanding.

'What a very wise move, for one so young,' she said. 'You retreated from the conflict and gave yourself time to think, and maybe even pray.' She was now smiling broadly. 'Following the example of Our Lord, we might say, when the Spirit drove him into the wilderness.' She paused and winked. 'You weren't there, up at that lake, for forty days and forty nights by any chance, being tempted by Satan?'

They both laughed gently. Anamar had never met a nun or a priest who spoke or acted quite like this, for whom religion was such a natural, practical, joyful part of life.

Anamar made a point of spending some time with Sister Teresa every day, sometimes helping with the invalids, understanding more about the draw of Lourdes with every visit.

The days passed quickly, each busy as they followed a strict programme. On the second day they went to Mass in the late afternoon to the house of the Poor Clare Nuns. From the bridge at the front of the Domain, the convent looked like a little fortress. The chapel was a haven of peace from the noise of the busy street outside. It was cool inside, almost cold at this time of year, mirroring the austere life of the nuns. As an enclosed community, their only work was prayer, so they depended on charity for their daily needs. Mass was still at an hour laid down by Saint Clare in the 13th. century. The community sang the office. The Blessed Sacrament was in a covered chalice. The nuns remained behind the grill. It was a place without time, as if the passage of the years had been diverted somewhere else.

The Irish pilgrims crowded into the confines of the chapel. This was so different to the huge, euphoric spaces of the Domain and the dramatic grandeur of the Church of the Rosary. There was the contrast of scale, but even more, there was the constancy of the devotions in this place, day and daily down the decades, as if no one had ever thought to count the years.

The effect, for Anamar, was even more powerful than the great processions of the pilgrimage. It was as if until this moment they had been involved in the public demonstration of faith. Now, within the chapel of the Poor Clares, it was time for the private reckoning, each person here alone with God.

They trooped out into the sunshine of the street and back into the busy life of the pilgrim in Lourdes.

Anamar was thinking of Sister Teresa. Unlike the visiting pilgrims and helpers, for whom the time here was a pause in the journey of life, this was her whole life. Anamar smiled, remembering how Sister Teresa had called it her 'work', in the kind of tone which would have brooked no argument. And she amused the sister by telling her about Hank's version of the Benedictine motto…

'Labore est orare, sed potare clarior,' and his translation, 'Work is prayer, (or as good as prayer) but drinking is better.'

Sister Teresa laughed quietly,

'Now that's one I'll have to remember,' she said. 'You never know when it might come in handy.'

On the Sunday morning, their fourth day in Lourdes, the Irish Pilgrimage made their own procession to the Domain. There was great excitement as Ellie and F. B. encouraged them to form up two deep outside the hotel. They were led by the priests with Father Brogan at the front, and guided by Anamar who went a little ahead through the streets. By this stage most of the party would have been able to find their way to the Domain, but to-day was different. They wanted to follow a route which they had seen other pilgrim groups use, and there must be no hesitation or mistake.

They were all so proud as they marched through the town, not the arrogant, egotistical pride of the Seven Deadly Sins but the pride in being able to bear witness for one's faith, the pride of valuing one's own worth. They paraded around the Domain, pausing at the Grotto for a short time for prayer and stopped on the steps of the Church of the Rosary in perfect time for High Mass. The timing was no accident. Ellie, F. B. and Anamar had stepped it out the previous day. 'Best not to leave anything to chance,' F. B. had said beforehand and as usual in such matters, F. B. had been right.

During Mass, Ellie was in a good position to see Father Brogan and he was so pale she thought he might be ill. Then she realised that this man, who always seemed so calm, so much in control of himself, was visibly moved by the experience of the day.

On the way back to the hotel they were no longer together, no longer needing to be. F. B. was looking for a chance to speak to Anamar alone. After his proposal had been rejected he had spent a sleepless night, so troubled he was not sure whether he was sad or angry. Did Anamar have someone else in tow? Someone much younger? How could he face her back in the shop in Donegal. How should he face her now? Should he be reserved, distant, hiding his hurt feelings, bearing no ill-will? Would it be better if he asked her to leave his employment?

Half way back, he had the right opportunity and came straight to the point.

'I need a word with you, Miss Cassidy, that is if it's all right to speak to you privately.' He was trying to be friendly but sounded ill-at-ease.

'It's about the shop ... ' He began to say.

Anamar smiled her most winning smile and gently interrupted.

'Great minds think alike, Mr O'Boyle,' she said cheerily. 'I was just thinking about the shop too. I've greatly enjoyed working for you but I think it's time for me to move on. I hope it won't inconvenience you but I'm sure it'll be for the best.'

F. B. felt a great sigh escape from his chest. He was so relieved that Anamar had made the move. Coming from him it was bound to have sounded like sour grapes. Her consideration only proved how thoughtful a person she was. Their time together, in what he liked to call 'dual harness', had been very good for the business. They would have made a great couple.

'You're very understanding, Miss Cassidy,' he said. 'I hope this doesn't leave you out on a limb.'

'Not a bit of it,' said Anamar. 'Now that the farm's sold and my father's away, I'll be needing time to sort out my affairs, then I think I'll be off on my travels again.'

F. B. held out his hand and gripped hers a little more firmly than usual.

'I won't forget this trip, Miss Cassidy,' he said. 'And for all the right reasons. We owe it all to you. Mrs McGinley makes no bones about that. It was you who set her off on the road to Lourdes and we all followed.'

Their last full day in Lourdes was a Monday and after Mass Anamar led them, at Ellie's request and without explanation of where they were headed, beyond the Baths to the bottom of a steep bank. Amongst a few trees was a statue in bronze of a formidable woman in ancient attire. The inscription read, 'St. Margaret, Queen and Patroness of Scotland - Pray for Us - 1929'. A garland of flowers had been woven through the railings around the foot of the plinth.

Surrounded as they had been for the past few days by French, Italian and Spanish pilgrims, it was a relief to come upon this evidence that others came here too, from nearer home. Father Brogan expressed himself surprised and explained that Margaret had been of Saxon descent and had done much to establish the pilgrimage to Iona in the Western Isles of Scotland.

But there was one more visit before they went back to the hotel. Anamar took them to the site of the Celtic cross erected by the Irish Pilgrimage of 1913. As they gathered around F. B. whispered to Father Brogan.

'We came here in '24,' he said, unable to hide his excitement. As Father Brogan spoke to the party, remembering everything they had done together since they had arrived in Lourdes, he thanked Ellie for her inspiration and hard work. He mentioned Anamar and F. B. and how important their previous experience here had been.

'Without them to lead us, like three biblical shepherds, we would have been as lost sheep bleating in the wilderness,' he said, and they all smiled.

Ellie felt a hot flush in her cheeks and turned away to hide her embarrassment. F. B. smiled and nodded in acknowledgement, rocking gently back and forth on his heels and toes. One way and another, he felt that this trip would be the making of him. Not for him, ever again, would it be discomfiting to do something in the public eye. A man like him had his place in Catholic society, and single or married, he intended to take it.

He looked across to Anamar to salute her part in the pilgrimage but she had gone to Ellie and put an arm around her shoulders. They were not yet at the end of their time in Lourdes but this was an emotional moment for everyone. Hands were grasped and shoulders patted and hugs exchanged. Jerome and Danny reached out to each other. Danny had virtually no strength in his fingers and Jerome held his hand like a newly-born baby's. There were tears in their eyes.

'Nobody can take this away from us,' said Jerome loudly, defiantly, for all to hear.

It was a moment none of them would ever forget.

Father Brogan said nothing. He recognised the power of the personal experiences and let each one of them have his or her own privacy. When it was time to go, they walked back slowly towards the hotel in small groups, silent or chatting quietly amongst themselves.

Anamar found herself alone for a moment and although she still had the same doubts about the child Bernadette's visions and the healing miracles as she had felt when she was here the previous year, she was now sure of the reality of the experience of Lourdes. Every day she had seen the regeneration of faith, in the processions, at the Grotto, in the Baths, at Mass. And Sister Teresa's thoughts, prayers and stories, her truly Christian work and life, were undeniable.

It was seeing the people here and feeling their response which bridged the gap between incredulity and acceptance.

Suddenly a weight of depression, which she had borne on her shoulders since F. B. had proposed, was lifted. She felt lighter on her feet, far lighter in her spirit than she had known since she and Hank had shared their last meal together in the Pyrenees, and since the moment she had been sure he had turned away from death towards life.

She tripped back to the hotel, skipping along like a child on an outing. When she reached the street she saw a smart sports' car parked near where Ellie was standing in the doorway of the hotel.

She had just started to say.

'That wee car is the spittin' image of …'

When there was a loud knock on the window of the hotel and there was Deirdre Ryan herself, looking out, 'dressed to kill', as Ellie would say later, waving with both arms, waiting for Anamar to return.

Vert-Vert the Parrot

Deirdre could hardly contain herself. Her face was a picture, her eyes sparkling, a grin from ear to ear.

The day after the Pilgrimage party had left the town, and taking advantage of the Easter school holidays, she had set out on her own journey. It had to be kept a secret in case it would have taken away from the pilgrimage preparations, but once they were away, she had packed the car and headed off for France. The boat trips across the Irish Sea and the English Channel had been enjoyable and she had taken her time on the long journey south to Lourdes. Now she had until the following week-end to get back to Donegal.

'I couldn't resist it,' she said. 'You were all trooping off to my favourite foreign country and there was me stuck at home, missing out entirely.'

They hugged and held each other by the arms as Anamar excitedly recounted the highlights of their time in Lourdes. She was so pleased to see Deirdre now the pilgrimage group was ready for home. It was as if she needed to tell the whole story, to talk about her experiences to someone outside the group who would understand. There was no question but that Deirdre was the ideal person. She would listen to what Anamar was really saying.

That evening, Deirdre joined the group on the Torchlight Procession, carrying a large candle with its little shield for the flame. She was staying at an hotel beside the railway station in the High Town and invited Anamar and Doctor Corr to have dinner with her there. They ate in a large, airy room which was part of the hotel bar and decorated in the elegant French style of the thirties.

'This place in quite famous,' Deirdre said when they were seated. 'The official surrender of the German army occupying this region took place on the pavement outside.'

It was so different from the pilgrimage party's hotel. The room was spacious, the dining tables laid with white cloths and silver cutlery. None of the staff spoke English and Doctor Corr felt he should leave the ordering to Deirdre.

The meals at the pilgrimage hotel were adequate and served quickly but they were hardly French cooking at its best. In this hotel, there was the prospect of something special. Having been on her own for a few days Deirdre seemed to be doing all the talking. She was asking about the pilgrimage, what they had done, how the group had reacted to the foreign food, how the pilgrimage arrangements had worked out.

'Well, Wilson,' said Deirdre to Doctor Corr. 'It's time to come clean. I suppose you'll be telling us that you hated the food and have been half-starved since you left Ireland.' She looked at Anamar and shook her head. 'He has very unsophisticated culinary tastes,' she said. 'I've tried my best, but you could take him nowhere.'

Wilson Corr was laughing.

'Never mind the grub,' he said. 'Just give us the benefit of your carefully-cultivated nose for wine to help me order a decent bottle or two. I'll eat anything you put in front of me.'

It was a meal which fittingly marked the end of the rigours of the pilgrimage for Anamar. In spite of local shortages, the food was excellent, the staff friendly and the service leisurely. Deirdre ordered *Crudités* as their first course and it came on a huge plate with separate sections for an arrangement of asparagus tips, celery, mild scallions, little florets of cauliflower, a huge succulent tomato sliced thinly and two kinds of mayonnaise, one with a distinctive garlic flavour.

She asked the waiter about the main course and took his advice, ordering *Coq au Vin*, for the three of them. From the wine list she chose a dark red from Madiran and a white from the nearby region of Jurançon which was a beautiful, greenish-gold colour in the glass.

'Happy now?' Deirdre asked, when she saw the look of ecstasy on Doctor Corr's face as he sipped the Maridan.

Since she had first come to France, Anamar had been in awe of French cuisine. It seemed that the cooks could make something special from the simplest ingredients. Before they had left home, Deirdre's interest and skill as a cook had helped Anamar recognise the French way. The secret was in the quality of the raw provisions. Food was obviously important to the French and they treated it with due respect. They proved to be discerning shoppers for fruit, vegetables and meats. They demanded quality produce and prepared it with loving care. And French cooks expected their food to be taken seriously.

When it was time for dessert, Doctor Corr let the sweet trolley pass him by with studied reluctance, but Anamar and Deirdre chose a *Mousse au Chocolat* and a *Tarte aux Fraises.* Later Deirdre ordered Benedictine liqueurs for the three of them. Anamar said that Sister Teresa, of the Lourdes Domain, had been amused when she recounted Hank's version of the Benedictine motto.

'Labore est orare sed potare clarior… Work is prayer but drinking is better.'

Even Deirdre was impressed.

'I expect you could translate the Latin,' she said to Wilson Corr. 'But I doubt if your Protestant education stretched to the lore of the Benedictines.'

It was a memorable meal and when Anamar said so, Deirdre's eyes twinkled.

'Thank you, my dear,' she said in her grand voice, which always made Anamar smile. 'To be worthy of such praise, a meal must be shared by good company, so Wilson and I appreciate the compliment.'

Wilson Corr responded with a formal incline of the head and a little bow to Anamar. She had never seen a man so much at ease, so able to show his enjoyment of the occasion. He pushed back his chair and rose to his feet.

'I hope you'll both permit me to offer you a toast,' he said gently, and raised his glass. 'Here's to two special ladies, the Smart Pilgrim and the True Traveller. May your joy be in your quest.'

Anamar could see that all the other diners were looking in their direction, smiling. Without knowing what was happening, the other patrons were obviously aware of the happiness at their table. She and Deirdre clapped, almost silently, and she could have sworn that Doctor Corr was blushing as he sat down.

'And now to business,' Deirdre said firmly. 'I too am leaving to-morrow for home but intend to spend a few days driving back in leisurely fashion, to arrive in Donegal at the week-end, just in time for the start of school on Monday. I'd like to be able to invite you both to join me, but as Wilson can't leave his patients in transit and anyway, he'd never be comfortable in the Dicky-seat of the car, it has to be you.'

She pointed a finger at Anamar and smiled.

'So I'm hoping you'll join me on a short Grand Tour of France, now your pilgrimage is over.'

Wilson Corr was grinning from ear to ear.

'And didn't I guess as much at the very start of this fine meal,' he said and gave Anamar a wink. 'You don't know this blade as well as I do. There's never such a thing as a free dinner. If she's not asking you to sit for a portrait for her Rogues' Gallery, she'll be wanting to whisk you off for a skite around France. I'm not sure the pair of you should be let loose on the poor unsuspecting Frenchies.'

Anamar was so surprised she could make no reply for a few moments. She sat back in her chair and took a deep breath.

'I'd love to go with you,' she said. 'And I'm sure it will be all right but I would need to speak to Ellie, and Father Brogan, of course.'

'That's easily done,' said Deirdre. 'When we're finished here I'll walk to the hotel with you both and take a taxi back when we've spoken to them.'

It was a great evening, so good-humoured, so friendly and relaxed that Anamar nearly told them about F. B's proposal of marriage. At the last moment, however, she suddenly realised that she would only be doing so for their entertainment, and that would hardly be fair to F. B. She stopped herself just in time and instead, she and the Doctor regaled Deirdre, imitating the comments of the Irish pilgrims at mealtimes in the French hotel.

'Wouldn't you think they'd have learned to make a decent cup of tea, it's only dish-water you'll ever get here.

'Have they never heard tell of H.P. sauce?

'I still can't believe it. Some days we didn't even have spuds with the dinner.'

'And do they never have decent breakfasts in this country? Where's the rashers and the two fried eggs and the black pudding? I swear to God I could murder half a dozen Halfners' pork sausages.'

'With the mercy of God I'll be back and I'll have the full rations with me, and I'll land into the kitchen and cook them myself.'

When they reached the pilgrims' hotel, Ellie and Father Brogan were sharing a pot of tea, standing at one end the bar. They listened intently to Deirdre's plan.

'What a wonderful idea,' said Ellie and she hugged Anamar. 'Father Brogan and I were just saying we owed so much of the success of the pilgrimage to you. Isn't it your due reward.'

Father Brogan was smiling. He shook hands with Anamar and Deirdre.

'Go with our blessing,' he said, then he laughed and allowed himself a twinkle in his eye. 'I was going to say, 'Go and enjoy yourselves', but thought the better of it. You pair don't need that class of advice from the likes of me.'

Wilson Corr was smiling too. He winked at Ellie and Father Brogan.

'We might even enjoy ourselves a little too,' he said. 'Now that we're on the home run, as you might say.'

The hotel staff telephoned for a taxi to take Deirdre back to her hotel and she arranged to meet Anamar at the railway station the next morning, so that they might see the others off.

The Donegal Town and District Pilgrimage arrived at the station by bus next day, on the first stage of their journey home. No one had ever seen Father Brogan in better form. He came striding across to Deirdre and Anamar, who were saying 'Good-bye' to Ellie. He took a map from his coat pocket and opened it out so that they all could see.

'I've had an idea. It came to me in bed last night,' he said excitedly. 'The mother house of St. Bernadette's order is in the town of Nevers, and the Saint herself is buried there'. He found Nevers on the map and drew a ring around it in pencil.

'Now if you could make a visit there on your way back to the English Channel,' he said, trying not to seem too forceful. 'Wouldn't it be a truly fitting benediction on all of us, at the end of our pilgrimage?'

Deirdre smiled and traced a curving line on the map from Lourdes to Paris.

'We could, of course,' she said. 'I had planned for us to visit Albi and then drive north to Chartres. Nevers is almost on our direct route.'

Ellie was so delighted she almost hugged Deirdre. Instead she shook her hand.

'Like it or not,' she said. 'You're now part of this pilgrimage.'

Deirdre laughed and nodded her head.

'And you and I and Father Brogan know who I have to thank for that.' And they all looked at Anamar, who half-turned away with embarrassment.

Then she saw Sister Teresa standing behind them, smiling, and she went across to speak to her. She felt her eyes prickling, as if she might cry. It seemed as if everyone was trying to make this moment special.

'I'll be back to Lourdes,' Anamar said quietly. 'And I hope you won't mind me writing to you in the meantime.'

Sister Teresa's eyes twinkled.

'I'll take both of those as promises,' she said. 'I couldn't help overhearing your plans, so, in your first letter, you can tell me all about your visit to our Mother House in Nevers.'

Father Brogan saw F. B. supervising the luggage and rushed over to tell him about Anamar's and Deirdre's trip. There was no need to tell anyone else. The story would reach everyone's ears before the train had travelled fifty miles. F. B. would do his duty, even though the very mention of Anamar's name made him feel dispirited.

Danny and Jerome were parked nearby, not in the least concerned that their wheel-chairs might be in F. B's way. They had overheard Father Brogan telling him the news. Danny caught Deirdre's eye.

'Are ye not taking anybody with you for a wee bit of company?' he said loudly. 'Me and Jerome are fancy-free. We could be easily persuaded.'

Ellie waved a finger at Danny in mock admonition.

'Get away with you,' she said. 'Here was me thinking that you both fancied me. You're a pair of fickle oul cods!'

And everybody joined in the laughter. Danny and Jerome were popular members of the group. Through their good spirits and wit they had both given much more to the pilgrimage than they had taken in the form of help, and that was recognised by all.

Deirdre and Anamar watched the baggage being loaded and the party boarding the train. Maureen was the last to get on. She lowered the window and leaned out to kiss Anamar as the train pulled out. Deirdre and Anamar stayed on the platform, waving, until the last carriage was out of sight. Then they carried Anamar's luggage across the road to stow it in Deirdre's beautiful dark-green sports-car, parked in front of her hotel.

They bought some food for a picnic and left Lourdes half an hour after the train. It was dull and overcast, so the soft top had to be unfolded and clipped into place. Deirdre wore her leather driving gloves with mesh backs and Anamar had the map on her knees. She was to do the navigating and she was a little nervous.

'Many's the good friendship has foundered on the rocks of poor route finding,' said Deirdre, using her stern, school-mistress voice but when Anamar looked across at her she was smiling.

'Don't worry yourself,' she said. 'All you have to do is tell me whether we go left, right or straight on. However, the secret is to tell me before we reach the junction!' She was laughing, enjoying the driving but it was different for Anamar. The first town would be an anxious time for her.

When they had successfully negotiated their way through Tarbes, Anamar let her breath out in a great sigh and felt she had passed the first test.

'Well done!' said Deirdre. 'But you'll have to get used to the aggravation. Drivers always give their navigators a hard time.'

The roads were good, with long straight, tree-lined stretches and steeply banked bends, the surface blackened with tyre rubber as the vehicles kept the speed up rounding the curve.

After lunch, Deirdre drove slowly through Toulouse. At one major junction there were no signs and she stopped beside the policeman directing the traffic. She wound down her window and asked for directions to Albi. The policeman stepped back to admire the car and pointed to a road to the right. With a raised arm he imperiously stopped the rest of the traffic, saluted smartly and waved them on their way.

'I'd love to think that happened because he appreciates my charm,' Deirdre was pretending to be coy. 'But I'd have to admit that it's the car he fancies, not me.'

They arrived in Albi and found accommodation in a pension near the centre. Their room was on the second floor. It was large and airy with two single beds against opposite walls. In between there was a settee, an arm-chair and a low table, forming a sitting area with a view through a large window across the roofs of the town.

Deirdre could hardly wait to take Anamar on a tour of Albi. She had been here only very briefly before the war, but having Anamar with her heightened the anticipation. Last time, her father had been the guide, now she would be able to share the experience with someone else who would understand.

They went to the cathedral first. Anamar stopped in amazement when they turned a corner and she saw the huge structure for the first time. It was a massive red-brick edifice, more like a castle than a cathedral. At the far end was a mighty tower. Directly in front of them the walls rose above a plinth like a cliff face, sheer for fifty feet, unbroken, without a foothold for even the most agile of the attacking hordes.

Deirdre could see the look of surprise on Anamar's face.

'Say nothing just yet. Wait until we're inside,' she whispered and pointed at a rounded tower which was part of the walls. 'That's called a *donjon*, built to withstand a siege. Let's find the door and see if it's open.'

The porch over the fortified doorway was elaborately carved. The walls were five feet thick. Inside, there were chapels within massive buttress walls. But what was incredible was that this was the interior of the same structure. It was a truly astonishing sight, rising grandly in great arches, so light and airy, so elegantly decorated, the stone-work so delicately carved, and yet within such a mighty stronghold.

They sat down on chairs within the preaching hall, each with her own thoughts.

'Can you hear the Bishop, Bernard de Castanet, here in the 13th century, railing against the heretics?' Deirdre was speaking quietly, almost talking to her self.

'And what must it have been like a few years before that, when the Grand Inquisitor was preaching in this very place against the sect they called the Albigensians? Like the Knights Templar two hundred years later, the Albigensians were cruelly suppressed, their men, women and children massacred in the cause of eradicating heresy. And what was one of their principal errors? Women were allowed to play a part in the pastoral work of the church. In fact, a woman was often the senior elder within a parish.'

Deirdre shook her head. This house of God filled her with dread.

'I still keep the faith,' she said sadly. 'But it's no wonder I've never had much confidence in the all male hierarchy of the Church.'

Anamar found herself confused. The Cathedral was such a magnificent building, but it was impossible for her to relate its splendid interior to the spectacular fortress of its exterior. When she sat down in the great hall, she had no feeling of it being a religious place. The tiny chapel attached to the ancient inn in the Pyrenees had aroused a sense of the spiritual, a mystical feeling of being connected to all those who had worshipped here on their way across the mountains.

They walked in silence to the bishop's palace beside the cathedral to see some of Henri de Toulouse-Lautrec's most important paintings. But Anamar was not able to concentrate on the pictures. Her mind was still inside the cathedral, thinking of the Albigensians, once a sect of the Church, now merely a dark shadow in its history.

Deirdre tried to encourage Anamar to taken an interest but it was no use. They walked on to a house in one of the town's picturesque streets.

'This is it,' said Deirdre. 'Your man Toulouse-Lautrec was born here. It's a little museum with some of his earliest work. It'll cheer you up to see how Henri triumphed over his disability. He managed to paint so evocatively of Paris in the last century and enjoy himself at the same time.'

Deirdre was right. As well as the fine pictures, the sketches and lithographs, the scribbles, the quickly drawn figures and faces delighted Anamar and, as they left to walk back to the pension, they were both in good humour again.

At dinner that evening Anamar confided to Deirdre her confusion about the cathedral. Deirdre nodded her head in understanding.

'There is no point in seeking a logical explanation,' she said. 'Perhaps, like me, it was the way the officers of the Church destroyed the Albigensians, but your spirit was troubled even before you had heard their story.

The meal at the pension was simple French country cooking. The chicken, salads, the four cheeses on a wooden platter were delicious and the bread fresh, crisp and crusty. The red wine was served in a jug and, to Anamar's surprise, it was filled up again as soon as they had drunk a few glasses.

'I have a story for you,' said Anamar, feeling warmed and relaxed by the food, the wine and Deirdre's company. She started straight into it.

'Before you arrived in Lourdes, F. B. O'Boyle proposed to me.'

Deirdre fell back in her seat, her mouth open, the glass of wine half-raised to drink, sprinkling a few drops on her napkin.

'I knew you wouldn't believe me,' said Anamar. 'But it's true. He gave me his version of his prospects, then he said, as if it would be a fore-gone conclusion, 'Miss Cassidy, I wish you to consider a proposal of marriage'.'

Deirdre began to laugh, her whole frame shaking gently.

'I'm sorry, my dear,' she said. 'I don't mean to be rude but, dear God, I can just see the cut of him rising on his toes and doing you the honour.' Suddenly she was serious.

'You turned him down? Tell me you turned him down.'

It was Anamar's turn to laugh but she did so hesitantly, out of relief at being able to tell Deirdre, but not wanting to make a joke of F. B.

'It wasn't easy,' she said earnestly. 'He wouldn't let me get a word in edgeways. He was for organising the whole thing right away, without me having the chance to say 'Yes' or 'No'. He took it for granted that I would be delighted. I almost had to be rude to stop him in his tracks.'

Deirdre held out both her hands across the table and grasped Anamar's.

'I didn't mean to make fun of him either,' she said gently. 'It's a big moment in a girl's life when someone asks her to marry him, even if she does turn him down. I should know. It's happened to me twice. The first was the right man at the wrong time in my life and the second had no right to ask anyone to marry him. He already had a wife.'

She turned her face away from the light. The good-humoured banter about F. B. had gone. She could not conceal the surge of sadness which made her catch her breath. It was easy to predict that Anamar would have other proposals but, in Irish terms, she knew that others saw her as an old maid. She drew herself up in the chair. Luckily, she loved the freedom of the single life, she told herself, and smiled at Anamar, releasing her young friend from the embarrassment of cheering her up.

Back in their big room they sat on the easy chairs, in the almost dark, and looked out over the roofs of the town, silhouetted by the street lights. The tower of the cathedral was just visible at one end of the view and Anamar felt that their visit to it had been days before, not that very afternoon.

Deirdre read the paragraph about it in her guidebook.

'After the Albigensian Heresy had been eradicated the imperious cathedral of St. Cecile was built in 1277 to replace the original building which had been undermined by wars and heretics. It is one of the finest Gothic cathedrals in France and the 15th century fresco, 'The Last Judgment', is the largest picture in the country.'

'It's the best time to read about places like this,' Deirdre said gently. 'After you've made your first visit, not before.'

And Anamar was sure she was right. Hearing the words from the guidebook had reminded her that this was history, not to be forgotten. How could it be? The huge edifice would ensure that it was not. But she was aware that, in a strange perverse way, this massive cathedral would stand as a monument to the massacred Albigensians, as well as being a manifestation of the great power of the Church in medieval times.

The beds were soft and comfortable, with deep feather pillows, but they both woke early next morning. Deirdre had explained that their drive had only been one hundred and fifty miles from Lourdes to Albi but that their next overnight stop, Nevers, was over one hundred miles further.

The Riley sports' car, with the hood down, ran smoothly on long straight roads between trees, then wound through wooded valleys, climbing steadily. Anamar could see that Deirdre was enjoying the driving, chatting away about the countryside as she drove. Then she would stop talking, or even listening, to concentrate on steering the car or changing gear before a bend or on a steep ascent. On the straight sections they would reach sixty-five or seventy miles per hour on the speedometer, but the car seemed always to be well within the driver's control.

'I know what you're thinking,' Deirdre said slyly. 'You'd love to be able to take the wheel. Anamar was smiling. It was exactly her thought at that moment.

'Don't worry your wee head,' Deirdre continued. 'I'll teach you to drive before the summer and the next time you and I slip off on our holidays like this, I'll sit back in the passenger seat, sipping champagne, and you can do chauffeuse. We'll get you the peaked cap and jacket. When we stop you can nip round the car to open my door for me.'

They laughed, Anamar was remembering her first ride in the car to Slieve League for the picnic and Deirdre was already planning their next trip. They stopped for coffee in a village and sat at a table on the pavement. They bought some food for lunch and picnicked beside the River Dordogne. Late in the afternoon they coasted down from the hills to the upper reaches of the River Loire and the town of Nevers.

They found the Convent St. Gildard, the mother house of the Sisters of Charity, without difficulty on the appropriately named, Rue de Lourdes. Half an hour later they were installed in the guest house, in two tiny rooms the size and shape of nun's cells, neat, clean and comfortably furnished.

There were a few other guests, all of them women and they ate at the same large table and attended mass together.

Shortly after they arrived, one of the older nuns brought the group of guests to see the uncorrupted body of St. Bernadette of Lourdes, displayed in its bronze and glass coffin. The nun was most interested to hear about the Donegal Town and District Pilgrimage and delighted when Anamar said that she had met Sister Teresa in Lourdes.

When they were around the coffin, Deirdre seemed uncomfortable and stayed at the back of the group. Anamar wondered what was wrong. It was not until the next morning when they were speeding away from Nevers, on a good road beside the beautiful Loire, that Deirdre had a chance to say something.

'I knew it was important for you to visit the convent,' she said. 'But I'm just not at ease with relics like the uncorrupted bodies of saints.'

Anamar was nodding her head in agreement.

'I understand that, of course,' she said. 'But I needed to be there to be able to tell the others about it when we get home. I hope it didn't spoil your visit.'

Deirdre was laughing gently.

'Not at all,' she said. 'That nun who showed us the coffin could see I was a bit put out, so she told me one of the convent's stories to cheer me up. It appears that the nuns had a parrot here, two hundred years ago, called Vert-Vert. And this parrot was so well up in religious doctrine that the monks from Nantes wanted to borrow him. However, on the river journey, the boatmen on the Loire taught Vert-Vert such blasphemy, that when he arrived at the monastery the monks put him in solitary confinement. Poor old Vert-Vert died of loneliness and indigestion, probably cursing the cruel Brethren of Nantes with his last breath.'

'I don't think we'll bother visiting the brothers at Nantes,' said Anamar. " You might just happen to mention the famous Vert-Vert and get us shown the door. And how could I explain that to Father Brogan when I got back home?'

The low spirits were gone. The scenery along the Loire surprised them at every turn in the road. They were now on the famous N7, the Route National from Paris to Marseilles, and the traffic was much heavier. Deirdre said very little, she was concentrating on the driving but obviously still enjoying herself.

They turned off the N7 for Orléans and Chartres and Anamar found herself fully occupied with the route finding. As Deirdre had warned her, the secret was to use the map to look ahead, anticipating changes of direction, so that the driver could be told well in advance. Then they made a mistake.

After the large town of Orléans everything had gone to plan. Anamar was beginning to think that the navigating was easy. Then they came to the much smaller Bonneval. She knew they should be turning right but could see no signs and they missed the turn.

Deirdre said nothing as she swung the Riley around in the road and drove back to the junction. A furniture van was parked in front of the signs, making it impossible for them to be seen from their previous direction of approach. She smiled. All was forgiven and Anamar breathed out a great sigh of relief.

They arrived in Chartres before noon, bought food for their picnic lunch stop later, and had coffee at a pavement café looking up at the facade of the great cathedral. Once again Deirdre told Anamar nothing about the building but she was watching her young friend's face as they talked

Anamar was spellbound. She walked ahead of Deirdre, up the steps and through the carved south portal, with its finely worked stone figures on either hand. Inside, a simple wedding was in progress, the ceremony almost over, the small group of guests keeping together in an alcove, inconspicuous, almost unnoticed within the vast interior. Anamar and Deirdre sat down in the main body of the church in silence.

It was an experience for Anamar, in total contrast to Albi. She could never have explained why it was so different, but here she felt in harmony with the place. There was the same spiritual feeling she had been aware of in the tiny chapel at the inn in the Pyrenees. One of these houses of God, so small, perched in the wilds of the mountains, the other so spectacularly splendid, set at the very heart of Christendom. They were at opposite ends of the same spectrum. In both, Anamar felt at ease. Her sense of place had turned her away from Albi but here she was at peace, as she had been in the Pyrenean chapel.

They must have sat for almost half an hour before Deirdre spoke.

'I knew you would be glad to come,' she said. 'I may not believe in a way that would be guaranteed to please Father Brogan, but when I'm here I know I believe in God. It's easy to see why historians regard the building of Chartres Cathedral as the great awakening of European civilisation. Have you heard of Peter Abelard?'

Anamar shook her head.

'He was one of the great medieval philosophers, a brilliant teacher, reputed to be invincible in argument. At a time when other philosophers would say, 'I must believe in order that I may understand.' Abelard taught, 'I must understand in order that I may believe.'

Deirdre looked closely at Anamar before continuing.

'I think I agree with Peter Abelard,' she said gently. 'Though that nearly got him excommunicated. He was only saved by the power and influence of the Benedictine Order. But I feel safe here. Chartres helps me understand.'

They left the town and had a long, leisurely picnic lunch in a field beside a river. They could hear the faint rumble of the traffic on the road some distance away but the scene before them was rural France at its most peaceful. There were still pools in the river, where the reflection of the trees in the water was brighter than the original. It was sunny, but never so hot that they thought of seeking shade.

Once they were back on the road they reached the outskirts of Paris quickly. A stop on the verge let them plan a route towards the centre. Deirdre had a hotel in mind in Montmartre. Half an hour later, she turned right from a narrow street into a square, and parked in front of a hotel beside a huge building.

'That's the Sorbonne,' she said, pointing at the building and speaking in a matter-of-fact tone, although she was relieved to find herself in exactly the right place. 'It's the University and this is the Hotel Select. It's mainly used by foreign students and, this being holiday time, they should have a spare room.'

The hotel seemed very large to Anamar. It was simple, comfortable and friendly. Once again they had a big room, this time on the first floor and with a view across the square.

'This is where we change gear,' said Deirdre, as she unpacked a few clothes from her suitcase. 'We have to leave for the channel port to- morrow after lunch, so this afternoon we're tourists. It's up the Eiffel Tower for you m'girl. To-night we'll eat where the locals eat and stroll along the Left-Bank in the evening.'

Anamar was excited by the very idea of it. She had passed through Paris before, but here with Deirdre they would see the sights, admire the style, become Parisiennes for a few hours.

In twenty minutes they were off to the Eiffel Tower. They travelled by Metro, Anamar taking her cue from Deirdre, who seemed completely at ease amongst the crowds on the escalators, buying tickets, travelling on the smart underground trains.

There was a short queue for the lift at the base of the Eiffel Tower and a breathtaking ascent to the viewing balcony. It was an awe-inspiring place to be, perched so high above the ground, the tower swaying gently, the view stupendous. Here, directly below their feet the whole of the city was laid out in tiny detail, as if on a huge map. And beyond, a vast terrain of surrounding countryside stretched back towards a hazy, indistinct skyline.

Deirdre's face was pale. She was gripping the hand rails.

'I should have warned you that I feel very strange up here,' she said wanly. 'It's hard to explain because I seem to have a good head for heights when I'm in the mountains. I was last here when I was seventeen, and it feels as bad to-day as it did then.'

Anamar knew that Deirdre was only here because she didn't want her to miss the experience. She tried to be reassuring, but she was as excited as a child. She traced the course of the river through the city. Deirdre's eyes were tightly closed but with her directions, Anamar spotted the Cathedral of Notre Dame on an island in the middle of the Seine and the Arc de Triomphe.

When they reached the ground again, Deirdre looked shaken and they walked to a nearby café for coffee and pâtisseries.

'I needed that coffee and the big bun to steady my nerves,' Deirdre said, sounding much more like herself. 'These places are always too dear. You pay for the privilege of sitting outside. It's like having a seat in the stalls at the theatre. But here the actors are the passers-by.'

In the evening they went to a restaurant in a side street near the hotel. At eight o'clock a small crowd was waiting for the doors to open.

'It's a secret the Parisians keep from the tourists,' Deirdre said confidentially. 'This place doesn't take bookings, but we're here at the right time. The locals reckon it's the best food in the Latin Quarter.'

A girl in a huge apron opened the doors and the good-natured patrons filed in, to be shown seats at long wooden tables. There were red-checked table-cloths and big napkins to match. Deirdre and Anamar found themselves seated beside a group of five women in their thirties who seemed to be regulars.

The menu was written up on large black-boards. There were two starters, one soup, two main courses and a choice of the cheese board or one of five desserts. For her first course Deirdre had *Rognons d'Agneau*, lambs' kidneys in a wine and cream sauce and then Canard *a l'Orange*, duck in an orange and wine sauce. Anamar was feeling hungry so she had a huge platter of dressed salad, the onion soup and *Andouillette*, a large, wonderfully tasty sausage stuffed with tripe pieces and pork chitterlings.

Without intruding, the French women spoke to them from time to time, assuming they both understood French. They complimented them on their choice of dishes and wine, discussed the food, and were obviously pleased to see that Anamar and Deirdre were enjoying the meal so much.

'That was a wonderful experience,' said Anamar as they strolled down the street towards the river Seine. 'And not just the food. I thought Parisians were supposed to be unfriendly to foreigners. They couldn't have been nicer to us. I wish now I'd tried the kidneys. How do you know about places like this?'

Deirdre smiled and the look on her face betrayed a very happy memory.

'After my mother died, my father often took me with him on his trips abroad. We drove the length and breadth of France. We climbed in the Alps in the summer and skied there in the winter. We always stayed in Paris for a few days on the way home. I was in my 'teens and twenties at the time and we were friends, as well as father and daughter.'

They reached the river and browsed amongst the stalls selling books and pictures. A bridge took them to the island in the middle of the river, the Ile de la Cité, and they sat down on a wooden seat to look at the facade of Notre Dame. Deirdre put her hand on Anamar's arm.

'I won't let on to the pilgrimage crowd if you resist the urge to rush inside,' she said confidentially. 'Like me, you've probably seen enough of the inside of churches to do you for one trip.'

Next morning Anamar went to early Mass in Notre Dame and returned for a leisurely breakfast with Deirdre. They crossed the Seine and walked to the art gallery called the Jeux de Paume at the other end of the Tuileries Gardens.

'We've only time for one art gallery on this trip,' Deirdre said firmly. 'So it has to be this one. It's famous for its collection of Impressionist paintings.'

'Yes, Miss Ryan. Whatever you say, Miss Ryan,' said Anamar, with the confidence now to tease Deirdre gently, the way Deirdre sometimes teased her.

Deirdre smiled and shook her forefinger at her.

'Now you just behave yourself, Missy,' she said. 'We've come here to further your education, and I intend to see that it's done properly.'

They were still laughing as they climbed the steps and paid at the entrance. Deirdre explained that this beautiful art gallery had once been, as its name indicated, an indoor hand-ball court, and suggested that they separate for half an hour to give Anamar a chance to wander around on her own.

Anamar was enthralled. There were so many paintings by famous artists, Manet, Monet, Renoir, Degas. She had seen good reproductions of some of them in the books in Deirdre's library at home, but it was a very different experience to see the actual paintings.

Looking at the pictures, she felt she could understand what the painter had seen in his mind as he painted, even though she had no idea how he had managed to convey that to her. But it was the power of these artists to illustrate their vision which was staggering. It was easy to see now, why they felt they had to revolt against traditional methods of painting.

When she and Deirdre met again, she suggested that they each take the other to see a painting.

'You first,' said Anamar. 'You've been here before.'

Deirdre took her to a side gallery, to a picture of a bare room where three workmen were preparing a wooden floor.

'It's called *The Parquet Planers,*' she said quietly. 'By a man called Caillebotte. He was never as famous as some of the others but he acted as patron to the Impressionists. Each time I come here, it seems to draw me back. I couldn't live with many of the great paintings here but this one is different. I'd find a place for it on my walls anytime.'

Anamar led the way into the main room and pointed to the one picture on the back wall. It was of a girl on a couch, naked except for a black velvet band around her throat. Then she turned to the left-hand wall, where there was a picnic scene in a forest glade. Two men were sitting, fully clothed beside a naked woman, with a second woman, scantily dressed, stooping behind them.

'They aren't my favourite pictures,' she said. 'But these two stopped me in my tracks.'

'What a choice,' said Deirdre. 'They're both by Manet. Experts might call them pre-Impressionist. This picnic scene, *Le Déjeuner sur l'herbe,* is regarded as the foundation stone of modern art. The other one of the girl, *Olympia*, caused the greatest scandal ever in art, when it was first exhibited.'

They walked to the Champs Élysées and saw the huge bulk of the Arc de

Triomphe in the distance. At lunch, in a bar in a side street, Anamar had two helpings of a delicious strawberry tart with cream called, *Tarte aux Fraise Chantilly,* while Deirdre watched.

'It's well for you,' she said enviously. 'You can eat what you like and it never shows.'

At four o'clock they were on their way out of Paris, heading north towards the coast. It was only four days since they had left Lourdes, but Anamar found that hard to believe. She had seen so much of France. It felt as if the pilgrimage had ended weeks before. Deirdre broke the silence.

'You're very quiet,' she said. 'But don't worry your little head about keeping me entertained while I do the driving. You and I have enough to keep us in chat for the rest of the year.'

Anamar felt like laughing. She had been quiet only because she needed time to think. Deirdre was right. It had been a memorable trip, an adventure they would recall over and over again in the months to come.

Arriba! Arriba!

On their last night in France, they stayed in an hotel in Dieppe. Deirdre took Anamar to a small restaurant called Madame Lola's, near the waterfront. They were early and the dining room was almost empty, the tables and chairs packed so tightly they had to squeeze through to get to their places.

Deirdre saw Anamar eyeing the friendly woman who had shown them to their table and knew she was wondering how such a substantially-built figure could be eased so effortlessly through the crowded furniture.

'That's Madame Lola, herself,' she said softly. 'I love this place.'

She ordered a bottle of white wine from Alsace and discussed the menu with Madame, as if asking her to share her confidences.

'Let me order to-night,' she said to Anamar. 'I know it's not the done thing to have shell-fish for the first two courses but here it has to be the mussels, and the famous scallop dish, Coquilles *St. Jacques.*'

'When we're talking about this trip next winter,' Anamar said excitedly, as if the idea had just come to her. 'There will be one particular memory which will bring back each place in every detail. For Albi, it will be the shock of first seeing that massive fortress of a red-brick cathedral. I'll remember Nevers for the story of the parrot Vert-Vert. For Chartres, I'll see the wedding in the cathedral, and for Dieppe, of course, it must be Madame Lola's.'

Deirdre smiled happily.

'Your great asset as a companion, little traveller,' said Deirdre. 'Is that you love the journey. You enjoy the sights, the people and the places, the food and the wine. I'm not sure I should tell you this, in case it goes to your head, but it's your enthusiasm which has made this tour for me.'

Next morning on the ferry across the English Channel, Anamar sat quietly, going over in her mind every stage of the journey she and Deirdre had made in France. Towards the end of the long drive through England and Wales, she suddenly remembered the pilgrimage. It had been so far from her mind for the past five days, she almost felt guilty.

The ferry across the Irish Sea docked in Dun Laoghaire in the early morning

183

and the drive north to Donegal went smoothly. They were both very quiet. 'Talked out,' as Anamar's mother would have said.

They reached Ballyshannon and the last few miles to Donegal Town seemed to take such a long time to cover, although Deirdre was driving as fast as ever.

When the car drew up in the yard of the farm which had once been Anamar's home, Maggie, the woman of the house now, and Ellie, Maureen and Eamon came out to meet them. They had been waiting, and had heard the car in the lane. There were hugs and handshakes and good-natured teasing between the girls.

Maggie brought Deirdre and Ellie into the house and Maureen and Eamon helped Anamar with her luggage across the field to her cottage. The fire there was lit and there was turf and logs in the basket. The food cupboards were stocked with bread, porridge meal and vegetables. In the food safe with the wire-mesh sides, outside on the wall which never got the sun, there was milk, butter, eggs and potted herrings in a dish.

'Survival rations,' said Eamon, looking embarrassed when Anamar tried to thank them. 'I hear I missed a great trip.'

Anamar was so pleased to find such a welcome, she hid her tears by hugging them both.

'Well, well, m'girl,' Maureen said to Anamar, adding to her brother's embarrassment, 'Eamon has no excuse now he knows that the way to your heart is through a well stocked food cupboard and a good fire. I'll leave the pair of you to it if you like.'

But when the three of them walked back to the farm-house together to join the others for tea, Anamar was in the middle, linking arms with both her friends.

It was well into the evening when Deirdre made a move to go home.

'It's all right for you lot,' she said. 'But I've got to get myself together for school in the morning.'

In her own bed, in her own cottage, Anamar slept soundly. In the morning she went into the Town by car with Maggie and her husband. She shopped, called on Doctor Corr and found people who had been on the pilgrimage with her appearing from around every corner, all delighted she was home again safely.

She called on F. B. O'Boyle at the shop and, although he seemed pleased enough to see her, F. B. kept his distance and spoke to her like a customer rather than a friend. Before she left the Town, she bought a bottle of dry sherry and two glasses and, on the way home, left a note at Deirdre's inviting her to come for a meal that evening.

When Deirdre arrived, Anamar hung the big iron griddle from the crane and swung it over the turf fire. She fried eggs on the hot griddle and cooked four small lamb chops, serving them with a lettuce and scallion salad and fresh home-made bread.

When they had finished eating, Deirdre produced a bottle of Benedictine from her bag and poured them each a small measure.

'I loved that story of yours about the motto of the Benedictine monks,' she said. 'I'm sure they're right about the proper place of work, prayer and drinking.' She raised her glass.

'Here's to the next time!' and they both smiled. Deirdre was hoping there would be a next time but had lived long enough not to take that for granted. Anamar was certain there would be. She knew life should have times like this.

Early next morning Anamar wrote to Sister Teresa, telling her about the trip back. She described their visit to the Convent St. Gildard in Nevers and enjoyed reminding the sister of the story of Vert-Vert the parrot.

Later she left the envelope with Maggie for posting and set off to walk up to Lough Belshade. The day was cool, dry, overcast, without the slightest breath of wind and she walked quickly up the track towards the gorge and the Doonan Waterfall.

She was not able to resist the urge to follow Eamon's secret path along the bottom of the cliff to the rocks below the waterfall. Sitting on a dry stone, just beyond the spray, she watched the river tumbling down from the ledge above, fluming as it struck a rock, falling deeply into the pool at her feet.

The sound was the muted roar of water cascading down against rock, dropping free into water. 'The most restful of all sounds,' was Anamar's thought, beyond music or gentle wind or soft words or even bird song. But what was that she could hear behind the water's rumbling? Was it the first cuckoo of Spring, as she had heard with Maureen and Eamon on their first visit here?

Anamar climbed back up to the track and walked on. She stopped at the first cairn where the Corabber River met the tributary stream. It was steady climbing now, avoiding the worst of the boggy patches, keeping close beside the river cascading down in a series of rapids and miniature waterfalls.

And then she reached the crest and Lough Belshade. She put another stone on the second cairn at the mouth of the lake and sat for a long time looking across to the tiny beach near her shelter stone cave.

Like the last part of the drive back from France, it seemed to take a long time to skirt the lake and reach the cave. When she got there, it was dry and undisturbed, as if no one had been since her last visit.

It began to rain and she sat cross-legged in the mouth of the cave and ate her soda bread sandwiches, filled with the potted herring from the dish Maureen had left for her.

There were so many thoughts jostling in a disorderly queue for her full attention, the solitary days and nights she had spent here by Belshade, the stream of visitors, her father pacing on the ridge, waiting for her to come towards him before he made a move.

The rain stopped and the sun came weakly through to warm the valley. Anamar sat on a stone down at the beach and listened to the lap of tiny wavelets on the coarse sand. Her mother's illness pushed its way to the front of her mind. That they had come to understand each other at the last seemed even more important now. And after the death there had been the birth of the pilgrimage, to give her new hope and opportunity.

Her impressions of the pilgrimage were dominated by the silent fervour of the crowds around the Grotto and surreptitiously infiltrated by F. B's proposal of marriage, of course. She still had not recovered from the shock of it. But most of all, her memories of Lourdes were the sharing of thoughts with Sister Teresa.

It was clear now to Anamar, that her power to change the world was the power to change her own world. It was not being able to control her life in every detail. But there were moments when she could choose. And an opportunity taken did lead to others. Only the adventurous were able to explore life. There might be mistakes, like her taking the wrong track in the Pyrenees but, for those who ventured, the great reward was in the journey.

Her time in the Pyrenees and her stay at Lough Belshade had changed everything. She had been enabled to be herself. Her friends, new and old, had understood. For the first time in their life together, she and her mother had been able to tell each other their thoughts. She knew now what she believed.

Woven through her experiences was a silver thread connecting her to the people in her life, from her visitors at Belshade to her mother at the last, from her old friends like Maureen, Eamon and Deirdre to her new friend Hank. It was as if they were the better for knowing her and she for knowing them. But there was one missed stitch, like the deliberate fault in the patch-work quilt. She and her father were still strangers.

Wandering back towards the cave, she climbed above it and suddenly spotted a silhouette on the skyline ridge near the mouth of the lake.

Someone was pacing to and fro, as her father had done when last she was here. The figure moved like a man, waved with both arms and began to come towards her, travelling quickly, almost running. She knew that loping walk. She had seen it before in the mountains.

It only took a few seconds to pick up her bag and begin to walk slowly towards him. He disappeared behind a ridge, but fifteen minutes later he was on a crest ahead, his arms raised, yelling to her. She strained to catch the words.

'Arriba! Arriba! ... Anamar! ... Arriba!'

It was Hank, calling her.

She had gone to the Pyrenees and had met him in his mountains. Now he had come to the Blue Stacks to meet her in hers.